HISTORY

OF

THE TRANSMISSION OF ANCIENT BOOKS TO MODERN TIMES

TOGETHER WITH

THE PROCESS OF HISTORICAL PROOF

HISTORY

OF THE

Transmission of Ancient Books to Modern Times

TOGETHER WITH

THE PROCESS OF HISTORICAL PROOF

OR

A CONCISE ACCOUNT OF THE MEANS BY WHICH
THE GENUINENESS OF ANCIENT LITERATURE GENERALLY, AND THE
AUTHENTICITY OF HISTORICAL WORKS ESPECIALLY
ARE ASCERTAINED
INCLUDING INCIDENTAL REMARKS UPON
THE RELATIVE STRENGTH OF THE EVIDENCE USUALLY ADDUCED
IN BEHALF OF THE HOLY SCRIPTURES

BY ISAAC TAYLOR

A New Edition, Revised and Enlarged

HASKELL HOUSE PUBLISHERS LTD.
Publishers of Scarce Scholarly Books
NEW YORK, N. Y. 10012
1971

First Published 1875

HASKELL HOUSE PUBLISHERS LTD.
Publishers of Scarce Scholarly Books
280 LAFAYETTE STREET
NEW YORK, N. Y. 10012

Library of Congress Catalog Card Number: 79-163893

Standard Book Number 8383-1317-5

Printed in the United States of America

PREFACE.

Two books which appeared more than thirty years ago, and which have been long out of print, are brought into one in this volume. The second of them — the "Process of Historical Proof," was, in fact, a sequel to the first—the "History of the Transmission of Ancient Books to Modern Times." In now reprinting the two, as one, it has not been difficult to give continuity to the whole: this has been effected, partly by removing from each volume portions which seemed to be of secondary importance, and to be not closely related to the principal intention of the work; and partly by introducing several entire chapters of new material; and by the insertion of additional paragraphs throughout. What is new in this volume occurs chiefly in the mid portions of it, and at the end.

In the course of this thirty years, the labours of critics, combined with the researches of learned travellers, have thrown much light upon all parts of the subject which is compendiously treated in this volume. No reader who is fully informed in this department will need to be told that, within the limits of a volume such as this, nothing more than the most concise mention of these recent labours and researches could be attempted: they are referred to only in the way of suggestion and of sample. At the first, the two books above mentioned were intended to find a place in a course of general educational reading; and it is only as coming within the range of a purpose such as this, that the Reprint is now offered to the public.

In excluding from the Reprint some chapters of the two volumes which related expressly to the Biblical argument, or "Christian Evidences," I have been influenced by several reasons—such as these: The first of them is this, that what may be regarded as the *religious* aspect of the general subject has no direct claim to be included in the treatment of it. In the next place, I have believed—and think so decisively—that, for the very purpose of bringing the Biblical argument home, with the greatest force, to the convictions of intelligent young persons, the subject should be fully understood in its broadest aspect. When it is thus presented, and when it is thus understood, well-informed and ingenuous persons will see and feel, irresistibly, that, as compared with any other mass of facts belonging to literary antiquarianism, and to historic evidence, the Biblical evidence is many times more ample, and various, and is more unquestionably certain, than even the best and the surest of those masses of facts.

There is yet another reason that has induced me to retrench, in this Reprint, much that, thirty years ago, might seem proper to the treatment of the subject. In this course of time a great change has had place upon the field of argument touching Christianity and its origin. Although disbelief may have spread widely of late, the argument concerning Christianity has been narrowed on every side of it. Much that, a while ago, was thought to need the production of proof, has, within a few years, quite ceased to be spoken of as questionable. Several elaborate and ingenious endeavours to bring, first, the *documents* of Christianity, and then, the *historic import* of those documents, into doubt, have signally failed, and in fact they are abandoned as nugatory and hopeless. It would, therefore, be a superfluous labour at this time to defend positions which have ceased to be assailed.

The course of adverse thought, at this time, in relation to the religion of Christ—the only religion concerning which any question can be raised—has this tendency, namely, to divert attention by all means, and as much as possible, from the *past;* and to engage all attention, and to concentrate it, upon the *present moment,* and upon its tangible and secular interests. This is now the aim of those writers, in the departments of Philosophy—physical and abstract, who would subvert Christianity, and who labour to do so by drawing the thoughts of the educated classes away from it—away from its neighbourhood. If it be so, then it must be well for those who take the other side, to do what they may for calling back the same classes, and for challenging them to acquaint themselves anew with History, and to assure themselves of its incontestible certainty.

STANFORD RIVERS,
February, 1859.

CONTENTS.

CHAPTER I.
INTENTION OF THE PRESENT ARGUMENT . . . . PAGE 1

CHAPTER II.
STATEMENT OF THE CASE, AS TO THE AUTHENTICITY OF ANCIENT BOOKS 9

CHAPTER III.
THE DATE OF ANCIENT WORKS, INFERRED FROM THE QUOTATIONS AND REFERENCES OF CONTEMPORARY AND SUCCEEDING WRITERS 27

CHAPTER IV.
THE ANTIQUITY AND GENUINENESS OF ANCIENT BOOKS MAY BE INFERRED FROM THE HISTORY OF THE LANGUAGES IN WHICH THEY ARE EXTANT 35

CHAPTER V.
ANCIENT METHODS OF WRITING, AND THE MATERIALS OF BOOKS 39

CHAPTER VI.

CHANGES INTRODUCED IN THE COURSE OF TIME IN THE FORMS OF LETTERS, AND IN THE GENERAL CHARACTER OF WRITING - - - - - - - - - - - - - - 50

CHAPTER VII.

THE COPYISTS; AND THE PRINCIPAL CENTRES OF THE COPYING BUSINESS - - - - - - - - - - - - 58

CHAPTER VIII.

INDICATIONS OF THE SURVIVANCE OF ANCIENT LITERATURE, THROUGH A PERIOD EXTENDING FROM THE DECLINE OF LEARNING IN THE SEVENTH CENTURY, TO ITS RESTORATION IN THE FIFTEENTH - - - - - - - 73

CHAPTER IX.

THE REVIVAL OF LEARNING IN THE FOURTEENTH CENTURY. 92

CHAPTER X.

SEVERAL METHODS AVAILABLE FOR ASCERTAINING THE CREDIBILITY OF ANCIENT HISTORICAL WORKS - - - - 97

CHAPTER XI.

EXCEPTIONS TO WHICH THE TESTIMONY OF HISTORIANS, ON PARTICULAR POINTS, MAY BE LIABLE - - - - - 113

CHAPTER XII.

CONFIRMATIONS OF THE EVIDENCE OF ANCIENT HISTORIANS, DERIVABLE FROM INDEPENDENT SOURCES - - - - - 125

CHAPTER XIII.

GENERAL PRINCIPLES, APPLICABLE TO QUESTIONS OF THE GENUINENESS AND AUTHENTICITY OF ANCIENT RECORDS 152

CHAPTER XIV.

RELATIVE STRENGTH OF THE EVIDENCE WHICH SUPPORTS THE GENUINENESS AND AUTHENTICITY OF THE HOLY SCRIPTURES - - - - - - - - - - - - - - 168

CHAPTER XV.

ILLUSTRATIONS OF THE PRECEDING STATEMENTS: A MORNING AT THE BRITISH MUSEUM - - - - - - - - 194

CHAPTER XVI.

FACTS RELATING TO THE CONSERVATION, AND LATE RECOVERY, OF SOME ANCIENT MANUSCRIPTS - - - - - 216

CHAPTER XVII.

THE PROCESS OF HISTORIC EVIDENCE EXEMPLIFIED IN THE INSTANCE OF HERODOTUS - - - - - - - - - - 257

CHAPTER XVIII.

METHOD OF ARGUING FROM THE GENUINENESS, TO THE AUTHENTICITY OF THE HISTORY OF HERODOTUS - - 293

CHAPTER XIX.

EXAMPLES OF IMPERFECT HISTORICAL EVIDENCE: HERODOTUS 325

CHAPTER XX.

RECENT EXPLORATIONS, CONFIRMATORY OF THE TRUTH OF ANCIENT HISTORY: HERODOTUS AND BEROSUS - - - 347

CHAPTER XXI.

INFERENTIAL HISTORIC MATERIALS - - - - - - - - 360

CHAPTER XXII.

THE MODERN JERUSALEM—A VOUCHER FOR THE LITERATURE OF ITS ANCIENT OCCUPANTS - - - - - - - - - 387

HISTORY.

OF THE

TRANSMISSION OF ANCIENT BOOKS.

CHAPTER I.

INTENTION OF THE PRESENT ARGUMENT.

THE credit of ancient literature, the certainty of history, and the truth of religion, are all involved in the secure transmission of ancient books to modern times. Many of the facts connected with the history of this transmission are to be found, more or less distinctly mentioned, in every work in which the claims of the Holy Scriptures are advocated. But these facts are open to much misapprehension when they are brought together to subserve the purposes of a single argument. It is the intention of this volume therefore to lay them before general readers, as they stand apart from controversy, and as if no interests more important than those of literature were implicated in the result of the statements we have to make.

Nothing can be more equitable than that the genuineness and authenticity of the Jewish and Christian Scriptures should be judged of by the rules that are applied to all other ancient books; nor is anything more likely to produce a firm and intelligent conviction of the validity of the claims advanced for the Holy Scriptures, than a clear understanding of the relative value of the evidence which supports them. To furnish the means therefore of instituting a comparison, so just in itself, and so necessary to a fair examination of the most important of all questions, is the design of these pages.

As this volume makes no pretension to communicate information to those who are already conversant with matters of antiquity, literary or historical, whatever might seem recondite, or what is still involved in controversy, has been avoided. Nor will these pages be encumbered with numerous references, which, though easily amassed, would increase the size of the volume without being serviceable to the class of readers for whom the author now writes. No facts are adduced which may not readily be substantiated by any one who has access to a library of moderate extent. But a few works, not often met with in private collections, are named at the foot of the page where special information has been derived from them.

The principal facts of ancient history, and the authenticity of the works from which chiefly our knowledge of antiquity is derived, are now freely admitted, after a few exceptive instances have been set off, which are unproved, or doubtful.

Yet on this subject, as well as upon some others, there often exists, at the same time, too much faith, and too little; for, from a want of acquaintance with the details on which a rational conviction of the genuineness and validity of ancient records may be founded, many persons, even though otherwise well informed, feel that they have hardly an alternative between a simple acceptance of the entire mass of ancient history, or an equally indiscriminate suspicion of the whole. And when it happens that a particular fact comes to be questioned, or when the genuineness of some ancient book is argued, such persons, conscious that they are little familiar with the nature of the evidence on the strength of which the question turns, and perceiving that the controversy involves many recondite and uninteresting researches, or that it rests upon the validity of minute criticisms, either recoil altogether from the argument, or they accept an opinion, without inquiry, from that party on whose judgment they think they may most safely rely.

And it is true that such controversies may, for the most part, very properly be left in the hands of critics and antiquarians, whose tastes and acquirements qualify them for investigations that can scarcely be made intelligible to the mass of readers. Nor are the facts involved in these controversies often of any importance to the general student of history; for they do not extensively affect the integrity of that department of literature to which they belong. Yet it must be allowed that the *principles* on which such questions are argued, and the facts connected with the transmission of ancient literature to modern times, are in themselves highly important; and that they well deserve more attention than they often receive. Nor are these facts, when separated from particular controversies, at all abstruse, or difficult of apprehension. Indeed, much of the information that bears upon the subject is in itself curious and highly interesting, as well as important.

Even in relation to those works of genius, the value of which consists in their intrinsic merits, and which would not be robbed of their beauties, though they were discovered to be spurious, an assurance of their genuineness is felt by every reader to conduce greatly to the pleasure they impart. But a much stronger feeling naturally leads us to demand this assurance in the perusal of works which profess to have reality only for their matter :—Truth is the very subject of History :—the adducing of satisfactory evidence, therefore, of the integrity of its records may well be deemed an indispensable preliminary to a course of study in that department of knowledge.

Besides its peculiar propriety in connection with the study of history, the argument in support of the genuineness and authenticity of the existing remains of ancient literature is singularly fitted to afford a useful exercise to the reasoning faculties; and perhaps, better than any other subject, it calls into combined action those powers of the mind that are separately employed in mathematical, physical, or legal pursuits, and which, in the actual occasions of common life, can subserve our welfare only so far as they move in unison.

But reasons of still greater moment recommend the subject of the following pages to the attention of the reader; for it is certain that every one, whether or not he is contented to admit, without inquiry, the authenticity of *profane* history, has the highest personal concern in the truth of that particular portion of ancient history with which the Christian religion is connected; and, therefore, every one should think himself bound to convince himself of the genuineness of the books in which its principles are contained. And as the facts on which this proof depends are precisely of the same kind in profane, as in sacred literature, and as the same principles of evidence are applicable to all questions relating to the genuineness of ancient books, it is highly desirable that the proof of the genuineness of the Sacred Writings should be viewed—in *its place*, as forming a part only of a general argument, which bears equally upon the entire literary remains of antiquity. For it is only when so viewed, that the comparative strength and completeness of the proof which belongs to this particular case, can be duly estimated. When exhibited in this light it will be seen that the integrity of the records of the Christian faith is substantiated by evidence in a tenfold proportion more various, copious, and conclusive, than that which can be adduced in support of any other ancient writings. If, therefore, the question had no other importance belonging to it than what may attach to a purely literary inquiry, or if only the strict justice of the case were regarded, the authenticity of the Jewish and Christian Scriptures could never come to be controverted, till the entire body of classical literature had been proved to be spurious.

Many—perhaps most persons, in perusing works on the evidences of revealed religion, are apt to suppose that the sacred books only, or that these books, more than any others, stand in need of laboured argumentation in support of their authenticity; while, in truth, these books, less than any other ancient writings, need a careful investigation of their claims; for the proof that establishes them is on all points obvious and redundant. Indeed this very redundancy and variety of evidence—especially if it be unskilfully adduced, may actually produce confusion and hesitancy, rather than an affirmed conviction, in unpractised minds; and this perplexity is likely to be increased by the very idea of the serious importance of the subject. Thus it may happen that those very facts which, if compared with others of a similar kind, are susceptible of the most complete proof, are actually regarded with the most distrust.

In presenting to the reader, what might be called—the History of the Records of History, we shall put him in position for tracing the extant works of ancient authors *retrogressively*, from modern times, up to the age to which they are usually attributed; and then it will be seen on what grounds—under certain limitations—the contents of these works are admitted to be authentic, and worthy of credit. In attending to the facts which we have to adduce it will appear that we are well warranted in accepting certain works as having been written in the age to which they are usually assigned, and by the authors to whom they are commonly attributed; and also in believing that they have not suffered material corruption in the course of transcription.

Further than this we may advance, and go on to show the grounds of our belief that such or such an author wrote what he believed to be true, and that he possessed authentic information on the subject of which he treats. The proof in this case must be drawn from the style and character of the work itself; from the circumstances that attended its first publication; from the corroborative evidence of contemporary writers; and from the agreement of the narrative in particular instances with existing relics of antiquity.

Evidence in support of the first part of this assumption will prove that the works in question are not *forgeries :*—evidence establishing the *second*, will show that they are not *fictions*.

It is obvious that these assumptions are not only distinct, but that they are independent of each other :—for one of them may be conclusively established, while the other is either disproved, or may remain questionable. A book may contain a true narrative of events, though not written by the author, or in the age, that has commonly been supposed. Or, on the other hand, it may undoubtedly be the production of the alleged author, but may deserve little credit as a professed record of facts. Thus, for example, the Cyropædia is, on good evidence, attributed to Xenophon; but there is little reason to suppose that it deserves to be considered as better than an historical romance :—the *genuineness* of the work is certain; but its authenticity as a history is, at the best, questionable. Yet the first of these propositions is more independent of the second, than the second can be of the first. For when the antiquity and genuineness of an historical work has been clearly demonstrated, it is seldom difficult to fix the degree of credit that is due to the author; or to discover those particular points on which there may be reason to suspect his veracity, or to question the soundness of his judgment, or to doubt the accuracy of his information.

It is then for the purpose of rendering these arguments and inferences intelligible, and more satisfactory also, than otherwise they would be, that, after giving a brief statement of this argument, we shall proceed to bring forward what relates to the manipulative and mechanical methods of multiplying copies of books, and to the diffusion and preservation of these copies, in ancient times;—that is to say, in all times anterior to the invention of Printing, in the fifteenth century.

CHAPTER II.

STATEMENT OF THE CASE, AS TO THE AUTHENTICITY OF ANCIENT BOOKS.

THE antiquity and genuineness of the extant remains of ancient literature may be established by three lines of proof that are altogether independent of each other; and though, in any particular instance, one, or even two out of the three should be wanting, the remaining one may alone be perfectly conclusive:—When the three concur, they present a redundant demonstration of the facts in question.

The *first* line of proof relates to the history of certain copies of a work, which are now in existence.

The *second*—traces the history of a work as it may be collected from the series of references made to it by succeeding writers.

The *third*—is drawn from the known history of the *language* in which the work is extant.

For understanding what belongs to the first of these three lines of evidence we ought to be acquainted with various particulars relating to the modes of writing practised among ancient nations, and to the materials employed, and to what may be called the business-system by means of which an ancient writer placed himself in communication with his readers.

In many, or in most of these particulars ancient and modern usages are very dissimilar. But something more should first be said indicative of the purpose with a view to which these facts are brought forward.

It need scarcely be said that the antiquity and integrity of a book can be open to no question, if in any case the existence of any one copy of it can be traced back, with certainty, to the time of its first publication. If, for example, a manuscript of a work in the author's handwriting were still extant, and if the fact of its being such could by any means be proved, our argument would be concluded, and any other evidence must be deemed superfluous. There are, however, few such unquestionable *autographs* to be found, even of modern works, and none, of any ancient one. Yet the circumstances attending the preservation and transmission of manuscripts are, in some instances, as we shall see, such as to prove the antiquity and genuineness of a work with little less certainty than as if the very first copy of it were in existence.

But before we enter into the particulars of this proof it should be mentioned, especially as we intend to follow the order of time *retrogressively*, that the history of *manuscripts* need not be traced through any later period than that of the early part of the fifteenth century, when most of the classic authors passed through the press. For the invention of printing has served, as well to ascertain, beyond doubt, the existence of books at certain dates, as to secure the text from extensive interpolation and corruption. A printed book is not susceptible of subsequent interpolation or alteration by the *pen*: it bears also a date, and the issuing of different editions of the same work from distant places, would render any falsification of date in one of them, or any material corruption of the text by an editor, a nugatory attempt. For example, there are now extant, printed copies of the history of the Peloponnesian war, dated "Venice, 1502;" other copies of an edition of the same work are dated "Florence, 1506;" others are dated "Basil, 1540;" and others, printed within a few years of the same time at Paris and Vienna. On being compared with each other, these editions are found to agree *in the main;* and yet to disagree in many small variations of orthography, syntax, or expression; so as to prove that they were derived independently from different manuscripts; and not successively from each other. These printed editions, therefore, sufficiently prove the existence of the work in the fifteenth century; and also that the text of the modern editions has not been materially impaired or corrupted during the last four hundred years.

But let it now be imagined, that there are no other means of ascertaining the antiquity and genuineness of the classic authors than such as may be collected from the history of existing manuscripts. Our object then will be to discover to what age they may clearly be traced; and to deduce from the facts some sure inference relative to the length of time during which those works have been passing through the hands of copyists.

The date of an ancient manuscript may be ascertained by such means as the following:—

1. Some manuscripts are known to have been carefully preserved in the libraries where they are

now found, for several centuries:—for not only have they been mentioned in the catalogues of the depositories to which they belong, but they have been so accurately described by eminent scholars of succeeding ages, that no doubt can remain of their identity. Or even if they have changed hands, the particulars of the successive transfers have been authentically recorded.

2. A large proportion of existing manuscripts are found to be dated by the hand of the copyists, and in such a manner as to leave no question as to the time when the copy was executed.

3. Many manuscripts have marginal notes, added evidently by later hands, which through some incidental allusion to persons, events, or particular customs, or by the use of peculiar forms of expression, indicate clearly the age of the notes, and therefore carry that of the original manuscript somewhat higher.

4. The remote antiquity of a manuscript is often established by the peculiar circumstance of its existing *beneath* another writing. These re-written manuscripts—palimpsests, or rescripts, as they are termed, afford the most satisfactory proof of antiquity that can be imagined. Parchment, which has always been a costly material, came to be greatly enhanced in price at the time when paper, manufactured from the papyrus of the Nile, began to be scarce, and just before the time when that formed from cotton—called " charta bombycina," was brought into general use. At the same period, owing to the general decline of learning, the works of the classic authors fell into very general neglect. Those, therefore, who were copyists by profession, and the monks especially, whose

libraries often contained large collections of parchment books, availed themselves of the valuable material which they possessed, by erasing, or washing out, the original writing, and then substituting lives of the saints, religious romances, meditations, or such other inanities as suited the taste of the times. Nevertheless, often, the faithful skin, tenacious of its pristine honours, retained the traces of the original writing with sufficient distinctness to render it still legible. These rescripts, therefore, offer to us a double proof of the antiquity of the work which first occupied the parchment; for in most cases the date of the monkish writing is easily ascertained to be of the twelfth, or even the ninth century. The writing which *first* occupied such parchments must, of course, be dated considerably higher; for it is much more probable that old, than that recent books should have been selected for the purpose of erasure. Some invaluable manuscripts of the Holy Scriptures, and not a few precious fragments of classic literature, have been thus brought to light.

5. The age of a manuscript may often be ascertained with little chance of error, by some such indications as the following:—the quality or appearance of the ink; the nature of the material; that is to say, whether it be soft leather, or parchment, or the papyrus of Egypt, or the bombycine paper; for these materials succeeded each other, in common use, at periods that are well known;— the peculiar form, size, and character of the writing; for a regular progression in the modes of writing may be traced by abundant evidence through every age from the remotest times;—the

style of the ornaments or *illuminations,* as they are termed, often serves to indicate the age of the book which they decorate. From such indications as these, more or less definite and certain, ancient manuscripts, now extant, are assigned to various periods, extending from the sixteenth, to the fourth century of the Christian era; or perhaps, in one or two instances, to the third, or second. Very few can claim an antiquity so high as the fourth century: but not a few are safely attributed to the seventh; and a great proportion of those extant were unquestionably executed in the tenth; while many belong to the following four hundred years. It is, however, to be observed, that some manuscripts, executed at so late a time as the thirteenth, or even the fifteenth century, afford clear internal evidence that, by a single remove only, the text they contain claims a *real* antiquity, higher than that even of the oldest existing copy of the same work. For these older copies sometimes prove, by the peculiar nature of the corruptions which have crept into the text, that they have been derived through a long series of copies; while perhaps the text of the more modern manuscript possesses such a degree of purity and freedom from all the usual consequences of frequent transcription, as to make it manifest that the copy from which it was taken, was so ancient as not to be far distant from the time of the first publication of the work.

Most, if not all, the Royal and Ecclesiastical and University libraries in Europe, as well as many private collections, contain great numbers of these literary relics of antiquity: and some of them could furnish manuscripts of nearly the entire body of ancient literature. There are few of the classic authors that are not still extant in *several* manuscript copies; and of some, the existing copies are almost numberless.

Although all the larger ancient libraries, such, for example, as those of Alexandria, of Constantinople, of Athens, and of Rome, were destroyed by the fanaticism of barbarian conquerors; yet so extensive a diffusion of the most celebrated works had previously taken place, throughout the Roman empire, and beyond its limits, that all parts of Europe and Western Asia abounded with smaller collections, or with single works in the hands of private persons. When learning had almost disappeared among the people, monasteries and religious houses became the chief receptacles of books; for almost every such establishment included individuals who still cultivated literature and the sciences with ardour; and who found no difficulty in amassing almost any quantity of this generally neglected property.

Happily for literature, religious houses were places of greater security than even the strongholds of the nobles, or the palaces of kings, which by conquest or revolution were, from time to time, violently rent from their possessors. Meantime, these sacred seclusions were usually respected, even by the fiercest invaders. Through a long course of ages, monasteries were occupied by an order of men who succeeded each other in a far more tranquil course of transition than has taken place in any other instance that might be named. The property of each establishment (and its literary property was always highly prized) passed down, from age to age, as if under the hand of a permanent proprietor, and it was therefore subjected to fewer dispersions or destructions than the mutability of human affairs ordinarily permits.

Every church, and every convent and monastery had its library, its librarian, and its other officers, employed in the conservation of the books. Connected with the library was the *Scriptorium*—the hall or chamber where the elder or the educated monks employed themselves in making copies of such books as were falling into decay; or of such as there was still some demand for, in the open world.

By means such as these it was that the literature of more enlightened ages has been preserved from extinction; and when at length learning revived in the fourteenth and fifteenth centuries, a large portion of those long-hoarded volumes flowed into the collections of the munificent founders of libraries, and there, having become known to the learned, they were speedily consigned to the immortal custody of the press.

The places in which these remains of ancient literature had been preserved, during the middle ages, were too many, and they were too distant from each other, and they were too little connected by any kind of intercourse, to admit of a combination or conspiracy having for its object any supposed purposes of interpolation or corruption. Possessing therefore as we do, in most cases, copies of the same author, some of which were drawn from the monasteries of England, others from those of Spain, and others collected in Egypt, Palestine, or Asia Minor, if, on comparing them, we find that they agree, except in variations of little moment, we have an incontestable proof of the care and integrity with which the business of transcription had generally been conducted. For it is evident that if the practice of mutilation, interpolation, and corruption, had to any considerable extent been admitted, the existing remains of ancient authors, after so long a time, would have retained scarcely a trace of integrity or uniformity. A licentious practice of transcription, operating through the course of a thousand or fifteen hundred years, must have resulted, not in giving us the connected and consistent works we actually possess, but only a heterogeneous mass of mangled fragments.

But now, if the general accordance of existing manuscripts attests the prevailing care, and even the scrupulousness of those through whose hands they passed, the peculiar nature of the diversities that do exist among the several copies of the same author, serves to establish a fact which, if we did not know it by other means, it would be of the highest importance to prove: namely, that these works *had already descended through a long course of time, when the existing copies were executed.* This fact is especially apparent in the case of the earlier Greek authors; for while some copies retain uniformly the peculiarities of the dialect in which the author wrote; in others, these peculiarities are merged in those more common forms of the language which prevailed after the time of the decline of the Greek literature. These deviations in orthography, or in construction, from the author's text, were evidently made by successive copyists in compliance with the tastes of purchasers of books in different countries; nor were they likely to have been effected by transcribers of *the middle ages*, when these books were no longer in use by readers to whom the language was vernacular, and to whom, alone, an accordance with the colloquial forms of the language could be a matter of any importance.

Books in a dead language, and which can be intended for the use of the learned only, will never be accommodated to the colloquial fashions of an intermediate period. Let us consider how it would be in an instance familiar to us. If, for example, in examining two editions of the poems of Chaucer, one of them should be found to retain the original peculiarities of orthography, proper to the author's time, while, in the other, those peculiarities are all softened down into the forms adopted in the reign of Elizabeth, we should certainly attribute the edition to *that* period rather than suppose the corrections to have been made by a modern editor.

Again :—some copies of ancient authors present instances in which, when a passage is compared with the same in another copy, it is easy to perceive that an early transcriber, having fallen into an error, more than one succeeding transcriber has attempted a restoration of the genuine reading; for the *last* conjectural emendation has plainly been framed out of two or three prior corrections.

Thus it is, then, that the existing manuscripts of the classic authors may be traced up, either by direct evidence, or by unquestionable inferences, very near to the age—and, in many instances—quite up to the age when these works were universally diffused, were familiarly known, and were incessantly quoted by other writers; and when, therefore, the history of each work may easily and abundantly be collected from the testimony of contemporary and succeeding authors. The various facts, above alluded to, serve to connect the literary remains of antiquity—now in our hands, with the period of their pristine existence:—we traverse the long era of general ignorance—that wide gulf which separates the intelligence and civilisation of antiquity from the intelligence and civilisation of modern times, and we land, as it were, upon the native soil of these monuments of Mind, and we once more find ourselves surrounded by that abundance of evidence which belongs to an advanced state of knowledge. We need not wish to trace the history of *manuscripts* further, than to the confines of that former world of learning and refinement.

Indeed we need not be solicitous to trace the history of these literary relics a step further than fairly into the midst of the dark ages. For even if all external and correlative evidence were wanting, and if nothing were known concerning the classic authors except this—that, such as they now are, they were extant in the tenth century, more than enough would be known to make it abundantly certain that these works were the product of a very different, and of a distant age. The men of those times might indeed have been the transcribers and conservators, and perhaps even the admirers, of Thucydides, of Xenophon, of Aristophanes, of Plato, of Virgil, of Cicero, of Horace, and of Tacitus; but assuredly they were not the *authors* of books, such as those which bear these names. The living pictures of energy, and of wisdom, and of liberty, which these monuments of taste and genius contain, could never have been imagined in the cells of a monastery, nor composed in an age when little was to be seen abroad but ignorance, violence, and slavery; and little found within but a dreaming philosophy, and a degrading superstition. It is not the prerogative of the human mind, however great may be its native powers, to trespass far beyond the bounds of the scene by which it is immediately surrounded, or to frame images of things which, in their elements, as well as in their adjuncts, belong to a system and an economy altogether unknown to the men of that time. To the genius of man it is given to imitate, to select, to refine, and to exalt; but not to create.

The general import of the facts that have thus been briefly stated, is this, namely, that the books now extant, and which are usually attributed to the Greek and Roman writers, have, such as we find them, descended from a very remote age. But this general affirmation must always be understood to include an exception of those smaller omissions, additions, and alterations in the text, which have taken place, either by design, or inadvertency, in the course of often repeated transcriptions.

The actual amount and the importance of these corruptions of the text of ancient authors is likely to be overrated by general readers, who seeing that the subject is continually alluded to in critical works, and knowing that criticisms upon "various readings" often occupy a space five times exceeding that which is filled by the text, and that not seldom they become the subject of voluminous and angry controversies, are led to suppose that questions upon which the learned are so long and so seriously employed, cannot be otherwise than weighty and substantial. With a view of correcting this impression, so far as it may be erroneous, we shall now briefly explain the general nature, the causes, and the extent of these variations and corruptions.

By far the greater proportion of all "various readings"—perhaps nineteen out of twenty, are purely of a *verbal* kind, and they are such as can claim the attention of none but philologists and grammarians: a few may deserve the notice of every reader of ancient literature; and a few demand the consideration of the student of history. But, taken in a mass, the light in which they should be regarded is that of their furnishing a significant and conclusive proof of the care, fidelity, and exactness with which the business of copying was ordinarily conducted. For it is certain that nothing less than a high degree, as well of technical correctness, as of professional integrity, on the part of those who practised this craft, could have conveyed the text of ancient authors through a period—in some instances—of two thousand years, with alterations so trivial as are those which, for the most part, are found actually to have taken place.

When the discrepancies of manuscripts of an author are such as materially to affect the sense of a passage in itself important, so as to demand the exercise of discrimination on the part of the student of history, it becomes necessary to understand, and to bear in mind, what were probably the most common sources of such diversities. The following may be named as the most common causes of the various readings which are met with in comparing several copies of the same ancient author.

1. Nothing can be more probable than that authors who long survived the first publication of their works, should, from time to time, issue revised copies of them; and each of these altered copies would, if the work were in continual request, and were widely diffused, become the parent, as we may say, of *a family* of copies. Thus it would be that, without any fault on the part of the transcribers, a considerable amount of such diversities would be originated, and perpetuated. A large proportion, perhaps, of those variations which occupy the diligence and acumen of editors and critics, and for the rectification of which so many learned conjectures are often hazarded, have, in fact, arisen from the author's own hand in revising the copies which, at intervals, he delivered to his amanuensis. The perpetual opportunity afforded for introducing corrections, when a book was continually in request, would not fail to encourage, in fastidious authors, the habit of frequent revision: meantime transcribers, in distant countries, might have no opportunity to collate the earlier with the later exemplars. This source of various readings seems to have been too little adverted to by critics; though it might serve to solve some perplexing questions relative to the genuineness of particular expressions or sentences, which have fallen under suspicion from their non-existence in certain manuscripts.

2. Some errors would, of course, arise from the mere inattention, carelessness, or the ignorance of transcribers; and yet fewer, probably, than may

at first be imagined; for besides that those who spent their lives in this occupation would generally acquire a high degree of technical accuracy of eye, ear, and hand, and that correctness and legibility must have been the qualities upon which, principally, the marketable value of books depended; it is known that in the monasteries, from whence the greater part of all existing manuscripts proceeded, there were persons, qualified by their superior learning for the task, whose office it was to revise every book that issued from the Scriptorium. Errors of inadvertency must, nevertheless, have occurred. If the author to be transcribed was read by one person, while several wrote from his voice, the process would be open, not only to the mistakes of the reader's eye, and to those of the writer's hand; but especially to those of the writer's ear; for words, similar in sound, might often be substituted, one for the other. Instances of this sort are of frequent occurrence, and the knowledge of the probable cause often serves to suggest the proper correction. If the writer read for himself, he would be liable to mistake letters of similar shape—to mistake the *sense* by a wrong division of words in his manner of reading, in consequence of which he might involuntarily accommodate the orthography or the syntax to the supposed sense. The frequent use of contractions in writing was a very common source of errors; for many of these abbreviations were extremely complicated, obscure, and ambiguous, so that an unskilful copyist was very likely to mistake one word for another. No parts of ancient books have suffered so much from errors of inadvertency as those which relate to *numbers;* for as one numeral letter was easily mistaken for another, and as neither the sense of the passage, nor the rules of orthography, nor of syntax, suggested the genuine reading, when once an error had arisen, it would most often be perpetuated, without remedy. It is, therefore, almost always unsafe to rest the stress of an argument upon any statement of numbers in ancient writers, unless some correlative computation confirms the reading of the text. Hence nothing can be more frivolous or unfair than to raise an objection against the veracity or accuracy of an historian, upon some apparent incompatibility in his statement of numbers. Difficulties of this sort it is much better to attribute, at once, to a corruption of the text, than to discuss them with ill-spent assiduity.

3. The assumption of short marginal notes into the text, appears to have been a frequent source of various readings. When such notes supplied ellipses in the author's language, or when they conduced much to the perspicuity of an obscure passage, the copyist would be very likely to incorporate the exegetical phrase, rather than that it should either be lost to the reader, or should deform the margin.

4. Transcribers frequently thought themselves free to substitute modern for obsolete words or phrases; and sometimes they consulted the wishes of their customers, by exchanging the forms of one dialect (of the Greek) for those of another; or, more often, for the common forms of the language. Alterations of this kind have often been the occasion of bringing authentic works under needless suspicion; for when the text has contained words or phrases which are known to belong to a later

age than that of the supposed author, such incongruities have seemed to afford proofs of spuriousness.

5. Intentional omissions, interpolations, or alterations, were unquestionably sometimes ventured on by transcribers. But so many are the means we possess for detecting any such wilful corruptions—drawn from a comparison of different manuscripts, or from the incongruity of the interpolated passage, that there is perhaps, altogether, more probability that, from some accidental peculiarity of style, genuine passages of ancient authors should fall under suspicion, than that any actually spurious portions should entirely escape suspicion and detection.

Of the above-mentioned sources of the various readings found in the text of ancient authors, it should be remembered that the operation of the *first* was confined to the short term of the author's life; nor indeed, whatever may be the amount or importance of variations arising from *this* source, must they go to swell the number of *corruptions* of the text. The *second* source of variations was indeed open during the lapse of many centuries; yet it has always been held in check by the diligent collation of copies, on the part of industrious critics, from age to age: and a large proportion of errors, arising from mere inadvertency, are either so palpable as to suggest the means of their own correction; or they are so trivial as to merit no attention, except from those who charge themselves with the responsibilities of an editor. There is, besides, reason to believe that not a few existing copies of the most celebrated authors, present a text that has passed through the process of transcription not oftener than once or twice; and that each time the copy has been executed with scrupulous exactness. Variations arising from the *third* and *fourth* sources, have perhaps occasioned to critics and editors more perplexity than those springing from any other cause; and yet these differences are rarely of any moment, so far as the sense of the author is concerned: they can be deemed important only when they tend to perplex the question of the date or the genuineness of a book. Corruptions of the *fifth* class must be acknowledged materially to affect the credit and value of ancient literature, so far as there can be any reason to suspect their existence; and every diligent student of history will think the investigation of cases of this kind deserving of his utmost attention.

CHAPTER III.

THE DATE OF ANCIENT WORKS, INFERRED FROM THE QUOTATIONS AND REFERENCES OF CONTEMPORARY AND SUCCEEDING WRITERS.

LET us now suppose, that the Greek and Latin authors are extant only in the printed editions—that is to say, that every one of the ancient manuscripts has long since perished, and that the facts that have been referred to in the preceding pages are out of our view, or unknown. Our business then would be, to collect from these works such a series of mutual references, as should both prove the identity of the works now extant with those so referred to ; and also fix the relative places of the several writers in point of time.

A single reference, found in one author, to the works of another, who, in his turn, needs the same kind of authentication, may seem to be a fallacious, or insufficient, and obscure kind of proof ; for this reference or this quotation may possibly be an interpolation ; or the reference may be of too slight or indefinite a kind to make it certain that the work now extant is the same as that so referred to. In truth, the validity of this kind of proof arises from its *amount*, from its *multifariousness*, and from its *incidental character*. For although a single and solitary testimony may be inconclusive, many hundred independent testimonies, all bearing upon the same point, are much more than sufficient to remove every shadow of doubt; some of these references may be slight and indefinite, but others are full, particular, and complete. If some are formal and direct, and such therefore as might be supposed to have been inserted with a fraudulent design, others are altogether circuitous and purely incidental. If some have descended to us through the same channels, others are derived from sources as far removed as can be imagined from the possibility of collusion.

But a work may happen to want this kind of evidence, and yet, on other grounds, it may possess a valid claim to genuineness. In fact, almost all the existing remains of ancient literature are abundantly authenticated by the numerous and explicit quotations from them, or descriptions of them, that occur in other works. And there are very few books that do not contain some direct or some indirect allusions to other works: so it is that the remains of ancient literature, taken as a mass, contains within itself the proof of the authenticity of each part.

The nature of the case gives to this body of references a pyramidal form. In the most remote age it is, of course, small in amount; in the next age it becomes much more ample and substantial; and in later periods, it spreads itself over the entire surface of literature.

The literature of the Greeks was national and original; they borrowed from their neighbours less in poetry, philosophy, and history, than in religion, or the arts: their *early* writers were not, in the modern sense of the term, men of learning; their works were composed at the impulse of genius, and of the moving spirit of the times. The habit of literary allusion and quotation had not then been formed, nor indeed was it congruous with this order of intellectual production; and yet the early Greek writers contain mutual references, which, if not numerous, are sufficient to establish and ascertain, in most instances, the genuineness of each.

The second period of Greek literature, dating from the times of Alexander, and reaching down to the overthrow of the Greek national independence by the Romans was, in the natural order of things, an era of learning, of criticism, and of imitation. The writers of this period, therefore, abound with references of all kinds to their predecessors and contemporaries. A second age of literature holds up a mirror of the first. Erudition, amplitude, comprehension, method, labour, take the place of spontaneous effort, and of intuitive taste. Commentators, compilers, and collectors, abound; and the writers of such an age seem to perform the functions of *caryatides* in the temple of learning; as if their only business was to sustain the pediment which chiefly attracts the admiration of spectators. Among writers of this class, therefore, we are to look for a copious harvest of quotations; and in their pages we shall rarely fail to meet with evidence bearing upon any question of the genuineness of an ancient writer.

The Romans borrowed everything but energy of character and practical good sense, from the Greeks. Their literature, from the first, was of a derived character; their writers added learning to what might be their native genius; and their works reflect the literature of their masters. Sufficiently ample allusions, therefore, to the most celebrated of the Greek authors, as well as to those of their countrymen, are found scattered throughout the Latin classics.

Both the Greek and Latin writers of later ages were well acquainted with the literature of brighter times; and they have left in their works ample means for bringing down the chain of references to the time of the decline of learning in Europe—to that time up to which we have already traced the history of existing manuscripts; so that the two lines of evidence unite about midway between the fifth and the fifteenth centuries.

The nature, extent, and validity of the evidence that may be derived from the mutual references of authors, will be best exhibited by a classification of its several kinds under the following heads:—

1. Literal quotations, whether the author cited is named or not. Such quotations serve the double purpose of proving the existence of the work quoted in the time of the writer who makes the reference, and of identifying, and sometimes even of correcting, the extant text. If, for example, in subsequent writers, we find only a dozen or twenty sentences, taken from different parts of an earlier work, the verbal coincidence is sufficient to prove that the work, such as we now find it, is the same as that quoted. When such quotations are numerous and exact, they afford the best means, either of restoring the genuine reading of authors, or of judging of the comparative purity of different manuscripts. For frequently these quotations seem to have suffered less in the course

of transcription than either the other parts of the work in which they are found, or than that from which they are taken. The reason of this difference may readily be imagined:—either the author himself quoted from a copy purer than any that are now extant; or the transcriber, meeting with a passage which he remembered to belong to a well-known work, consulted the original, of which he had a good copy, and the very circumstance of doing so would naturally induce somewhat more of care than in ordinary transcription.

2. Incidental allusions are often met with, either to the words or to the sense of an author, suf- ciently obvious to prove that the one writer was known to the other; and yet they are too incidental and remote to be regarded as an interpolation. In questions of apparent difficulty, such accidental references may be conclusive in proof of the existence of a work at a certain time. Among the ancient historians, there are instances in which two writers, who do not mention each other, narrate the same facts with so many coincidences of method, or of details, embellishments, or reflections, as to make it certain either that both narratives were derived from the same source; or that the one was copied from the other. And if the one narrative has altogether the air of originality, and is in accordance with the writer's style and spirit, the other writer must be held to be the quoting party, and therefore he establishes the prior existence of the work from which he has borrowed.

3. Nearly every one of the principal authors of antiquity has been explicitly mentioned, or criticised, or described, by later writers. Lists of their

works have been given, with summaries of their contents ; or they have been made the subjects of connected commentaries, by means of which the mass of the original work may be identified, and collated, with existing copies. Books of this secondary class are usually fraught with references to the entire circle of literature that was extant in the writer's time. There are also extant several works containing the lives of ancient authors, with accurate lists of their works. These biographical pieces, while they have on one hand afforded a security against the production of spurious works, on the other hand have given occasion to such attempts; for if some treatise, known to have been written by a celebrated author, was believed to have perished, an opportunity was presented for composing one which should correspond with the description given of it. But such spurious works must always be deficient in positive evidence, nor will they fail to betray the imposition by some glaring inconsistencies in style, or in matter. The lives of statesmen and warriors often contain such allusions to the writers of the same age, as suffice to prove the time when they flourished. All the information we possess on this head is, in many instances, derived from allusions of this sort.

4. A copious fund of quotations is contained in some ancient treatises on particular subjects, in which all the authors who have handled the same topic are mentioned in the order of time.

5. Controversies, whether literary, political, or religious, have usually occasioned extensive quotations to be made from works of all classes ; and, on the spur of an acrimonious disputation, many obscure facts have been adduced, which, by some

circuitous connection with other facts, have served to determine questions of literary history.

6. Among all the means for ascertaining the antiquity and genuineness of ancient books, none are more satisfactory or more complete than those afforded by the existence of early translations. Indeed, if such translations can be proved to have been made near to the time at which the author of the original work is believed to have lived, and if they correspond, in the main, with the existing text—and if they have descended to modern times through channels altogether independent of those which have conveyed the original work—and if, moreover, ancient translations of the same work, in *several languages*, are in existence, no kind of proof can be more perfect, or more trustworthy. In such cases every other evidence might safely be dispensed with. Ancient translations serve also the important purpose of furnishing a criterion by which to judge of the comparative merits of manuscripts, and by which also to determine questions of suspected interpolation.

Although the genuineness of by far the greater part of ancient literature is established by a redundancy of testimonies, such as those here described, there will of course be some few instances of works which, though probably genuine, are so destitute of external proof that they must remain under doubt; and there are also some few which, though probably spurious, possess just so much plausible proof of genuineness as serves to maintain a place for them on the ground of controversy. The two together, therefore, will yield some number of disputable cases. The controversies that have actually been carried on relative to such doubtful works have served to show the exceedingly small chance which any actually spurious work can have of escaping suspicion and detection. And thus these discussions furnish, implicitly, the strongest grounds for relying upon the genuineness of those works against which even a captious and whimsical scepticism can maintain no plausible objection.

CHAPTER IV.

THE ANTIQUITY AND GENUINENESS OF ANCIENT BOOKS MAY BE INFERRED FROM THE HISTORY OF THE LANGUAGES IN WHICH THEY ARE EXTANT.

A LANGUAGE is at once the most complete, and it is the least fallible of all historical records. A poem or a history may have been forged; but a language is an unquestionable reality. The bare circumstance of its existence, though it may long have ceased to be colloquially extant, proves, in substance, what it is which history has to communicate. If we did but possess a complete vocabulary of an ancient language, and if we were to digest the mass in accordance with an exact principle of synthesis, we should frame a model of the people that once used it—a model more perfect than any other monuments can furnish: and on this ground we need fear no falsifications, no concealments, no flatteries, no exaggerations. The precise extent of knowledge and of civilisation to which a people attained—nothing more and nothing less, is marked out in the mass of words of which they were accustomed to make use.

A language, if the comparison may be admitted, might be called a *cast* of the people who spoke it —a cast, taken from the very life; and it is one which represents the world of mind, as well as the world of matter. The common objects of nature—

the peculiarities of climate—the works of art—
the details of domestic life—political institutions
—religious opinions and observances—philosophy,
poetry, and art—every form and hue of the external world, and every modification of thought,
find their representatives in the language of the
people.

In any case, therefore, if we have a complete
knowledge of a language—that is to say, of the
words of which it consists—we possess a mass of
facts by aid of which to judge of the claims to
authenticity of every work in which that language
is embodied. And if, in addition to a knowledge
of its vocabulary, the laws of its construction also,
and the nicest proprieties of its syntax and style are
known; and if, moreover, the changes that have
taken place from age to age in the sense of words,
and in modes of expression, are understood, we
then possess ample and exact *data* with which to
compare any book that pretends to antiquity. A
writer who employs his native language must be
expected to conform himself to its usages; and we
should find him adhering, more or less strictly, to
the peculiarities of the age in which he writes:
his vocabulary, moreover, will include that compass
of words which his subject demands, and which
the language affords.

It is true that such a degree of skill in a dead
language may be acquired as may enable a writer
to use it with so exact a propriety as shall deceive,
or at least perplex, even the most accomplished
scholars. But the difficulty of avoiding every
phrase of later origin, and all modern senses of
those words which are continually passing from a
literal to a metaphorical meaning, is so great, as to

leave the chances of escaping detection extremely small. Yet, as such a chance still remains within the range of possibility, this line of evidence cannot be reckoned absolutely conclusive, but must only be employed as subsidiary to those other evidences that bear upon questions of authenticity.

The minute changes which are continually taking place in most languages, and the history of which, when known, serves often to ascertain the date of ancient books, are of two kinds; namely, those which result necessarily from actual changes in the objects represented by words, and those which are mere changes in the use and proprieties of language itself.

Language being a mirror, reflecting all the communicable notions of the people who use it, every mutation in the condition of the people must bring with it, either new terms, or new combinations of words; and as the particular circumstances which introduce such additions or alterations are often known, their occurrence in an author may serve to fix the date of the book, almost with certainty.

Moreover, there is a progression in language itself, independent of any alterations in the objects represented by words. Whenever a vocabulary affords a choice of appellatives, even for immutable objects or notions, the caprices of conversation or of literature—affectation perhaps, or excessive refinement, will, from time to time, occasion a new selection to be made. In all those terms, especially, which either bring with them ideas too familiar to accord with the proprieties of an elevated style, or which are in any degree offensive to delicacy, there will take place a continual, and sometimes, even a rapid, substitution of new for old phrases —not because the new are in themselves more dignified, or more pure than the old; but because, when first introduced, they are untainted by gross associations or vulgar use.

Every language, therefore, copious specimens of which are extant, and of which the progress is known, contains a latent history of the people through whose lips it has passed, and furnishes to the scholar a series of recondite dates, by means of which literary remains may almost with certainty be assigned to their proper age. This sort of evidence bears the same relation to the history of *books*, which that derived from the successive changes known to have taken place in the mode of writing bears to the history of *manuscripts.* It is of a subsidiary kind, and from its very indirectness it often deserves peculiar attention.

We have now seen on what grounds it is, generally, that with reasonable confidence the extant works of ancient authors may be accepted as being such in truth. In presenting this statement of the case, nothing more has been attempted than to offer an outline or brief summary of the argument before us. Certain parts of this argument, as the reader will at once perceive, would admit of much amplification; and in any instance in which the genuineness of a particular manuscript, or the authenticity of an ancient work were alleged to be questionable, every part of the evidence would require to be brought forward in all its details, and to be narrowly scrutinised.

CHAPTER V.

ANCIENT METHODS OF WRITING, AND THE MATERIALS OF BOOKS.

As our present inquiry relates to *Books*, it will not be expected to include anything concerning ancient methods of engraving inscriptions upon marbles, metals, or precious stones. Yet it should be remembered that a knowledge of inscriptions is often highly important, as furnishing subsidiary and independent means of determining the age of manuscripts, as indicated by the character of the writing. For as there are extant almost innumerable specimens of writing upon the more durable materials, and as these specimens belong to every age from the very earliest times, and as such inscriptions usually contain, either an explicit date, or some allusion to public persons or events, they serve to determine, beyond doubt, the successive changes that have taken place in the form of letters, and in the modes of writing.

MATERIALS OF ANCIENT BOOKS.

No material for books has, perhaps, a higher claim to antiquity than the skin of the calf or goat, tanned soft, and which usually was dyed red or yellow: the skins, when thus prepared, were most often connected in lengths, sometimes of a hundred feet, sufficient to contain an entire work; or one *book* of a history or treatise, which then formed a roll, or *volume*. These soft skins seem to have been more in use among the Jews and other Asiatics than among the people of Europe. The copies of the Hebrew Scriptures, found in the synagogues of the Jews, are often of this kind: the most ancient manuscripts extant are some copies of the Pentateuch, on rolls of crimson leather.

Parchment—Pergamena, so called long after the time of its first use, from Pergamus, a city of Mysia, where the manufacture was improved and carried on to a great extent, is mentioned by Herodotus and Ctesias, as a material which had been from time immemorial used for books. It has proved itself to be, of all others, except that above mentioned, the most durable. The greater part of all those manuscripts, now in our hands, that are of higher antiquity than the sixth century, are on parchment; as well as, generally, all carefully written, and curiously decorated manuscripts, of later times. The palimpsests, mentioned in a preceding chapter, are usually parchments.

The practice, which is still followed in the East, of writing upon the leaves of trees, is of great antiquity. The leaves of the mallow, or of the palm, were those the most used for this purpose; sometimes they were wrought together so as to form larger surfaces; but it is probable that so fragile and inconvenient a material was employed rather for ordinary purposes of business, letter-writing, and the instruction of children, than for books, intended for preservation.

The inner bark of the linden or teil tree, and perhaps of some others, called by the Romans *Liber*, by the Greeks *Biblos*, was so generally used as a material for writing, as to have given its name to *a book*, in both languages. Tables of solid wood called *codices*—whence the term *codex*, for a manuscript, on any material, has passed into common use—were also employed; but this was chiefly for legal documents, on which account a system of laws came to be called—a Code. Leaves or tablets of lead, or of ivory, are frequently mentioned by ancient authors as in common use for writing. But no material or preparation seems to have been so frequently employed, on ordinary occasions, as tablets covered with a thin coat of coloured wax, which might be readily removed by an iron needle, called a *style;* and from which the writing was as easily effaced, by applying the blunt end of the same instrument.

But during many ages the article most in use, and of which the consumption was so great as to form a principle branch of the commerce of the Mediterranean, was that which was manufactured from the papyrus of Egypt. Many manuscripts written upon this kind of paper in the sixth, and some even so early as the fourth century, are still extant. It formed the material of by far the larger proportion of all books from very early times till about the seventh or eight century, when it gradually gave place to a still more convenient manufacture—our modern paper.

The papyrus, or reed of Egypt, grew in vast quantities in the stagnant pools that were formed by the annual inundations of the Nile. The plant consists of a single stem, rising sometimes to the height of ten cubits: this stem, gradually tapering from the root, supports a spreading tuft at its summit. The substance of the stem is fibrous, and the pith contains a sweet juice. Every part of this plant was put to some use by the Egyptians —so ingenious and so industrious as they were. The harder and lower part they formed into cups and other utensils; the upper part into staves, or the ribs of boats: the sweet pith was a common article of food; while the fibrous part of the stem was manufactured into cloth, sails for ships, ropes, strings, shoes, baskets, wicks for lamps, and, especially, into paper. For this purpose the fibrous coats of the plant were peeled off, throughout the whole length of the stem. One layer of fibres was then laid across another upon a block, and being moistened, the glutinous juice of the plant formed a cement, sufficiently strong to give coherence to the fibres; when greater solidity was required, a size made from bread or glue was employed. The two films being thus connected, were pressed, dried in the sun, beaten with a broad mallet, and then polished with a shell. This texture was cut into various sizes, according to the use for which it was intended, varying from thirteen, to four fingers' breadth, and of proportionate length.

By progressive improvements, which were made especially when the manufacture came into the hands of the Roman artists, this Egyptian paper was at length brought to a high degree of perfection. In later ages it was made of considerable thickness—perfect whiteness, and an entire continuity and smoothness of surface. Nevertheless, it was, at the best, so friable, that when durability was required, the copyists inserted a page of parchment between every five or six pages of the papyrus. Thus the firmness of the one substance defended the brittleness of the other; and great numbers of books, constituted in this manner, have resisted the accidents and decays of twelve centuries.

Three hundred years before the Christian era, the commerce in the paper of Egypt had extended over most parts of the civilised world; and long afterwards it continued to be a principal source of wealth to the Egyptians. But at length the invention of another material, and also that interruption of commerce which ensued in consequence of the conquest of Egypt by the Saracens, banished the Egyptian paper from common use. Comparatively few manuscripts on this material are found of later date than the eighth or ninth century; although it continued to be occasionally used long afterwards.

The "charta bombycina," or cotton paper, which has often improperly been called *silk* paper, had unquestionably been manufactured in the East as early as the ninth century, and probably much earlier; and in the tenth century it came into general use throughout Europe. Not long afterwards, this invention was made still more available for general purposes by the substitution of old linen, or cotton rags, for the raw material; for by this means both the price of the article was reduced, and its quality greatly improved. The cotton paper manufactured in the ancient mode is still used in the East, and is a beautiful fabric; it is also extensively used in the United States.

From this account of the materials successively employed for books, it will be obvious, that a knowledge of the changes which these several manufactures underwent from age to age, will often make it easy, and especially when employed in subservience to other evidence, to fix with certainty the date of manuscripts; or at the least, to furnish infallible means for detecting fabricated documents.

The preservation of books, framed as they are of materials so destructible, through a period of twelve, or even fifteen hundred years, is a fact which might seem almost incredible; especially so as the decay of far more durable substances, within a much shorter period, is continually presented to our notice. Yet so it is, that while the massive walls of the monasteries of the middle ages are often seen prostrate, and their materials fast mingling with the soil, the manuscripts, penned within them, or perhaps at a time when these stones were yet in the quarry, are still fair and perfect, and glitter with their gold and silver, their cerulean and their cinnabar.

It must be remembered, however, that the materials of books, although destructible, are so far from being in themselves perishable, that so long as they are defended from positive injuries, they appear to suffer scarcely at all from any intrinsic principle of decay, or to be liable to any perceptible process of chemical decomposition. "No one," says Mabillon, "unless totally unacquainted with what relates to antiquity, can call in question the great durability of parchments; since there are extant innumerable books, written on that material, in the seventh and sixth centuries; and some of a still more remote antiquity, by which all doubt on that subject might be removed." It may suffice here to mention the Virgil of the Vatican Library, which appears to be of more ancient date than the fourth century; and another in the King's Library little less ancient: also the Prudentius, in the same library, of equal age; to which you may add several, already mentioned, as the Psalter of S. Germanus, the Book of the Councils, and others, which are all of parchment.

The paper of Egypt, being more frail and brittle, might be open to greater doubt; and yet there are books of great antiquity, by which its durability may be established.

Books have owed their conservation, not merely to the durability of the material of which they were formed; but to the peculiarity of their being, at once precious, and yet (in periods of general ignorance) not marketable articles; they were of inestimable value to a few, while absolutely worthless in the opinion of the multitude. They were also often indebted for their preservation, in periods of disorder and violence, to the sacredness of the roofs under which they were lodged.

THE INSTRUMENTS OF WRITING, AND INKS.

The instruments used for writing would, of course, be such as were adapted to the material on which they were to be employed. For writing upon the brazen, leaden, or waxed tablets, above mentioned, a needle, called a style, was used, the upper end of which, being smooth and flat, served to obliterate the marks on the tablet, as occasion might require. These styles were at first most often formed of iron or brass; but afterwards of ivory, bone, or wood. Indeed a fatal use having been, on several occasions, made of these pointed weapons by angry partisans in the public courts, the use of iron styles was prohibited; Cæsar, when attacked by the conspirators, is said to have used his iron style as a dagger, and with it to have pierced the arm of one of them: and the story of the Christian schoolmaster, Cassianus, is well known, who is said to have been killed by his scholars, armed with their styles: other similar instances are recorded.

For the purpose of writing with fluid ink, a calamus, formed generally from a reed of the Nile, was used. Persons of distinction often wrote with a calamus of silver. The use of quills seems to have been of ancient date; but long after the time when the fitness of the quill for the purpose of writing had become known, the calamus of reed continued to be preferred. The scalpel, or knife employed for trimming the pen, the compasses, for measuring the distances of the lines, and the scissors, for cutting the paper, are always seen on the desk of the writers in the decorations attached to many ancient manuscripts.

The ink most used by the ancients has been said, but on rather uncertain authority, to have consisted of the black liquor found in the cuttle fish. But it has been proved by chemical analysis that an opaque ink, very different from the mere dye or stain used at present, was commonly employed by the transcribers of books. This opaque ink seems, like the China ink, to have been formed from the finest soot of lamps, in which the purest combustibles were burnt. The coal of ivory, or

of the finer woods, powdered, was also in use;
these, or similar substances, mixed with gums,
and diluted with acids, formed a pigment that
was much more durable than our modern ink;
but it was also far less fluent, and therefore less
adapted to a rapid and continuous movement of
the pen.

"The ink," says Montfaucon, "which we see in
the most ancient Greek manuscripts, has evidently
lost much of its pristine blackness; yet neither
has it become altogether yellow or faint, but is
rather tawny or deep red, and often is not far
from a vermilion." This appears in many manuscripts of the fourth and following centuries. Yet
there are some written with an ink more skilfully
composed, which have preserved their first blackness. It has happened also, when the surface of
the parchment, instead of being polished, was
spongy, that the ink has become yellow. In all
the bombycine manuscripts, owing to the nature
of the material, a separation of the parts of the
ink has taken place; the grosser part standing on
the surface, while the finer has penetrated the substance of the paper.

Inks of various colours, especially red, purple,
and blue, and also gold and silver inks, were much
used by the ancients: few manuscripts are destitute of some such ornamental diversities of colour;
and many are splendidly recommended to the eye
by these means. There was a purple ink, which
was appropriated to the use of the emperors,
and was called the sacred encaustic; but a dye,
not easily distinguished from that which appears
upon some imperial charters, is very commonly
found in ancient books. And it is said that they

must have had a nice sight who could so distinguish between the two as to have detected a violation of the law on this subject. The subscription commonly seen at the end of Greek manuscripts, containing the name of the transcriber, with the year, month, day, indiction, and sometimes the hour when the copy was finished, are most often written in the imperial colour, especially in the times of the lower empire; or if not in that ink, in one that cannot now be distinguished from it.

The titles of chapters were frequently written alternately in red and cerulean: marginal notes, most often in the latter colour. Books of a later date often have all the capitals of a bright green. The Greeks, more frequently than the Romans, used golden ink; and many Greek manuscripts are extant in which, not the titles and capitals only, but whole pages, are elegantly written in a pigment of the precious metals: but it was rather upon ecclesiastical than profane literature that this honour was bestowed. The works of the Fathers, chiefly, were so adorned, and sometimes the Gospels: there is extant a copy of the four Evangelists, written upon purple parchment, in letters of gold throughout. The practice of using gold and silver inks was so common, that the manufacture of them became a distinct business; and those who were skilled in this sort of writing seldom followed any other employment than that of inserting the titles, capitals, or emphatic words, in copies that had been executed by inferior hands. Several curious recipes for the preparation of the precious pigments are given by the later Greek writers.

Those who have been long accustomed to inspect and examine ancient manuscripts acquire a certain tact in judging of the age of a book from the condition of the ink, its colour and composition, which cannot be explained to others, and for the exercise of which no rules can be laid down. But in cases where a fraud is suspected, this nice habit of the eye often detects at once the imposition. It is perhaps more practicable to give to a picture, than to a manuscript, the hue of antiquity by artificial means.

CHAPTER VI.

CHANGES INTRODUCED IN THE COURSE OF TIME IN THE FORMS OF LETTERS, AND IN THE GENERAL CHARACTER OF WRITING.

An exact uniformity in the shapes of letters, and in the general appearance of writing, is hardly maintained for so long a period as fifty years in any language, especially if it be widely diffused. Within that space of time, the fashion of our own typography has undergone several changes, so perceptible as to afford a tolerably certain criterion of the date of books. No person, for example, who is familiar with books, would find it difficult, merely from the character of the type, to discriminate the age of works published at the several periods of 1775, 1800, 1825, and 1855. On similar grounds a knowledge of the successive changes introduced by caprice, accident, or a regard to convenience, in the ancient modes of writing, affords an almost certain means of determining the age of manuscripts.

The knowledge requisite for the exercise of this discrimination is derived, in part, from incidental allusions to modes of writing which occur in some ancient authors; but principally from an extensive comparison of manuscripts themselves, and from a comparison of manuscripts with inscriptions upon marbles, brazen tablets, or coins.

STYLE OF WRITING.

From these sources may be collected a sufficiently precise idea of the character or fashion of writing prevailing in each century, from the second to the fifteenth, of the Christian era.

The oldest Greek manuscripts that are extant differ little in the form of the letters, or the general appearance of the writing, from inscriptions belonging to the corresponding periods. They are written in capitals, called uncials, without division of words, and without marks of accentuation or punctuation. About the seventh century, the custom of affixing the accents and aspirates appears to have been introduced; at the same time a greater degree of precision was observed in the formation of the letters, and also in the directness and the parallelism of the lines. To these improvements was added a change in the form of those letters which most impeded the rapid movement of the pen.

In the eighth and ninth centuries a mode of writing, which had been long before practised by notaries and by the secretaries of public persons, was adopted by the transcribers of books. This was a kind of running-hand, those who invented, or who most used it, being called tachygraphoi— swift writers. To adapt the Greek letters to the purpose of public business and common life, the square forms had been changed for curves, and uprights for slopes: and while a radical resemblance to the primitive character was preserved, facility and freedom were obtained.

The uncial character was not, however, altogether abandoned by the copyists; but modifications of it were introduced with a view to obtain greater facility: for the unconnected and upright squares formerly used, seemed still more operose in execution after the running-hand had been adopted. The copyists of the eighth century introduced the practice of commencing books or chapters with a letter of large size, which they usually distinguished by grotesque decorations, somewhat in the manner seen in the printed books of the sixteenth century.

Those who gained their living by copying books found so great an advantage in the adoption of the swift, or tachygraphic character, that they presently sought to improve it by every device that might favour the uninterrupted movement of the pen; not content with joining the letters of each word, they combined them in forms that often bore little or no resemblance to the component characters. The books of the tenth and following centuries abound with these contractions, abbreviations, and symbols. Many entire words of common occurrence were indicated by single turns of the pen. A great part of these contractions were adopted by the first printers, and many of them continued in use until a very recent date.

The manuscripts of the twelfth and thirteenth centuries are distinguished by a degeneracy in the mode of writing, and by a growing abuse of the principle of celerity and facility. To these symptoms of the influence of a mercantile motive, put into activity by an increasing demand for books, may be added the practice of discharging the writing of old parchments, which prevailed at the same period more extensively than heretofore. A vast number of books of this sort, written upon erased parchments, are to be met with, executed in the twelfth, thirteenth, and fourteenth centuries.

In most instances, the first writing is utterly obliterated; yet the marks of the erasure are still evident. Thus in a MS. above described, not a letter, not a point, of the ancient writing remains; but on many of the leaves may be discerned ruled lines, either transverse or perpendicular, which having been deeply impressed upon the parchment could not be effaced; so that those old lines often crossed the new writing. Other pages of the same MS. present no such indications; the leaves having probably been taken from different books. In another MS., executed in the year 1186, though the ancient writing is generally obliterated, yet in a few places, if closely inspected, the ends of the letters may be perceived. In a word, if all the books of the thirteenth and fourteenth centuries are examined, there will appear to be almost as many written upon erased, as upon new parchments.* I am of opinion, that many authors extant in the time of Photius, and even in that of Porphyrogenitus, were utterly destroyed by the prevalence of this pernicious practice. This plague, as it may be termed, spread its devastation among ancient books first in the twelve century, and continued its ravages during the thirteenth and fourteenth. The same thing is rarely to be observed in bombycine manuscripts: I have met with one book only of this material in which the first writing had been erased, and a second induced. The Greek writers of these times ordinarily erased a better work for the sake of substituting a worse; either one of their own inane productions, or those works of which there is no scarcity among MSS. The extremest ignorance must

* Montfaucon.

certainly have pervaded Greece in those times, when what related to ancient history, or to polite learning, was not valued a straw by the writers, who rather than purchase new parchment, destroyed, without scruple, ancient books.

A progression similar to that which took place in Greek writing, distinguishes manuscripts in the Latin language, and affords a like criterion of antiquity. Several manuscripts believed, on good evidence, to belong to the third and fourth centuries, are extant, which present a style of writing nearly allied to that which appears in the inscriptions of the same period. But the uncial character gave place to the small letter at an earlier date among the Roman, than among the Greek copyists; yet they seem to have availed themselves of the change in a much less degree for the purposes of celerity. Indeed, there is little more of continuity, or of abbreviation in the small, than in the large character. Towards the tenth century the Latin scribes adopted a square and heavy character, similar to that which is seen in legal documents. This wide and full-faced letter was so much exaggerated by the writers of the fourteenth century, as almost to blacken the page with its massiveness. Still, a handsome regularity and a fair degree of legibility were maintained. There are, indeed, some manuscripts of this period extant which, for mathematical exactness and beauty, might almost challenge comparison with printed books.

Nothing less, it is obvious, than a long-continued and extensive examination of ancient manuscripts, can confer upon any one such a degree of skill in discriminations of this kind, as might warrant his

STYLE OF WRITING. 55

giving an opinion in a case of difficulty. Yet the mere inspection of a small number of these relics of antiquity may convince any one of the reality and distinctness of those progressive changes in the modes of writing upon which such discriminations are founded. The architecture of different periods is not more characteristic of the age to which it belongs, than is the style of writing in manuscripts; nor is there less certainty in determining questions of antiquity in the one case, than in the other. Particular instances may perplex or deceive the best-informed and the most acute observers; but the greater number of cases admit of no question.

FORM OF ANCIENT BOOKS, AND THEIR ILLUMINATIONS.

The mode of compacting the sheets of their books remained the same among the Greeks during a long course of time: little, therefore, pertinent to our argument, is to be gathered on this head. The sheets were folded three or four together, and separately stitched: these parcels were then connected nearly in the same mode as is at present practised. Books were covered with linen, silk, or leather.

Sometimes the page was undivided; sometimes it contained two, and in a few instances of very ancient manuscripts, three columns. A peculiarity which attracts the eye in many Greek manuscripts, consists in the occurrence of capitals on the margin, some way in advance of the line to which they belong; and this capital sometimes happens to be the middle letter of a word. For when a sentence finishes in the middle of a line, the initial of the text is not distinguished, that honour being conferred upon the incipient letter of the next line; as thus—

          THEGREEKSENTERING
          THEREGIONOFTHEMA
          CRONESFORMEDANAL
          LIANCEWITHTHEM.AS
T   HEPLEDGEOFTHEIR
          FAITHTHEBARBARIANS
          GAVEASPEAR.

The Greeks, especially in the earliest times, divided their compositions into verses; or into such short portions of sentences as we mark by a comma, each verse occupying a line; and the number of these verses is often set down at the beginning or end of a book. The numbers of the verses were sometimes placed in the margin.

Much intricacy and difficulty attends the subject of ancient punctuation; nor could any satisfactory account of the rules and exceptions that have been gathered from existing manuscripts be given, which should subserve the intention of this work. Generally speaking, and yet with frequent exceptions, the most ancient books have no separation of words, or punctuation, of any kind; others have a separation of words, but no punctuation; in some, every word is separated from the following one by a point. In manuscripts of later date a regular punctuation is found, as well as accentuation. These circumstances enter into the estimate when the antiquity of a book is under inquiry; but the rules to be observed in considering them cannot be otherwise than recondite and intricate.

Few ancient books are altogether destitute of decorations; and many are splendidly adorned with pictorial ornaments. These consist either of flowery initials, grotesque cyphers, portraits, or even historical compositions. Sometimes diagrams, explanatory of the subjects mentioned by the author, are placed on the margin. Books written for the use of royal persons, or of dignified ecclesiastics, usually contain the effigies of the proprietor, often attended by his family, and by some allegorical or celestial minister; while the humble scribe, in monkish attire, kneels and presents the book to his patron.

These illuminations, as they are called, almost always exhibit some costume of the times, or some peculiarity which serves to mark the age of the manuscript. Indeed a fund of antiquarian information, relative to the middle ages, has been collected from this source. Many of these pictured books exhibit a high degree of executive talent in the artist, although labouring under the restraints of a barbarous taste.

CHAPTER VII.

THE COPYISTS; AND THE PRINCIPAL CENTRES OF THE COPYING BUSINESS.

It is a matter of some importance to know by what class of persons, chiefly, the business of copying books was practised; and it gives no little support to our confidence in the genuineness of existing manuscripts, to find that individuals of all ranks, influenced by very different motives, were accustomed to devote themselves to this employment. From the earliest times in which literature flourished, there were, in all the principal cities of Greece and its colonies, great numbers of professional scribes; that is to say, persons who gained their subsistence by copying books. Labourers of this class, it may well be supposed, aimed, in general, at nothing but to gain custom by the fairness and the fidelity of their copies. But it appears to have been not uncommon for persons of rank and leisure to occupy themselves in this employment. Thus it is that in the list of copyists we find the names of the nobles of the Constantinopolitan empire. Some created their libraries for themselves by transcribing every book that came in their way. To persons of a sedate temper, or who by indisposition were confined to their homes, this occupation may be imagined to have been highly agreeable. Nor was it a wasted labour to those who had leisure at command; since the high price of books made the collection of a library, by purchase, scarcely practicable, except to the most opulent.

The influence of Christianity very greatly extended the practice of private copying; for motives of piety operated to stimulate the industry of very many in the good work of multiplying the sacred books, and the works of Christian writers. The highest dignitaries of the Church, and princes even, thought themselves well employed in transcribing the Gospels and Epistles, the Psalter, or the homilies or meditations of the Fathers; nor were the classic authors, as we shall see, entirely neglected by these gratuitous copyists.

But from the third or fourth century downwards, the religious houses were the chief sources of books, and the monks were almost the only copyists. The employment was better suited than any other that can be imagined, to the rules, and usages, and to the modes of feeling peculiar to the monastic life. The mental and bodily inertness which the spirit and rules of the conventual orders tended to produce, when conjoined, in individuals, with some measure of native industry, would find precisely a field for that lethargic assiduity which it needed, in the business of copying books. In many monasteries this employment formed the chief occupation of the inmates; and by few was it altogether neglected.

Various appellations occur in the Greek authors, by which the several orders of writers were designated. Among the scribes or notaries attached to the service of public persons, there were always some who were eminent for the rapidity with which they wrote, and who therefore bore the title of *tachygraphoi*, or "swift writers." But those who followed the business of copying books, in which legibility was the chief excellence, generally called themselves *kalligraphoi*, or "fair writers." Yet these appellations are often used interchangeably.

The copyists usually subscribed their names at the end of every book, with the year in which it was executed: to which they often added the name of the reigning emperor; sometimes, though rarely, the name of the patriarch of Constantinople, for the time being, is added to the subscription of the copyist. Manuscripts written in Sicily, bear the name of its kings; those executed in the East, mention the Arabian or Turkish princes. The Greeks of the early ages commonly dated from the creation of the world, which they placed 5508 years before Christ. Sometimes they reckoned time from the death of Alexander the Great; sometimes from the accession of Philip Aridæus; sometimes from the accession of Diocletian; and, occasionally, they give some notice of the signal events of their times. From these incidental references much important historical information has often been collected. These signatures are usually written by the hand of the transcriber of the book.

Besides the signature of the copyist, the margins of many manuscripts contain notes—often very trivial or absurd, from the hands of successive proprietors of the book; each accompanied with some date or reference to persons or events, serving to fix the time of the annotator, and, by inference, proving the antiquity of the manuscript. In a few instances the transcribers copied the subscription of the transcribers of the book from which they wrote; and if that former subscription bears a date, we have a double indication of antiquity.

The fidelity of the copyists, and the genuineness and integrity of ancient manuscripts, have been warmly and learnedly defended by the laborious Father Mabillon, on every occasion throughout his great work, *De Re Diplomatica*.* The leading motive which impelled the indefatigable author to the prosecution of the researches of which this work gives the result, seems to have been the desire to establish the genuineness and integrity of ecclesiastical, and especially of monastic charters. In the course of his inquiries, he brings forward a vast variety and amount of information relating to the modes of writing practised in the monasteries, and in the courts of the French kings, during the middle ages. These facts are of course most available in arguments that relate to the genuineness and antiquity of existing manuscripts in the *Latin* language; but there is so much of the substance of the argument touching the genuineness of all ancient writings in the following passages, that they may well be placed before the reader. The work itself is little likely to come under the eye of those for whom this volume is intended.

* DE RE DIPLOMATICA, Libri vi. in quibus quidquid ad veterum instrumentorum antiquitatem, materiam, scripturam et stilum; quidquid ad sigilla, monogrammata, subscriptiones ac notas chronologicas; quidquid inde ad antiquariam, historicam, forensemque disciplinam pertinet, explicatur et illustratur. Op. et Stud. JOH. MABILLON.—Fol. Paris, 1709.

This learned writer says:—" Before I conclude this supplement, I think it may be proper to say something concerning the integrity and authority of ancient books, which some persons dispute. For assuredly, if the genuineness of charters and public deeds is doubted, the authority of ancient manuscripts in general is also called in question; and, if these doubts can be substantiated, it will appear that those who employ themselves in collating the printed editions of the Fathers, or other sacred books, with ancient manuscripts, spend their labour in vain. And hence, too, we must believe, contrary to the opinion of all learned persons, who think the world greatly indebted to the labours of the monks in transcribing books, that they toiled to no good purpose. Such persons, to give colour to their opinion, affirm that the existing ancient manuscripts were executed by ignorant men, whose blunders are easily perceived by the learned; and on this prejudice they have founded the decision, that manuscripts having been written for the most part, by unskilful hands, and derived many from one, are of little avail in understanding or restoring an author.

"But if this principle were admitted, our confidence in the printed editions, as well as in the ancient manuscripts, must fall to the ground. Neither the acts of councils, the works of the Fathers, nor the Holy Scriptures, would retain any authority. For whence, I ask, proceeded the printed editions, both of profane and sacred writers? were they not derived from ancient manuscripts? If, therefore, these are of no authority, those can have none; and thus, by this paradoxical opinion, the foundations, both of

CENTRES OF THE COPYING BUSINESS. 63

literature and of religion, are torn up. And, on this principle, there would be no force in the argument used by St. Augustine against the Manichæans, who calumniously affirmed every place of Holy Scripture, by which their errors might be confuted, to be falsified and corrupted. But Augustine, in reply to Faustus, reminds him that whoever had first attempted such a corruption of the Scriptures, would have immediately been confuted by a multitude of ancient manuscripts, which were in the hands of all Christians.

"On this principle the labours of the Fathers, Jerome, Augustine, and others, in collating ancient books with modern copies, would have been fruitless. In vain the appeals of councils to such authorities for the determination of controversies; in vain the costs and cares of princes and kings in collecting manuscripts from the remotest countries. And if the case be thus, the Vatican, the Florentine, the Abrosian, and the royal (French) libraries are nothing better than useless heaps of parchment. And it was to no purpose that the Roman pontiffs and the kings of France, as well as other prelates and princes, sent learned men to the farthest parts of the East to obtain ancient books in the Latin, Greek, Hebrew, and other languages. And then the ancient transcribers must lose their credit, and especially the monks, who devoted themselves entirely to the copying of books; such were the disciples of St. Martin, among whom, according to Sulpicius, no art but that of writing was practised. For they thought they could not be better imployed than while at once edifying themselves in the continual perusal of the Holy Scriptures, and spreading the precepts of the

Lord far and wide by their pens. Of this opinion was the pious Guigo: 'As we cannot preach the word with our lips,' says he, 'let us do it with our hands; for as many books as we transcribe, so many heralds of the truth do we send forth.' And thus also Peter the venerable, writing to Gislebert, a recluse, exhorts him to diligence, in this exercise: 'For so you may become a silent preacher of the Divine Word; and though your tongue be mute, your hand will speak aloud in the ears of many people. And in future times, after your death, the fruit of your toils will remain, even as long as these books shall endure.'

"If it is affirmed that the manuscripts we possess were, for the most part, written by unlearned persons; are they therefore undeserving of regard? In the first place, I deny that they were generally written by the unlearned. Certainly the blessed martyr Pamphilus, who wrote out the greater part of the works of Origen, was not unlearned; nor was Jerome unlearned, nor Hilarius. Of Fulgentius, the celebrated bishop (of Ruspa), it is reported that he was famed for his skill in the writer's art. The same praise was earned by those holy men Lucianus, Philoromus, and Marcellus; also by the blessed Plato and Theophanus. The blessed Marcella the younger, as says Jerome, wrote quickly and without fault. The venerable Bede, Radbert, Raban and others among our learned men, discharged the function of copyists, not of their own works only, but of those of others.

"And even if the greater part of manuscripts were written by unlearned men, they are not therefore to be accounted unskilful copyists, provided they read and copied accurately. Experience proves every day that those compositors are not the most correct who understand Latin, but that such are commonly the most faulty; especially in attempting to correct that which they do not properly understand, and which those who know nothing of the language set up accurately. But let it be granted that the copyists were unlearned: we know that the printed editions are not derived from a single copy, but from a comparison of many: the most careless scribe does not always err, and where he does, his mistakes are amended by the collation of the copies of others.

"In a word, there were in all well-ordered churches and monasteries, not only learned writers who transcribed books themselves, but learned correctors, who compared the copies made by others with the originals, and amended whatever was erroneous. 'A devoted scribe,' says Trithemius, 'when he has carefully written a book, compares it anew with the original, and subjects it to a diligent revision.' Many instances might be adduced in proof of this revision and correction of manuscripts. One or two may suffice. In the library of the Vatican there is a manuscript written towards the close of the fifth, or in the beginning of the sixth century, containing the books of St. Hilary on the Trinity, which has been collated with an older copy by some studious person, as appears by a note at the end. Again, Paul Warnefrid, deacon and monk of Casina, having copied the epistles of Gregory the Great, sent the book to Adalhard, abbot of Corbeia, requesting him to revise the copy; but the abbot, fearing lest he might alter the genuine text of so learned a doctor, contented himself with placing a mark in the margin at every place where there appeared to him to be an error.

"But it is affirmed that there are many faulty, and many falsified manuscripts. That there are not a few faulty books I grant; but that there are many falsified manuscripts I stoutly deny. The difference between a *faulty* and a *falsified* book is essential: of the former sort are those which, from the mistakes or negligence of the writer, contain some blemishes: of the latter kind are those which have been wilfully corrupted. Many, indeed, may appear to be falsified which are not so really, nor are even faulty. Which I may thus explain.—It could not but happen that the copyists in transcribing large works, should sometimes wander from the true reading—putting perhaps one word for another. When they observed their error, they might rectify it in two ways, either by erasing the word and inserting the genuine reading; or by inserting the true word beneath the other which they marked with points. Now some persons, not understanding this, or purposely putting upon it an unfavourable construction, found upon the first case a charge of *erasure,* and in the second, place both words in the text of the author, though the pointed word ought to be omitted. Sometimes also it happened that words or initials written in vermilion, having grown pale, were renewed by a later hand, which alterations have occasioned an unfounded suspicion of falsification."

The pens of the monastic scribes were chiefly occupied in transcribing religious books, the Holy Scriptures, the works of the Fathers, the lives of saints, books of meditations and prayers; yet the classic authors were not neglected. "The Monastery of Pomposia has been much improved since the time of its founder Guido [about 1025], renowned for sanctity. Incited by the fame of his piety great numbers assumed the sacred habit in his church; marquesses, counts, and sons of noblemen have laid aside the pomps and pleasures of the world to follow there the duties of religion. Among these my master Jerome, afterwards abbot, was trained up from his earliest years to follow the monastic life, and made great proficiency in grammar and logic. He, for the edification of the brotherhood, set himself to collect the works of learned men; in order that amidst the variety, all might meet with the information they sought for. Bonus—good—both in name and life, who was first a hermit and afterwards a monk, was his librarian, a man esteemed by all as a perfect scholar, and so eager in the acquisition of books that he purchased all he met with, however indistinctly they were written; for the abbot determined to have them all transcribed for his library: and by his care almost all are now copied. He is ever inquisitive for religious books of all kinds, so that the church of Pomposia is become the most renowned in Italy. Thus by the goodness of God our thirst of knowledge is increased by knowing. Indeed the abbot's desire of enriching his church with these treasures is unbounded. But envious persons may ask, Why does this reverend abbot place the heathen authors, the histories of tyrants, and such books, among theological works? To this we answer in the words of the apostle, that there are vessels of clay as well as of gold. By these means the tastes of all men are excited to study—the intention of the gentile writings is the same as that of the Scriptures, to give us a contempt for the world and secular greatness." *

By these or similar apologies those of the monks, and there were some such in most houses, who possessed taste and learning, excused, to the more devout, the attention they bestowed upon the works of the profane authors. That the Greek and Latin classics were known and studied during what are called the dark ages, is capable of abundant proof, as we shall presently see. And those whose taste led them to be conversant with these writings took care, by the labours of their hands, to perpetuate the works they most admired.

During the flourishing period of the Grecian republics, that is, from the defeat of Xerxes to the time of Alexander the Great, many of the Greek colonies almost equalled, or even surpassed, the mother country in wealth, refinement, and intelligence. In the neighbouring islands of the Ægean Sea—in Asia Minor—in Italy and in Sicily, literature and philosophy were as eagerly cultivated as at Athens. Many of the most distinguished writers and philosophers were natives of the colonies; and if Greece itself was the principal seat of learning, and the fountain head of books, whatever was there produced quickly found its way to distant settlements; for to every city along the shores of the Mediterranean, and of the Euxine, there was a constant exportation of books: in many of these remote cities libraries were collected, and the business of copying was extensively carried on.

* Italian Diary.

After the time of Alexander, Grecian literature flourished nowhere so conspicuously as at Alexandria in Egypt, under the auspices of the Ptolemies. Here all the sects of philosophy had established themselves; numerous schools were opened; and, for the advancement of learning, a library was collected, which was supposed, at one time, to have contained 700,000 volumes, in all languages. Connected with the library there were extensive offices, in which the business of transcribing books was carried on very largely, and with every possible advantage which royal munificence on the one hand, and learned assiduity on the other, could insure. Nor did the literary fame of Alexandria decline under the Roman emperors. Domitian, as Suetonis reports, sent scribes to Alexandria to copy books for the restoration of those libraries that had been destroyed by fire. And it seems to have been for some centuries afterwards a common practice for those who wished to form a library, to maintain copyists at Alexandria. The conquest of Egypt by the Saracens, A.D. 640, who burned the Alexandrian Library, banished learning for a time from that, as from other countries, which they occupied.

Attalus, and his successors, the kings of Pergamus, were great encouragers of learning; and the copying of books was carried on to so great an extent in their capital as to occasion the establishment of a vast manufacture of prepared skins (as mentioned above) which long continued to be a considerable article of commerce. The library of the kings of Pergamus is said to have contained 200,000 books.

During upwards of a thousand years, from the

reign of Constantine until the fall of Constantinople, in the fifteenth century, that city was the principal seat of learning, and the chief source of books. The Byzantine historians are frequent in their praises of the munificence of the emperors in purchasing books, and in providing for their reproduction. The manuscripts executed at Constantinople are often remarkable for the great beauty of the writing, and the splendour of the decorations. Besides the imperial libraries, the churches and monasteries of the city were enriched with collections, more or less extensive, and in all of them the business of transcription was constantly and actively pursued.

A large number of existing manuscripts are dated from the monasteries of the country immediately surrounding the metropolis of the eastern empire; and many also, from those of Asia Minor, from the islands of the Ægean Sea, and especially from Cyprus.

But no spot was more famed for the production of books than Mount Athos—the lofty promontory which stretches from the Macedonian coast far into the Ægean Sea. The heights and the sides of this mountain were almost covered with religious houses, rendered by art and nature, and by the universal opinion of the sanctity of the monks of the "holy mountain," so secure that neither the meditations nor employments of the recluses were disturbed by the approach of violence. The chief occupation of the inmates of these establishments is affirmed to have been the transcription of books, of which each monastery boasted a large collection.

Many extant manuscripts prove that the copying of books was practised extensively during the middle ages in the monasteries of the Morea, in those of the islands of Eubœa and of Crete. This latter island seems indeed to have been a place of refuge for men of learning during the latter periods of the eastern empire, who found in its monasteries, both shelter, and the means of subsistence.

Fifty religious establishments in Calabria, and the kingdom of Naples, are mentioned, from which proceeded a large number of books afterwards collected in the libraries of Rome, Florence, Venice, and Milan.

In the monasteries of western Europe also, and especially in those of the British Islands, this system of copying was carried on. Though there were considerable diversities in the rules and practices of the monks of different orders, the elements of the monastic life were in all orders and in every country the same; and generally speaking, wherever there were monasteries, there was a manufacture of books. Yet, in some houses, these labours of the pen were much more worthily directed than in others. For while the monks of one monastery employed themselves in transcribing missals, legends, or romances, others enriched their libraries with splendid copies of the Fathers of the Church, and of the Holy Scriptures; and some, though a smaller number, took care to reproduce such of the classic authors as they might be acquainted with.

The monastic institution seemed as if it were framed for the special purpose of transmitting the remains of ancient literature—sacred and profane, through a period in which, except for so extraordinary a provision, they must inevitably have perished. In every country a large class of the community—freed from the necessity of labour, and excluded from active employments, was constrained to seek the means of allaying the pains of listlessness; and nothing could answer this purpose so well as the transcription of books. And to this employment, congruous as it was with the physical habits that are induced by an inert mode of life, and compatible, too, with the observance of a round of unvarying formalities, was attached an opinion of meritoriousness, which served to animate the diligence of the labourer. "This book, copied by M. N. for the benefit of his soul, was finished in the year ——, may the Lord think upon him." Such are the subscriptions of many of the manuscripts of the middle ages.

> "Meanwhile along the cloister's painted side,
> The monks—each bending low upon his book
> With head on hand reclined—their studies plied;
> Forbid to parley, or in front to look,
> Lengthways their regulated seats they took:
> The strutting prior gazed with pompous mien,
> And wakeful tongue, prepared with prompt rebuke,
> If monk asleep in sheltering hood was seen;
> He wary often peeped beneath that russet screen.
>
> "Hard by, against the window's adverse light,
> Where desks were wont in length of row to stand,
> The gowned artificers inclined to write;
> The pen of silver glistened in the hand;
> Some on their fingers rhyming Latin scanned;
> Some textile gold from balls unwinding drew,
> And on strained velvet stately portraits planned;
> Here arms, there faces shone in embryo view,
> At last to glittering life the total figures grew."
> FOSBROOKE.

CHAPTER VIII.

INDICATIONS OF THE SURVIVANCE OF ANCIENT LITERATURE, THROUGH A PERIOD EXTENDING FROM THE DECLINE OF LEARNING IN THE SEVENTH CENTURY, TO ITS RESTORATION IN THE FIFTEENTH.

GENERAL epithets usually carry with them a meaning that oversteps the bounds of truth : we hear of "the dark ages"—"the period of intellectual night"—"the season of winter in the history of man"—and we are apt to imagine that during the times thus designated the human mind had become utterly palsied, and that all learning was extinct. But in fact throughout that period, reason, though often misdirected, was not sleeping: philosophy was rather bewildered than inert; and learning, although immured, was not lost.

In no part of the period that extends from the reign of Justinian, when Greek and Roman literature everywhere lay open to the light of day, till the fall of the Constantinopolitan empire, and the revival of western learning in the fifteenth century, do we lose the traces even of the classic authors, much less of those that belong to sacred literature; for in each of the intervening ages, and in every quarter of Europe, there were writers whose works, being still extant, give evidence of their acquaintance with most of the principal authors of more remote times.

Under the vague impression that has been created by certain loose modes of speaking, relative to the deep and universal ignorance said to have prevailed throughout Europe during a space of seven hundred years, the existence of a large number of manuscripts of the classic authors, undoubtedly executed during those very ages of ignorance, presents a great apparent difficulty: for, from what motive, it may be asked, or for whose use, were these works transcribed, so frequently as that they were found in all parts of Europe, on the revival of learning in the fifteenth century? The facts that are now to be mentioned, will furnish a sufficient solution of this question, by proving that, in the West and in the East, during those times of general intellectual lethargy, there were more than a few individuals who cultivated polite literature with ardour, and to whom the possession and preservation of books was a matter of the liveliest interest. The names about to be mentioned—as the well-informed reader will recollect—bear but a small proportion to the whole number that might be adduced: it is sufficient for our purpose to refer to one or two writers in each century.

But before naming individual men, whose extant writings give evidence of the continuity of literature, and therefore assure us of the safe transmission of ancient books to modern times, it will be serviceable to bring clearly into view what it is which is needed for constituting the LIVING MEDIUM of this transmission. Now, for bringing this matter home to the convictions and the consciousness of the reader, let him take up his own family history, and pursue it, retrogressively, inquiring how many individuals are needed—or let us rather say how *few*—to make up a chain of historical and literary conveyance, through any given track of time past; for instance, from this present time, 1858, into the mid-time of the Elizabethan era, as thus:—

I will now assume the fact—whether it be true or not does not signify to the argument—that my progenitors in a direct line were educated persons —or if not so—that each father in the line secured for his son an ordinary grammar-school education —instruction just sufficient for making him cognisant of the most noted persons and authors of preceding times; so that, in each case, if the father himself did not teach the son, the father's friend and townsman, the schoolmaster, did it, as for instance:—From my father's own lips I received the rudiments of general history, and of literary history, so that in my boyhood I came to be familiar with all the principal names of public men and authors, up from that time to times indefinitely remote. This process of paternal instruction carries me up to the last decade of the eighteenth century: say, to the time of the breaking out of the French Revolution. But then, my father had received, either from his father, or from his father's proxy, the schoolmaster, a like kind and amount of general information, by means of which we are carried up, without a break, to the times of Samuel Johnson, Oliver Goldsmith, Sir Joshua Reynolds; and in fact my father distinctly remembers, when a boy, seeing, and being in company with, some of these illustrious men, the friends of my grandfather. Then he had received —we will suppose—a similar initiation in literary and political history, and if so, then we are furnished with stepping-stones up to the times of Bentley, Pope, Swift, Addison, Watts, and although this last name would seem to stand beyond the limit of any immediate recollections, yet it is a fact that the "Divine Songs" have come to me by means of a single intervening person—from one who, as a favoured little girl, learned them, standing at the amiable doctor's knee. Thus it is that we travel safely, and with a distinct cognisance of the way, through more than a century of literary conveyance. At this rate, and if we may take this last preceding period of time as our gauge of centuries past, then we shall require the aid of only eight or nine persons, in series, to bring us into correspondence with Shakespeare and Ben Jonson. Fewer than this—we might take six long-lived men to put us into this position of proximity with the worthies of the Elizabethan era.

In making good our supposition, it is not necessary to assume the fact (which we can seldom certainly know) that there has been, in any one family, a continuous succession of fathers and sons —the father living long enough to instruct the son. We should rather take the case of the intellectual filiation of college life: we imagine the learned professor, during the last ten years of his official life, imparting his mental substance to a hundred or two of scholars, some two or three of whom, at least, will live to do the like, from the same chair, in behalf of their successors. On this ground the individual teachers need not be more than twelve, upon whose oral testimony, in succession, we rely in passing from an age of generally diffused intelligence, to the times of the revival of learning, and of printed books.

It will be remembered that—if indeed there were grounds of doubt concerning the safe transmission of ancient books to modern times, any such suspicions can attach only to the period that is usually designated as the "Dark Ages," and *these* need not be reckoned as more than seven, reaching back from the times of Dante, Petrarch, Chaucer, Wickliffe, to the pontificate of Gregory the Great, in whose times, as appears from their writings, the learning of the preceding ages was still familiarly known to more than a few.

The Sixth Century of the Christian era abounds with the names of writers in all departments of literature, many of whose works, having descended to modern times, present ample evidence of the scarcely diminished diffusion of general learning. Among many others, such were—Procopius, the historian of the reign of Justinian;—and Agathias, who continued that history, and was a learned man;—Boethius, author of what is regarded as the last specimen of pure Latinity—a poem on "the Consolations of Philosophy;"—Hesychius, the lexicographer;—Proclus, a platonic philosopher;—Fulgentius and Cassiodorus, ecclesiastical writers; —Priscianus, a grammarian;—Gildas the wise, an Anglo-Saxon historian;—Evagrius Scolasticus, an ecclesiastical historian;—Simplicius, the commentator upon Aristotle and Epictetus;—Marcellinus Ammianus, an historian and critic, whose works contain copious references to ancient literature; and Stephen, of Byzantium, a grammarian and geographer. We might take in hand the work of this last-named writer—ΠΕΡΙ ΠΟΛΕΩΝ, as furnishing, by itself, a sufficient mass of evidence in proof of the extensive book-learning of those times which immediately overlook the gulf—the dark ages. This Stephen, the geographer, in the course of his account of the cities and towns of the ancient world, cites, or makes some reference to, the works of more than three hundred authors, to which he had access at any moment, while compiling his own.

The Seventh Century produced fewer writers than perhaps any other period that can be named within the compass of literary history. Yet there are more than enough to serve our present purpose: such are—Theophylact of Simocatta, who has left a history of the reign of the emperor Maurice, not very highly esteemed indeed, but abounding in allusions to the literature of the times.

Isidore, bishop of Seville, a complete collection of whose works fills seven quarto volumes, is a writer very proper to be mentioned in relation to our present purpose. Confessedly the age of Mahomet was a dull time: few indeed are the writers whose mere names have come down to us;—and yet, even in such a time, a voluminous writer, who treats of all kinds of subjects—religion, Church history, grammar, poetry, astronomy, physical science, and treats some of these systematically, might not only employ himself in labours of this kind, but also find among his contemporaries, and the men of the next age, numerous readers, and admirers, and copyists too, who found their account in transcribing so vast a product of literary industry. The times of this bishop, therefore, dark as they might be, were nevertheless times of book knowledge: throughout the dim period there was a class of the learned, numerous and intelligent enough, to keep watch upon the intellectual treasures of brighter times, to conserve the rich inheritance of mind, and to do their office in transmitting it down, unimpaired, to after ages. This fact is all which just now we need think of.

What we have thus said of the seventh century —of its darkness and its light, might be affirmed with little difference, as to the next. Our countryman, the "Venerable Bede," flourished in the seventh, but lived far on into the eighth century. The writings of Bede—and we should remember that he passed his life in the seclusion of a remote monastery—St. Peter and St. Paul, on the Tyne, in the diocese of Durham—afford ample proof of a wide diffusion of books, in that age. Bede displays extensive, if not profound learning, the whole of which he had acquired from sources that were ordinarily within the reach of monastic students. Bede "was a man of universal learning, not less skilled in the Greek than the Latin tongue: a poet, a rhetorician, an historian, an astronomer, an arithmetician, a master of chronology and geography, a philosopher, and theologian." So much was he admired in his own times that it became a proverbial saying among the learned—"A man born in the farthest corner of the earth has compassed the earth with the line of his genius." "He was," says Bale, "versed in the profane authors beyond any man of that age. Physics and general learning he derived, not from turbid streams, but from the pure fountains; that is, from the chief Greek and Latin authors. Indeed, there is hardly anything of value in the compass of ancient literature, that is not to be met with in Bede, although he never travelled beyond the limits of his native land."

The conservative function was taken up by several of Bede's disciples; among them we may name Alcuin, who did much, by his learning and his influence at the court of Charlemagne, to aid the endeavours of that enlightened prince for the restoration of literature. He was skilled in the Latin, Greek, and Hebrew languages; gave lectures in all the sciences, and founded many public schools. His works, historical and theological, are in part extant, and they justify the reputation he enjoyed. In his letters he familiarly quotes the classic writers.

Charlemagne, himself tolerably well aquainted with Latin and Greek authors, zealously laboured to restore learning in the Church, and out of it. He invited learned men to his court, employed them in making Latin translations of the Greek classics and of the Fathers, founded public schools, and introduced regulations tending to make some degree of education indispensible to all who held office in the Church. Of the professors invited by Charlemagne to his court, as many came from the British Isles as from Italy. "We must not forget," says Muratori, "the praise of Britain, Scotland, and Ireland, which, in the study of the liberal arts, surpassed all other nations of the West in those times; nor omit to record the diligence of the monks of those countries, who roused and maintained the glory of letters which everywhere else was languishing or fallen."

Raban Maurus, a disciple of Alcuin, created archbishop of Mentz, in 847, had, before his elevation, taught theology, philosophy, poetry, and rhetoric at Paris, in the school established there by the Anglo-Saxon monks. "A man well versed in the Holy Scriptures, and thoroughly learned in profane literature, as his writings abundantly testify." He enriched the monastery of Fulda, on the Rhine, where he received his early education, with a large collection of books; and there he founded a school. Two hundred and seventy monks belonged to the establishment, who were trained by him in every branch of learning. Disciples flocked to him from all countries, and he reared for the Church a great number of ministers well furnished for its service. He died, 856.

One of the first professors in the University of Oxford founded (or restored) by King Alfred, was John Scot; he afterwards went into France, where he was honourably entertained at the court of Charles the Bald, at whose request he translated some Greek authors into Latin: but these versions, in which a literal adherence to the original was observed, were scarcely intelligible to those for whose use they were intended. His writings display, however, much various learning; they were condemned as heretical by the Church on account of his opinions relative to the Eucharist. Being driven from France by the order of the Pope, he took refuge in an English monastery; but there, at the instigation of the monks, he, it is said, like Cassianus, was killed by his scholars, with their iron styles.

Before the Danish incursions, the English monasteries and churches abounded with men of learning; but these establishments being broken up and the monks dispersed by the rude invaders, literature and the arts became almost extinct in the country. Alfred, himself a man of learning, and a various writer, effected, as is known, much towards their restoration, by the re-establishment of the ruined monasteries—the erection of many new ones—the endowment of schools—the foundation of lectureships at Oxford, and by the diffusion of his own writings, which, even if he had not been a king, would have perpetuated his name.

Contemporary with the last-named writer was Photius, with whom no author of that, or of several succeeding ages, can be compared: his works hold up a mirror of the literature that was extant in his times. Photius, educated for secular employments, and for some time engaged in the service of Michael III., was by that emperor forcibly invested with the dignity of patriarch of Constantinople (858) in the room of Ignatius. That he might pass regularly to this elevation, he was made monk, reader, sub-deacon, deacon, priest, and patriarch, in the course of six days. From the office thus violently assumed, he was, with little ceremony, expelled by Basilius, the successor of Michael. Once again, at the head of a band of soldiers, he possessed himself of the patriarchate, of which, by similar means, he was at length finally deprived; after which he retired to a monastery, where he ended his days. Before his elevation, he had composed the most useful and the most celebrated of his works, the *Myriobiblion*, which contains, in the form of criticisms, analyses, and extracts, an account of upwards of 270 works. This treasury of learning preserves many valuable fragments from authors whose works have perished, and affords important aid in ascertaining the genuineness of many of the remains of ancient literature.

Eutychius, an Egyptian physician, and afterwards (933) patriarch of Alexandria, wrote a universal history, which is still extant, and which, though it contains numerous fables, exhibits the various learning of the author, and of his times. Though so large a number of existing manuscripts as appear to have been executed in the tenth century, prove that a great degree of activity in the reproduction of books prevailed in that age, it presents the names of few authors whose works have descended to modern times.

The Eleventh Century is much richer in distinguished names, of which it may suffice to mention these:—

Avicenna, an Arabian physician and Mahometan doctor, reduced the science of medicine to a systematic form, including almost everything that had been written on the subject by his predecessors: he was versed in Greek literature, and is said to have committed Aristotle's Metaphysics to memory. The first conquests of the Saracens in Asia, Africa, and Spain, during the seventh and eighth centuries, were almost fatal to the interests of learning. But no sooner had they well established their power in the conquered countries, than the Caliphs sought to rekindle the light of knowledge. During two or three centuries, Bagdat in the East, and Cordova in the West, were the seats, not only of splendid monarchies, but of science, general learning, and great refinement. It was, however, chiefly the mathematical and physical sciences that were cultivated by the Arabians. They possessed imperfect and corrupted translations of several of the Greek authors, especially of Aristotle, Theophrastus, Euclid, and Dioscorides; and they had some general, though imperfect, acquaintance with the Greek historians. Some of the Latin translations, made by the order of Charlemagne, were derived from these Arabian versions.

Michael Psellus, a Greek physician, and a monk, wrote upon subjects of all kinds: "There was no science which he did not either illustrate by his comments, or abridge, or reduce to a better method.—A man celebrated for the extent of his acquirements in divine and human learning, as his many works, both printed and in manuscript, evince."

Lanfranc, by birth an Italian, was created archbishop of Canterbury by William of Normandy; he promoted learning among the clergy, and was himself reputed to be universally accomplished in the literature extant in that age.

Anselm, the disciple and successor of Lanfranc, in the see of Canterbury, was also in repute for general learning.

The works of Suidas, a Byzantine monk, like those of Photius, contain a vast store of various learning, singularly useful on points of criticism and literary history. The lexicon of this writer, besides the definition of words, contains accounts of ancient authors of all classes, and many quotations from works that have since perished.

Sigebert, a monk of Brabant, has left a chronicle of events from A.D. 381 to his own times, 1112, and a work containing the lives of illustrious men.

The name of Anna Comnena, daughter of the emperor Alexius Comnenus, and wife of Nicephorus Bryennius, distinguishes the early part of the twelfth century. She wrote an elegant and eloquent history of her father's reign. This work displays not only a masculine understanding, but an extensive acquaintance with literature and the sciences.

England produced during this century several eminent writers, who were accomplished in the learning of the age. Such were William of Malmesbury, Henry of Huntington, Geoffrey of Monmouth, and Joseph of Exeter—author of two Latin poems, on the Trojan war, and the war of Antioch, or the Crusade—and, somewhat later, Stephen Langton, archbishop of Canterbury, reckoned the most learned man of western Europe in those times.

Eustathius, archbishop of Thessalonica, flourished towards the close of the twelfth century. His commentaries on Homer, besides serving to elucidate the Greek language by many important criticisms, drawn from sources that have since been lost, contain, like the works of Photius and Suidas, innumerable references to the Greek classics, and thus furnish the means of ascertaining the integrity and the genuineness of the text of those authors, as they are now extant.

The brothers John and Isaac Tzetzes, critics and grammarians of Constantinople, are still consulted as commentators upon some of the Greek authors. John Tzetzes is a voluminous writer: his extant works give evidence at once of his vast acquaintance with literature, and of the literary facilities of that age, at least in cities such as Constantinople.

Robert Grostest (Greathead), bishop of Lincoln

was famed for his skill in the Latin, Greek, and Hebrew languages, as well as for the bold resistance he made to the exactions of the popes upon the English church. Camden says of him that "he was a man versed in the languages and in general literature in a degree scarcely credible, when the age in which he lived is considered; a terrible reprover of the pope, the adviser of his king (Henry III.), and a lover of truth."

Matthew Paris, one of the earliest of the English historians, displays in his works an acquaintance with ancient literature, as well as a familiar knowledge of the antiquities of his native country. Like the bishop last named, Paris vigorously opposed the papal usurpations in England; nor did he less courageously reprove vice in every rank at home. His reputation as a man of learning and virtue enabled him to effect a considerable reformation in many of the English monasteries. He died 1259. The "Historia Major" of this writer begins with the Norman Conquest, and is continued to the year of the author's death, 1259.

The works of Albert, called the Great, a Dominican friar, and afterwards, in 1260, bishop of Ratisbon, fill one-and-twenty volumes. They are chiefly on the physical sciences, but include a sort of encyclopædia of the learning of the age. "A man of wonderful erudition, to whom few things in theological science, and hardly any in secular learning, were unknown. On account of the extent and variety of his acquirements surnamed 'the Great'—an honour conferred upon no other learned man during life." Albert, like Roger Bacon, incurred among his contemporaries the suspicion of being a magician. Learning, in the restricted sense of the term, or the knowledge of books, though possessed by a comparatively small class of persons, was too frequent to excite wonder or envy; but Science, or a knowledge of nature, and this acquired, not from Aristotle, but from experiment, was so rare, that it seldom failed to engender both, and to occasion a dangerous accusation of correspondence with infernal spirits.

The revival of learning is usually reckoned to have commenced in the fifteenth century: but in the fourteenth a very decided advancement in almost every department of literature had taken place. That the ignorance which had prevailed in the preceding century was wearing away from the bulk of the community in several parts of Europe, and that the educated classes were acquiring a better taste and more expanded views, needs no other evidence than that which is so abundantly presented in the works of Dante, of Petrarch, of Boccatio, of Chaucer, and of Gower, which were not merely produced in that period, but were extensively read and admired.

Fewer instances than those given above might suffice to prove, that at no part of that tract of time, which extends from the decline of learning in the sixth century, to its revival in the fifteenth, was there anything which can be called an extinction of the knowledge of ancient literature. This proof, it must be acknowledged, is much more complete in reference to the Greek, than to the Latin authors; it is also more ample in relation to ecclesiastical and sacred, than to profane literature. Of all the extant manuscripts, executed in the middle ages, perhaps nineteen in twenty belong to the former class. The continuance of the eastern empire till the middle of the fifteenth century, afforded an uninterrupted protection to Greek learning during those periods in which western Europe was laid waste by the Gothic nations. Yet even those devastations were never universal either in their extent, or in their kind. At times when Italy was in ashes, the British Islands were secure. And if cities were sacked and burned, and if castles, palaces, and cathedrals were pillaged and overthrown, hundreds of religious houses, in strong or secluded situations, remained untouched; or if occasionally they were subjected to the violence of armies, or to the exactions of conquerors, they more often lost their chests, their cups and their salvers, than their books.

Learning and the sciences can *flourish* and advance only where there are the means of a wide and quick diffusion of the fruits of intellectual labour: but they may *exist* even under the almost total absence of such means. This was the case in Europe during the middle ages. Knowledge rested with the few whom the inward fire of native genius constrained to pursue it: and these few were often insulated from each other, and unknown beyond the walls within which they spent their lives; and often secluded also by their tastes, even from their fellows of the same society.

In every myriad of the human race, take the number where or when we may, there will be found a few individuals—born for thought; and if the vocation of nature is not always stronger than every obstacle, it is, for the most part, strong enough to overcome such as are of ordinary magnitude. Those who are thus endowed with the appetite for knowledge, will certainly follow the impulse, if the means of its acquirement are presented to them in early life. Now these means were everywhere interspersed among the nations of Europe during the middle ages, by the monastic system; and it may be questioned whether there were not then greater chances for drawing within the pale of learning the native mind of every district, than are afforded even by the present constitutions of society. The religious houses were so thickly scattered through every country, and the continual draught from the population for the maintenance of the numbers of their inmates (a standing rule of the monastic establishments enjoined that the original number of each congregation should be maintained) was so great, that they must have taken up many more than the gifted individuals of every neighbourhood; and yet such individuals would almost certainly be included within that enlistment; for whenever a youth displayed a fondness for learning, nothing better could be done for him, whether he was the son of a peasant or a noble, than to devote him to the service of the Church. The monasteries usually contained schools for the youth of their vicinities. From these schools the superiors of the house had the opportunity of selecting any who gave promise of intelligence.

In the very darkest times, learning insured to its possessor a degree of reputation; and the heads of religious houses, in most instances, sought to decorate their establishments with some particles of the honours of erudition, as well as to recommend them by the possession of relics; and many were eagerly ambitious to enhance the literary celebrity of their communities. With this view it would be their policy to afford the necessary means and encouragement to those who seemed most likely to support the credit of the society. "The education of a monk, at least in the fourteenth century, consisted of church music and the primary sciences, grammar, logic, and philosophy—obviously that of Aristotle. Some French and Latin must also have been included; for these were the languages the monks were enjoined to speak on public occasions. They were afterwards sent to Oxford or Paris to learn theology. Such indeed was the encouragement held out to literature, that in a provincial chapter of abbots and priors of the Benedictine order, held at Northampton, A.D. 1343, men of letters and masters of art were invited to become monks, by a promise of exemption from all daily services."*

Independently therefore of any more direct evidence, there would be reason to believe that many if not most of the monasteries and conventual churches, at all times, included an individual or two whose tastes led him to devote his life to study, and who would become the sedulous guardian and conservator of the books of the house, directing the labours of his less intelligent brethren in the work of transcribing such as might be falling into decay.

In the estimation of minds ruled by the love of books, even if incapable of discriminating the precious from the worthless—the worthless, by a principle of association, partakes, to a large degree, of the respect that belongs in reason only to what is intrinsically valuable. A BOOK, whatever be

* Fosbrooke.

its subject or its merits, is viewed with a fond covetousness by those whose passion it is to love books. This feeling must have been strong indeed in times when books were hardly to be purchased, and when their ideal value included a recollection of the toil of transcription. The spirit of the ruling superstition, which taught the attachment of an incalculable importance to objects intrinsically worthless, must also have favoured an undistinguishing reverence for books. We need not then be surprised to find that works of all classes, though altogether unsuited to the taste of the times, were reproduced, from age to age, by the monkish copyists.

While, therefore, all taste for instruction had disappeared from the face of society—while kings and nobles were often as ignorant as artisans and peasants, while even many of the clergy retained only some shreds of learning, the productions of brighter ages were still hoarded and perpetuated, and were made accessible to the few whose intellectual ardour carried them beyond the standard of their times.

The reader who would extend his acquaintance with the subjects so briefly referred to in this chapter will find the means of doing so amply supplied in the work of Mr. Maitland which so conclusively establishes the fact of the uninterrupted *continuance* of the intellectual life of Europe through those ages which too hastily have been spoken of by modern writers as times of universal ignorance.*

* The Dark Ages: a series of Essays, intended to illustrate the state of Religion and Literature in the ninth, tenth, eleventh, and twelfth Centuries. By the Rev. S. R. Maitland, &c.

CHAPTER IX.

THE REVIVAL OF LEARNING IN THE FOURTEENTH CENTURY.

MORE than half a century before the taking of Constantinople by the Turks, the learned men of that city, apprehensive of the approaching fall of the empire, had begun to emigrate into Italy, where they opened schools, and became the preceptors of princes and the guides of the public taste, which they directed towards the study of the classic writers of Greece especially, and even of Rome. But it was the fall of Constantinople in 1453 which filled the Italian cities with these learned strangers.

The Italians of that age needed only to receive this kind of direction, and to be aided by these means of study; for they had for some time been placed under those peculiar circumstances which have ever proved the most favourable to the advancement of the human mind. Throughout a number of independent states—crowded upon a narrow space, the same language, yet diversified by dialects, was spoken. The energy, the rivalry, the munificence that accompany an active commerce kept the whole mass of society in movement; while the influence of a gorgeous superstition, which sought to recommend itself by every embellishment that the genius of man could devise or execute, overruled the tendency of successful trade, and directed the ambition of princely merchants towards objects more noble and intellectual than are those which wealth usually selects as the means of distinction.

The formation of libraries, suggested or favoured by the abundant importation of manuscripts from Constantinople, was the means not only of making more widely known the works of those Greek authors which had never fallen into oblivion, but of prompting researches which issued in the recovery of the Latin writers also, many of whom had long been forgotten. The appetite for books having thus been quickened, neither cost nor labour was thenceforward spared in their accumulation; and learned men were despatched, in all directions, throughout Europe, western Asia, and Africa, expressly to collect manuscripts. In the course of a few years, most of the authors that are now known to us, were brought together in the libraries of Rome, Naples, Venice, Florence, Milan, Vienna, and Paris, where they were laid open to those who were best qualified to give them forth anew to the world.

Thus aided by the munificence and zeal of princes and popes, the scholars of the fifteenth century sedulously applied themselves to the discovery, the restoration, and the publication of the remains of Greek and Roman literature; and so it was that in the course of sixty or eighty years, most of the works now known had been committed to the press. Since that time some few discoveries have been made; but the principal improvements in classic literature, of later date, have consisted in the emendation of the text of ancient authors by means of a more extensive collation of manuscripts than the first editors had any opportunity to institute. This restoration of the remains of ancient works to their pristine integrity has not been effected, like that of a dilapidated building, or a mutilated statue, by the addition of new materials in an imagined conformity with the plan and taste of the original work; but by the industrious collection and replacement of the very particles of which it at first consisted.

The invention of printing, which virtually exempts books from the operation of the law that subjects all things mundane to the decays of time, has greatly promoted also the process of their renovation; for, by giving to the issue of an edition of a standard work a degree of importance, several hundred times greater than what belonged to the transcription of a single copy, it has called for the employment of a proportionably larger amount of learning, diligence, and caution in the work of revision; and then, by enabling each successive editor to avail himself of the labours of his predecessors, the advantages belonging to the concentration of many minds upon the same subject have been secured.

It is a fact therefore, the significance of which should be clearly understood, that, since the fifteenth century, the lapse of time, instead of gradually impairing and corrupting the literary remains of antiquity, has incessantly contributed to their renovation and purification. Indeed it may be affirmed that, in relation to the amount, the exactitude, and the certainty of our knowledge, we are not receding from remote ages, but are constantly approaching towards them. In a thousand instances what was unknown, or was doubtful, or imperfect, or corrupted, at the commencement of the fifteenth century, has been ascertained, restored, and completed in the nineteenth. The history and the literature of Greece and Rome— long inhumed in monasteries, were, at the period of their re-appearance, liable to uncertainties and to suspicions which not all the learning and industry of that vigorous age were able to dispel. But the learning and industry of the four centuries that have since elapsed, constantly directed towards the same objects, and constantly accumulating a various mass of evidence, have left exceedingly few questions of literary antiquity open to controversy.

Thus then, by the mention of some leading facts, we have traced the remains of ancient literature up to the time when they passed to the press, and when their history can no longer be regarded as obscure or questionable. Nor can it be thought that this body of literature is now liable to the hazards of extinction from political changes, or from the decline of learning in this or that country; for unless a universal devastation should take its course, at once, over every region of the civilised world, the literature now extant in books can neither perish, nor suffer corruption. A temple, a statue, a picture, or a gem is but *one;* and however durable may be the material of which it consists, it continually decays, and it is always destructible. The touch of the sculptor moulders from the chiselled surface; and the time will come when every monument of his genius shall have crumbled into dust, and when his fame—lost from the marble, shall live only in the works of the poets and historians who were his contemporaries.

Thus it is that the *written* records of distant ages, with the knowledge of which the intellectual moral, and political well-being of mankind is inseparably connected, are secured from extinction by a mode of conservation that is less liable to extensive hazards than any other that can be imagined. If Man be cut off from the knowledge of the past, he becomes indifferent to the future, and thenceforward sinks into the rudeness and ferocity of the sensual life. The redundant amplitude, therefore, of the means by which this knowledge is preserved, only bears a due proportion to the importance of the consequences that depend upon its perpetuation.

CHAPTER X.

SEVERAL METHODS AVAILABLE FOR ASCERTAINING THE CREDIBILITY OF ANCIENT HISTORICAL WORKS.

The facts referred to in the preceding chapters belong in common to ancient books of all classes, and they tend to prove that the works of the Greek and Roman writers—poets, dramatists, philosophers, critics, and historians—which issued from the press in the fifteenth and sixteenth centuries, may, by means of various and independent evidence, be infallibly traced up to the age in which they are commonly supposed to have been written.

The reader's attention is now to be directed to one class of those ancient works, namely, those which are professedly historical; and our object will be to ascertain on what grounds, and with what limitations, such works deserve our confidence as truthful narratives of facts.

The very same mode of inquiry which common sense suggests, on the most ordinary occasions, when we are called upon to estimate the value of testimony, is applicable to all cases of the like nature. Nor can the importance of the consequences that may be involved in the issue of the investigation, in a peculiar instance, render it invalid, or warrant our rejection of it as unsatisfactory.

In some lesser particulars the modes of estimating oral and written testimony must differ; but in substance the heads of inquiry will be the same. In the case with which we have now to do—namely, the credibility of the testimony of ancient historians, it is natural to consider the following points :—

1. The moral and intellectual character of the writer,—if this can be known;
2. The means of information he possessed;
3. The time and circumstances of the first publication of the work;
4. The exceptions it may be necessary to make to his testimony on particular points; arising either from the peculiar nature of the facts affirmed, or from the apparent influence of prejudice—personal, or national; and—
5. The agreement of the narrative in question with evidence derived from other, and independent sources.

In judging then of the authenticity of an historical work we have, in the first place, to form an estimate of the writer's moral and intellectual character and qualifications; supposing that the means of forming an opinion on these points are within our reach.

If the personal integrity of an historian has happened to be put to the proof by any well known and remarkable events, in which he was concerned, the reader whose own character may qualify him to feel the force of such proof, will seldom ask for better grounds of confidence; for such errors in matters of fact as a thoroughly honest historian may be liable to, will seldom be of vital importance. Even if no such proof of a writer's personal integrity exists, and if the circumstances of his life are altogether unknown, yet almost every writer leaves in his works sufficient indications of his moral dispositions. The characteristics of honesty are distinct enough to secure the confidence of candid minds; nor can an instance be adduced in which they have been so successfully counterfeited as to have stood the test of time. A perverse intention as certainly betrays itself in writing, as it does in personal behaviour. Nevertheless this sort of evidence, though it will be more satisfactory than any other to one reader, may be unperceived by another; for cold, feeble, and suspicious minds are destitute of the sympathies to which it appeals.

If the proofs of integrity and veracity in an historian are wanting, or are thought to be insufficient, we must descend to that sort of evidence which his works afford relative to his intellectual qualifications; and these may be such as fully to warrant a general confidence in his preference of truth to falsehood. As to the strongest minds, such minds attach themselves to truth by an instinctive movement: to acquire the knowledge of facts in their characteristic passion;—to promulgate this knowledge is the function they feel themselves born to fulfil. Nor can it happen that the falsification of facts—in which neither personal interests nor prejudices are involved—should present an adequate inducement to writers whose powers of narration enable them to command more attention in the direct paths of truth and reality, than they could hope to gain in the regions of fiction. Every gifted mind has its sphere; and there is a native talent for history, as well as a genius for poetry; and he who possesses eminently the former, will as certainly make himself conversant with realities, as he who may boast the possession of the latter will choose to live among the creations of fancy.

If therefore an historical work displays a healthy vigour of intellect—good sense—elevation of sentiment, and the specific talent for narration, these qualities may safely be held to afford a strong presumptive proof of the author's veracity, even though there should be no direct means of ascertaining his moral dispositions, or his integrity. Those writers who occupy a first rank among ancient historians may therefore safely be held to possess this presumptive proof of their veracity; for the reputation they have so long enjoyed is attributable, quite as much to their talent for narration, as to the interest or importance of the story that forms the subject of their works. These intrinsic merits contain, then, a tacit guarantee for the authenticity of the works that are thus adorned.

On this ground, the good sense, the simplicity, the ease, and the accuracy of Herodotus—the stern vigour, the elevation, and the dignity of Thucydides, the graceful simplicity of Xenophon, and the philosophic terseness of Tacitus, not only win the admiration of the reader, but, in different degrees, these qualities invite, or demand, his confidence.

There are moreover qualities of style which, though they may not entitle an author to a place in the first rank of writers, must secure for him a high regard as an authentic historian. Indeed, in this department of literature, those less brilliant and less attractive qualities which give security as to an historian's diligence, accuracy, and impartiality, may well be accepted in place of the brighter recommendations of genius, or eloquence, or powers of description. There is a specific taste for details, there is a passion for laborious researches, there is a superstitious regard to exactness, and an indefatigable industry, which, though they may tire the reader who seeks only for amusement, will secure the confidence and attention of the intelligent student of history. Thus, for example, the assiduity of Diodorus the Sicilian, the accuracy and good sense of Polybius, and the minuteness and amplification of Dionysius the Halicarnassian, give to their works a substantial value which goes far to compensate for the want of more shining excellences.

In those historical works which have necessarily been compiled from various documents, a sound judgment in the selection of materials must be considered as the principal merit of an author. In this quality some of the ancient historians were certainly deficient; and yet it must be added that to this very want of judgment we are indebted for the knowledge of innumerable particulars, in themselves curious, or perhaps important, which our modern notions of method, consistency, and propriety, would greatly have retrenched, or entirely have excluded.

Although, to a certain extent, the genius or talent of an historian may be held to vouch for his veracity; yet it is also true that a writer may possess a sort of genius which tends to bring his fidelity into suspicion. If, for example, he continually indulges his taste for scenes of splendour, or terror, or extraordinary action, or if he loves to exhibit images of magnanimity, or wisdom, surpassing the ordinary reach of human nature; if his principal personages are heroes, or if he seems pleased to find occasions on which to display his command of the nervous eloquence of vituperation, we may well conclude that his genius will have tempted him to relinquish the merit of being simply exact, or calmly just.

A consideration of personal and national prejudices enters, of course, into the estimate that is formed of an historian's moral and intellectual character. But these will be best adverted to when we come to mention the exceptions which it is necessary to make against the evidence of historians, on particular points.

We have next to make inquiry concerning the means of information which may have been possessed by an ancient historian.

The same kind of confidence that is due to an historian who narrates events in which he was personally concerned, cannot be claimed by one who compiles the history of remote times from such materials as he can collect: for in the former case, if we are assured of the writer's veracity and competency, there remains no room for reasonable doubt; at least in reference to those principal facts of the story for the truth of which his character is pledged. But in the other case, though we may think well both of the writer's veracity and judgment, the confidence we afford him must still be conditional, and will be measured by the opinion we form of the validity of his authorities.

The entire mass of ancient history, may therefore be considered as consisting of two kinds, namely, the *original* and *compiled.* In the first class may be comprehended, not merely those narratives that are strictly personal, such for instance as the history of the retreat of the ten thousand Greeks, by Xenophon; or again the Commentaries of Cæsar, which describe actions wherein the author was immediately concerned, and was, in fact, the principal actor; but those also which relate to the events of the author's own times and country, and concerning which he had the most direct and unquestionable means of becoming accurately informed. Such are the history of the Peloponnesian war by Thucydides; and the history of the Catiline conspiracy by Sallust, and much of the histories and annals of Tacitus, and the history of the reign of Justinian by Procopius; and that of her father's reign by Anna Comnena.

The credibility of historical works of this class must, obviously, be determined chiefly upon the grounds mentioned in the preceding section; that is to say, from those indications of integrity, impartiality, and good sense, which the work exhibits. Every reader of Thucydides, for example, feels that he may rely with confidence upon the general authenticity of the narrative:—the caution and the unwearied assiduity of the author in ascertaining the truth of whatever he affirms, his exactness in minute circumstances, his eminent good sense and fairness, and the dignity of his manner, all concur to stamp upon the work, for the most part, the seal of truth. In *original* histories the truth of the story and the veracity of the writer are inseparably linked together:—both must be admitted, or both should be denied.

But by far the greater part of all extant history belongs to the second class; and yet, among works that must rank as *compilations*, some wide distinctions are to be observed; for there are some of this kind of which the authenticity is little, if at all, inferior to that of the best original histories; while many are, in the ordinary sense of the term, compilations, and as such deserve only a qualified confidence. In regard to the nature and probable value of the authorities they have relied upon, each historian—and indeed almost every separate portion of the works of each writer—must be estimated apart. An example or two will be sufficient to show, as well the necessity, as the mode of exercising this discrimination.

The nine books of Herodotus afford instances of every degree of validity in regard to the probable value of the materials that were employed by the author. A reader who, in his simplicity, peruses that work, throughout, with an equal faith, will be in danger of having his indiscriminate confidence suddenly converted into undistinguishing scepticism, by discovering the slenderness of the authority upon which some portions of it are made to rest.

Diodorus the Sicilian, is reported to have employed thirty years in collecting materials for his universal history. Like Herodotus, he visited the countries of which he speaks—consulting public records—inspecting monuments—conversing with the learned, and collecting books. In fact his work exhibits many proofs of this assiduity; but yet when some of his statements are compared with those of other writers, who were better informed on particular subjects, it becomes apparent that he exercised too little caution in the selection of his authorities; and that therefore the discrimination of the reader, or of the learned annotator, must supply the want of judgment in the writer.

The universal history of Trogus Pompeius, which is extant only in the abridgment made by Justin, seems to have been compiled on a plan somewhat similar to that of the work last mentioned. It is evident that the author, in collecting his materials, employed considerable diligence and judgment; nevertheless, in what relates to remote nations, he shows himself often to have been egregiously misinformed. A striking instance of this kind is furnished in the account he gives of the history and religion of the Jews (Book xxxvi. cap. 2) ; for it is evident that the author—whether it be Trogus, or Justin, must have received his information—not from the source from which he ought to have derived it—the Jewish records ;— nor even from individuals of that nation; but from prejudiced and ill-informed men of the neighbouring countries of Asia or of Africa. The account given by Tacitus (Hist. Book v.) of the same people, is little more just than is that of Trogus. If these instances were to be taken as specimens of the accuracy of ancient historians in all similar cases, their descriptions of remote nations must be held to be of very little value. But there seems reason to believe that the history and institutions of the Jews were much less known, and were more misrepresented, than those of any other people bordering upon the Mediterranean.

Abundant evidence proves that, from the very earliest ages, and in almost all countries, there were persons employed and authorised by governments to digest the current history of the state. These annals contained, of course, the names of kings, and the records of their acts and exploits, their decrees and wars. Each city, as well as the capitals of empires, had its archives; and these public documents appear to have suggested the idea of a more comprehensive form of history. They were certainly consulted by those who, in later times, undertook the composition of historical works: by these means there was imparted to such works more of authenticity and exactness than may be generally supposed. Herodotus, Thucydides, Diodorus, Pausanias, Strabo, Dionysius of Halicarnassus, Plutarch, Arrian, Dion Cassius, the Elder Pliny, and others, evidently availed themselves with all possible diligence of such public records.

Ancient historians conversed extensively with official persons, wherever they travelled; and it must be granted they were often too ready to accept those oral communications as authentic. This is especially to be observed in reference to those accounts that were confessedly, or that seem to have been received from priests; for that class of persons, too much accustomed to think truth their enemy, and disception their business, would have thought themselves betraying the interests of their order in furnishing simple facts to an inquirer.

Every city of the ancient world, where civilisation had made any progress, was crowded with columns, statues, busts, monuments, inscriptions, by which every memorable event, and every illustrious personage, was perpetually presented to the regards of the people, and was retained in their recollection. It is certain that this monumental and sculptural mode of embodying a people's history obtained to a far greater extent in ancient cities than it does in those of our times. And so it was that to visit a city—to pace its public ways—to enter its temples and its halls, was to peruse its history. The meanest citizen— even a child, would be able to conduct an inquisitive stranger through the streets, and to explain to him these memorials of the past. It is difficult for us in these times, and in these inclement latitudes, to form an adequate notion of the extent to which the history of each people was familiarised to them by these means; or how much the living conversed with the dead, and identified themselves with whatever was heroic or wise in preceding times. These public monuments, when collated with the public records, and explained by the public voice, furnished historians with abundant materials; and so great was the importance attached to them, that there are instances in which historians made long journeys for the express purpose of examining the sculptures of a city, the history of which they had occasion incidentally to mention.

What was most wanting to give a higher value, in point of authenticity, to the materials so diligently collected by the ancient historians was— that general diffusion of information among neighbouring nations which would have subjected the fables and the boastful pretensions of each people to the animadversion of others, and thus have given room for a more ready and complete collation of discordant evidence on the same points. The Greeks were very little acquainted with the languages of the surrounding nations; and they were egregiously ignorant of facts in which they were not immediately concerned. If the literature of the Asiatic nations had been familiarly current in Greece, and that of Greece in Asia, both would have been purged of many errors and frivolities; and something more of that consistency, expansion, and good sense imparted on both sides, which were acquired by the Roman writers in consequence of their acquaintance with the literature of Greece. In the department of history, especially, such an interchange of light would have enhanced immensely the value, as well as augmented the amount of knowledge. Knowledge, like the vital fluid, corrupts whenever it ceases freely to circulate.

On this ground, the moderns possess, incomparably, an advantage over the ancients; and even if party interests and political prejudices act more forcibly in modern times, the means of correction are also vastly more efficient. European nations have, in relation to important subjects, a common literature:—all things are known by all: national misrepresentations are quickly noticed and chastised. The same corrective process is actively carried on within each community; and if particular falsifications abound, the ultimate probabilities of the prevalence of truth are still more abundant.

In estimating the credibility of ancient writers —historians especially, we have to consider the time and circumstances of the first publication of such works.

To ascertain the *antiquity* of historical works is peculiarly important, because when that point has been placed out of doubt, we obtain, in most instances, a conclusive proof of the general truth of the narrative. For if a history is known to have been published, and widely circulated, and generally admitted to be authentic, in the very age when the principal facts to which it relates were matters of universal notoriety, and when most of the lesser circumstances were perfectly known to many of the author's contemporaries, and when some of them stood personally related to the events, we have the best reasons for confiding in the substantial truth and accuracy of the history.

No pretended narrative, published under circumstances such as these, which was altogether untrue in its main elements, or which was grossly incorrect in its details, could, by any accident, or by any endeavours, have gained general and lasting reputation as an authentic work. No such book could endure, and survive, the scrutiny of contemporary antagonists; no such book could maintain its reputation through the next age, while the means of ascertaining the truth of the narrative were still extant, and after the interests and prejudices of the moment had subsided.

As in relation to the sources of information that were possessed by historians, it has been seen that historical works should be divided into two classes —the *original*, and the *derived;* so a similar, but not exactly an identical division must be made in relation to the circumstances under which such books were at first published. In the *first* class are to be included those histories of the truth of which the author's contemporaries, in general, were competent judges; and in the *second*, such, as having been drawn from rare, or recondite, or scattered materials—relating to events remote in time or place, could not be open to the test of public opinion, and could be estimated only by a few of the learned class.

Histories of the *first* kind may be termed—*popular;* those of the *second*—*learned.* It is evident that *learned* histories, although on different grounds, may deserve a high degree of confidence as to their authenticity and their accuracy; and, indeed, on the score of impartiality and comprehensive information, and exactness in details, they may greatly surpass any of the original narratives from which they may have been compiled. For it is manifest that a later historian, if he be industrious, judicious, and unprejudiced, has the opportunity so to collect and collate the various mass of subsidiary testimonies bearing upon particular facts, as shall impart much more of consistency to his narrative than can belong to any earlier work on the same subject.

But the direct proof of authenticity must belong *exclusively* to *popular* histories. A work of this class is, essentially, a condensation of the common knowledge of a nation or community; it is the universal testimony, arranged and compacted by one whose aim it is to found his personal reputation as a writer upon the consent and approval of his contemporaries. Let it be supposed that in passing through the crowded ways of a metropolis, we hear, in substance, the same account of some recent and public transaction, from a thousand lips, and from opposing parties; or we read a narrative of this event drawn up by a contemporary writer, whose veracity has been tacitly or explicitly assented to by the same parties. The validity of the evidence rests upon the same grounds in both cases: only that for accuracy and consistency, the accepted *written* narrative will be found to surpass the *oral* testimony.

We may take as an example the latter books of Herodotus, which, viewed with reference to the distinction above mentioned, may be reckoned as belonging to the class of popular histories, and may therefore deserve the confidence that is due to a narrative that has generally been accepted as true by those who were well acquainted with the facts it describes, and many of whom were personally concerned in the transactions it narrates. The history of the Peloponnesian war, by Thucydides, has a still higher claim to unimpeachable authenticity, inasmuch as the facts were more recent at the time of the publication of the work; and because, also, the strongest motives of national rivalry and civil discord were then in activity, and were in readiness to crush, on the instant, any attempted misrepresentation. The author's hope that his work should descend to posterity, rested directly upon such an adherence to truth, on his part, as should exclude the opportunity of giving any plausibility to a charge of extensive or wilful falsification.

Xenophon's history of Greece possesses, in part, a claim to credibility on the same ground. But the Cyropædia, on the contrary, is altogether destitute of authentication from this source; for the Greeks, at the time when the work was published, were far from being generally competent to judge of the truth of the story. The same author's account of the expedition of Cyrus, may, in this respect, take a middle place between the two above-named works. It was not composed, as there is reason to believe, till many years after the writer's return from Asia; and though the general facts were still matters of notoriety, the particulars could not then be universally recollected; especially as the scene of these transactions was so remote from Greece.

The works of Sallust, the Commentaries of Cæsar, the works of Tacitus, of Suetonius, of Polybius, claim, in whole or in part, the authority of popular histories, having been generally accredited as authentic by those who were well acquainted with the facts they contain.

But, excepting some small portions, or particular facts, the works of Diodorus, of Dionysius the Halicarnassian, of Nepos, of Ælian, of Paterculus, of Curtius, of Plutarch, of Arrian, of Appian, of Pausanias, and many others, are to be regarded only as learned compilations, the claim to authenticity of which is of an indirect kind.

CHAPTER XI.

EXCEPTIONS TO WHICH THE TESTIMONY OF HISTO-
RIANS, ON PARTICULAR POINTS, MAY BE LIABLE.

FROM the very nature of the case the authenticity of an historical work can be affirmed only in a restricted sense, and must be understood to be open to exceptions in particular instances. Such exceptions may be taken without impeaching the character of the writer for veracity, or even for general accuracy. It is easy to suppose that he may have been imposed upon in certain cases, by his informants; or he may have reported things that were currently believed in his time, without thinking himself personally pledged for their truth: he may not have thought himself called upon, as an historian, to discuss questions which might more properly be taken up by philosophers; or he may merely have been negligent—here and there, in the course of a voluminous work. Yet allowances of this sort must, as it is evident, be confined to cases of an accidental kind, and should only then be brought forward in the way of apology for a writer's mistakes, when he is giving an account of facts that were not immediately known to himself. For in a narrative of events, of which the writer professes to have had a personal knowledge, we must either admit his veracity, and with it the truth of the facts; or we must deny both.

The first point to be considered, when the affirmation of an historian in a particular instance is doubted, is—*The nature of the fact in question.*
1. If, for example, it be a question of numbers, measures, or dates, it is always to be remembered —as already remarked—that a peculiar uncertainty attaches to these matters, in ancient authors, owing to the method of notation *by letters*, which were easily mistaken, one for another. The numbers of which armies were composed—the numbers of the slain in battle—the population of cities —the revenues of states—the distances of places— the weight or measure of bodies, and computations of time, must, therefore, always be held open to question, as to what was actually intended and written by the author: this doubt may be entertained without in the least derogating from the credit of the work in which they occur. Besides the probable corruption of copies in such instances, it is to be remembered as to many of the particulars above named, that they are far more liable to uncertainty, or mistake, than other facts, so that scarcely any degree of diligence and care on the part of an historian, will entirely secure him from errors on such points.
2. Geographical details, descriptions of the objects of natural history, or accounts of natural phenomena, must also, generally, be considered as open to a degree of uncertainty, on account of the imperfect information upon such subjects, which was possessed by the ancients. And yet the names and relative distances of places in all the countries bordering upon the Mediterranean sea, as reported by ancient geographers and historians, have been to so great an extent authenticated by

the researches of modern scholars, that any apparent inconsistencies should not hastily be assumed as proofs of ignorance. But as to whatever relates to countries remote from Greece and Italy, or lying beyond the bounds of the Persian, Macedonian, Carthaginian, and Roman empires, it must of course be received with hesitation. Many of these descriptions of remote countries, when they come to be compared with the accounts of modern travellers, afford, at once, amusing instances of exaggeration, and striking attestations of the substantial authenticity of the works in which they occur. For the coincidence of these accounts, in many respects, with the facts, as they are now fully known, puts it beyond doubt that the historian had actually conversed with natives of those countries, or with travellers; while at the same time the distortion of the picture is precisely such as might be expected from the channels through which the information was derived.

3. The descriptions so frequently met with in ancient writers, of monstrous men or animals—griffins—dragons—hydras—pygmies—giants; or of trees bearing golden fruit, of fountains flowing with perfumed liquids, or even with the precious metals, may, in most cases, be now traced to their origin in actual facts, which, passing to the writer through the medium of ignorant, fanciful, or interested reporters, assumed the characteristic extravagance of fables. On occasions of this kind it is much more becoming to an intelligent student of history to make search, among the stores of modern science, for the probable source of such accounts, than to pass them by with the sneer of indolent scepticism. Some writers of the sixteenth

and seventeenth centuries took so much offence at certain passages of this sort in the history of Herodotus, as to treat the entire work of that industrious and generally accurate writer with contempt, as if it were little better than a repository of fables. But these rash censures now fall back upon themselves; for modern travellers, in visiting the countries described by the father of history, find frequent occasion for noticing the correctness of his statements, or their substantial truth, even in those descriptions or relations which may seem the most open to suspicion.

4. In narrating or describing natural phenomena, such as meteors, tempests, eruptions of volcanoes, earthquakes, eclipses, all that is needed is to remove from the narrative of the historian those explanations, or those decorative phrases, by which he endeavoured to accommodate such occurrences to the political events of the moment, at the suggestion of popular superstitions.

And here we may take occasion to point out a remarkable difference, which forms a characteristic distinction in comparing the Jewish writers with those of other nations, as to the nature of those marvellous or supernatural facts which they describe. The marvellous events reported by the Greek and Roman authors may, with few exceptions, be classed under two heads; namely—allegorical and poetical combinations, which were so obviously fabulous as to ask for no credence, and to demand no scrutiny; or they were mere exaggerations, distortions, or misapplications of natural objects or phenomena. But the Jewish historians and poets do not describe, *as actually existing*, any such allegorical prodigies; and their descriptions of real animals, are either simply exact, or they are evidently *poetical* (like those in the book of Job), but they are not *fabulous*. They do not throw a supernatural colouring over ordinary phenomena, or convert plain facts into prodigies. The supernatural events they record—as matters of history, are such deviations from the standing order of natural causes, as leave us no alternative between a peremptory denial of the veracity of the writers, or a submission to their affirmation of divine agency.

The freedom of the Jewish historians, poets, and prophets, from those admixtures of the marvellous and the natural, with which other ancient writers abound, is one of the most remarkable of their characteristics. Their descriptions of human nature are neither heroical, nor fantastic; their narratives of human affairs are of the simplest complexion, and they are strictly consistent with the known modes of the time and country. Nor is our assent taxed, on any occasion, except when an event is recorded which, unless it had actually taken place, could not have been affirmed by any but reckless impostors.

Besides those prodigies which are met with in profane historians, and that only require to be freed from exaggerations appended to natural events by ignorance, poetry, or superstition, there are other accounts which are not to be satisfactorily explained so readily, and which call for the exercise of some discrimination. They are of a kind that must be accounted either altogether false, or else must imply, in some sense, a supernatural agency. Of the former kind may well be reckoned all, or nearly all, those alleged supernatural occurrences which no doubt were contrived to give credit to an established superstition, or to subserve the designs of statesmen or commanders, and which, in most cases, rested exclusively upon the testimony of priests. On the other hand, there are recorded, in the pages of profane historians, some few facts, apparently beyond the range of natural causes, which cannot be rejected as untrue, unless we do violence to the soundest principles of evidence, and which will not be treated with uninquisitive contempt, except by a purblind scepticism, that is more nearly allied to credulity than to true philosophy. These peculiar cases demand a far more full and particular consideration than it is compatible with the design of this volume to bestow upon them.

5. The political habits and tastes of the Greeks and Romans, induced their historians to supply the personages of their story with formal speeches, on all remarkable occasions; for oratory was the spring and life of every political movement; and as the machine of government could not in fact be made to go without the impelling force of harangues, history must not seem to omit them. Yet there is little reason to believe that authentic reports of public speeches were often, if ever, in the possession of historians. Indeed, these brilliant portions of the history are often so much in the manner of the author, as to leave the reader in no doubt to whom to attribute them. Nevertheless it may be imagined that, on some memorable occasions, the very words of a short speech, or the general purport of an oration, was remembered and recorded, and so was worked into the speech, as framed by the historian.

A compliance with the taste of the times seems also to have led some writers to use means for diverting the attention of their readers, and for relieving the burden of the narrative, by introducing digressions, often of a trivial kind, which, though not announced as mere embellishments, and which perhaps were not purely fictitious, are evidently not entitled to an equal degree of confidence with the main circumstances of the story.

6. The secret motives of public men, or the hidden causes of great events, are not the proper subjects of history, which is concerned only with such facts as may be truly and fairly known. The disquisitions of an historian on such topics are therefore to be excepted against; for when he so forsakes his function, he must expect to be forsaken by his reader; his errors, on such points, do not impeach his veracity; although they lower our opinion of his judgment.

7. Very few facts of importance, such as form the proper subjects of history, rest entirely upon the testimony of a single historian, or are incapable of being directly, or remotely confirmed, by some kind of coincident evidence. Whenever therefore a question arises relative to the truth of a particular statement, recourse must be had, either to the testimony of contemporary writers, or to the evidence of existing monuments. But even if all such means of corroboration should fail, and if we meet with a perplexing silence where we might expect to find confirmation, we are by no means justified in rejecting the unsupported testimony, merely on the ground of this want of correlative support. Many instances may be adduced of the most extraordinary silence of historians relative to

facts with which they must have been acquainted, and which seemed to lie directly in the course of their narrative. Important facts are mentioned by no ancient writer, though they are unquestionably established by the evidence of existing inscriptions, coins, statues, or buildings. There are also facts mentioned only by some one historian, which happen to be attested by an incidental coincidence with some relic of antiquity lately brought to light; if this relic had remained in its long obscurity, such facts might (we see with how little reason) have been disputed.

Nothing can be more fallacious than an inference drawn from the silence of historians relative to particular facts. For a full, comprehensive, and, if the phrase may be used, a *business-like* method of writing history, in which nothing important—nothing which a well-informed reader will look for, must be omitted, is the produce of modern improvements in thinking and writing. The general diffusion of knowledge, and the activity of criticism, occasion a much higher demand in matters of information to be made upon writers than was thought of in ancient times. A full and exact communication of facts has come to be valued more highly than any mere beauties of style; at least, no beauties of style are allowed to atone for palpable deficiencies in matters of fact. The moderns must be taught—and pleased; but the ancients would be pleased, and taught. Ancient writers, and historians not less than others, seem to have formed their notions of prose composition very much upon the model of poetry, which, in most languages, was the earliest kind of literature. As their epics were histories, so, in some sense, their histories were epics. Such particulars, therefore, were taken up in the course of the narrative, as seemed best to accord with the abstract idea of the work—not always those which a rigid adherence to a comprehensive plan would have made it necessary to bring forward.

8. The influence of personal or party prejudices is indefinite; and as it may distort the representations of an historian almost unconsciously to himself, and without impugning his general integrity, so will it, in most instances, be difficult, especially after the lapse of ages, to discover the extent to which the operation of such prejudices should be allowed for. But if it cannot be ascertained how much of the colouring of the picture is to be attributed to the medium through which an historian exhibits his characters, yet the general hues of that medium will hardly escape the observation of an intelligent reader; and when once observed, the illusion is destroyed.

But in relation to the influence of prejudices of this sort, ancient historians unquestionably appear to advantage when compared with those of modern times. Instances of equanimity might be cited from the Greek historians to which few parallels could be adduced, drawn from the pages of modern writers. Like the sculptures of the same people, the works of the Greek historians, though not wanting in the distinctive characters, or the moving energy of life, present an aspect from which the sublimity of repose is never lost. These writers seem to have been conscious that they were holding up the picture of their times to the eyes of mankind in all ages: they forgot, therefore, the passions and interests of the moment.

With ourselves, the instantaneous diffusion of books through all ranks of the community, places a modern author too nearly in the presence of his contemporaries to allow him to think much of posterity. The clamour of public opinion rings around his seclusion: his situation, in its essential circumstances, is almost the same as that of the public speaker—the din of the crowd fills his thoughts, and he almost forgets the distant fame which his genius might command. This nearness of his audience offers therefore to a modern writer every excitement and every inducement to the indulgence of party misrepresentations. If it were not for the correcting influences of a free press, nothing worthy of the name of history would be produced in modern times.

9. That the Greeks were not in fact much inferior to the representations given of them by their historians, the existing monuments of their philosophy, of their poetry, and of their arts, sufficiently attest. Indeed if we pass from an examination of these monuments and remains to the perusal of Herodotus, Thucydides, and Xenophon, we shall be far from thinking that a tone of exaggerated encomium is to be charged upon those writers. From the pages of the historians alone, we should fail to form an adequate idea of the perfection that was attained in all departments of literature and art by the people whose political affairs they narrate. Scarcely half of the history of Greece, in a full and philosophical sense of the term, is to be gathered from its historians:—we must seek for it rather in the remains of its literature at large,— in museums, and cabinets, and among the ruins that still bespread its soil.

It is not therefore this sort of general misrepresentation that is to be suspected in the Greek historians; for more is made certain by other means than is explicitly affirmed by them. Yet it has been supposed that, in their accounts of military affairs, the Greek historians, in order to enhance the glory of their countrymen in repelling the Persian invasions, have exaggerated the power and extent of the Asiatic monarchy, and the numbers of the armies with which those of Greece had to contend. Some amount of misrepresentation, of this kind, may have been admitted. But yet the pictures given by the Greek writers of the wealth and resources of the Persian power—of the puerile ambition of its monarchs—of the countless hosts which they drove before them, by the lash, into Scythia, Egypt, and Europe—conquering nations rather by devastation than by military conduct—by the mouths, more than by the swords of their armies, are so strikingly similar to unquestionable facts in the later history of the Asiatic empires, that, as the one cannot be doubted, the other need not be deemed incredible.

10. The arrogance with which, under the term *barbarians*, the Greek writers speak of all nations that were not of Greek extraction, naturally suggests the belief that we must not expect to derive from them a just idea of the civilisation of the surrounding nations. In truth, not a few indications may be gathered from other sources, which authorise the belief that, in communities not very distant from Greece itself, or its colonies, a degree of intelligence and of refinement existed of which it was their shame to be ignorant, or their greater shame to have taken so little notice.

11. With the Romans it was perhaps less from mere national vanity, than from a dictate of that deep-plotted policy by which they supported their unbounded pretensions, that they were induced to misrepresent the resources and the conduct of the nations on whose necks they trampled. This policy would often produce misrepresentations of a contrary kind to those suggested by national vanity. That universal empire was the right of the Roman arms was the principle of the state: a reverse of fortune therefore was not simply a calamity—it was a seeming impeachment of the high claims of the republic. The nations must not think that their masters could anywhere find equals or rivals in courage or military skill. A defeat hurt the political faith of the Roman citizen more than it alarmed his fears; and he would rather waive the glory of having broken an arm of equal strength with his own, than confess that there was anywhere an arm of equal strength, to resist his will. He would choose to sustain the aggravated shame of having been beaten by an inferior, rather than redeem a part of his dishonour by acknowledging that he had encountered a superior. A writer therefore could not do full justice to the courage, conduct and successes of the enemies of Rome, without offering such an outrage to the common feeling as would have amounted almost to treason against the state. Modern historical criticism—exercised by such a writer as Niebuhr, has sufficed to remove from early Roman history a very large amount of the misstatements and the exaggerations which Livy and his predecessors had accumulated around it.

CHAPTER XII.

CONFIRMATIONS OF THE EVIDENCE OF ANCIENT HISTORIANS, DERIVABLE FROM INDEPENDENT SOURCES.

Most of the principal facts mentioned by ancient historians, as well as many particulars of less importance, are confimed by evidence that is altogether independent, both in its nature, and in the channels through which it has reached us. In truth, although the narratives of historians serve to connect and explain the entire mass of information that has descended to modern times, relative to the nations of remote antiquity, they are far from being the sole sources of that information:— perhaps they hardly furnish so much as a half of the materials of history. These independent sources of information may be classed under the following heads:—

1. The remains of the *general* literature of the nations of antiquity:—their poetry, and their oratory especially, and their philosophical treatises.

2. Chronological documents or calculations.

3. Facts—geographical and physical, which are unchanged in the lapse of time.

4. Those institutions, usages, or physical peculiarities of nations, which have been subjected to little change.

5. The existing monuments of ancient art— paintings, sculptures, gems, coins, and buildings.

The information derivable from these sources answers two distinct purposes, namely—in the first place, that of contributing to the amount of our knowledge of the state of civilisation among ancient nations; and then that of furnishing the means of corroborating or of correcting the assertions of historians on particular points. It is obvious that to go through the particulars that are comprehended under the general heads above-named, or to do so with any degree of precision, would greatly exceed the limits of this book; indeed, the object aimed at in it will be sufficiently attained by merely pointing out, in a few instances, what is the nature, and what is the value of this sort of corroborative evidence.

1. Corroboratory evidence, derived from books—coming as it does through similar, if not the very same channels with those through which we receive the works of historians, and being of the same external form—is likely to produce less impression on the mind than its real validity ought to command. And yet, when it comes to be examined in detail, nothing can be more conclusive than the proof which thus arises from coincidences of names and allusions, such as are found scattered through the works of dramatists, orators, poets, and philosophers, with the more formal statements of contemporary historians. If, for example, the Greek dramatic writings—those of Æschylus, Sophocles, Euripides, Aristophanes, and the Orations of Demosthenes, are collated with the narrations of Thucydides, Xenophon, Diodorus, and Plutarch;—or if the Epistles and the Orations of Cicero, and the Satires of Horace, and of Juvenal, are compared with the historical works of Livy, of Sallust, of

Tacitus, and of Dion Cassius, so many points of agreement present themselves, as must convince every one that these historical assertions, and these allusions, must have had a common origin in actual facts.

Yet it is not merely by presenting special coincidences, on particular points, that the remains of ancient literature confirm the evidence of historians; but it is also by furnishing such pictures of the people among whom they were current, as to all points of their political, religious, and social condition, as consist with the representations of historians. To exhibit the full force of this sort of evidence, let it be imagined that the names of men, and of cities, and countries, having been withdrawn from the works of the classical poets, orators, and philosophers, it were attempted to associate, as countrymen and contemporaries, Herodotus, Thucydides, and Xenophon, with Cicero, Horace, and Seneca; or Tacitus, Cæsar, and Suetonius, with Isocrates, Plato, and Æschylus: every page in the one class of writers, would present some incongruity with the accounts given of the people by the others. On the contrary, in perusing the contemporary writers of the same nation, whatever may be the diversities of their style or subject, we feel that they were all surrounded by the same objects, and that they were subjected to the same influences.

2. Those corroborative evidences that are derived from chronological inscriptions, or from astronomical calculations, have served in some notable instances to confirm or to correct, the testimony of ancient writers, in a very conclusive manner. It should be remembered that ancient historians,

being destitute for the most part of sufficiently precise chronological information, and being themselves also less observant of dates than the modern style of historical composition demands, leave the subject open to many difficulties; and to these difficulties is added that uncertainty which belongs peculiarly, as we have before remarked, to whatever relates to numbers, in the text of ancient authors. It must not however be supposed that ancient chronology is altogether unfixed; for though it may be impossible now to determine the precise time of many events, the results of different lines of calculation are seldom so widely discordant as to be of much importance in the general outline of history.

3. Those inequalities of the earth's surface which have undergone no great change within the historic period, and also the course of rivers, and the peculiarities of climate, and the vegetable and animal productions of each country, though they are not absolutely immutable, have not, even in the lapse of many ages, undergone any such changes as to perplex us in fixing the identity of ancient and modern names. There are now open to our observation, the same scenes, and the same physical appearances which were described, or alluded to, by historians, twenty centuries ago; and finding, as we do, their accounts of these permanent objects to accord with present and well-known facts, we accept such coincidences as a pledge of the general accuracy and authenticity of the writings in question: for if an historian is proved to have been careful to obtain correct information on points that were indirectly connected with his subject, it is but just to believe that he was at least equally

exact in regard to events, and to what belongs more immediately to his narrative.

We have already adverted to the geographical accuracy of Herodotus, and have remarked that the descriptions he gives of countries, and of their productions, are such, for the most part, as to put it beyond doubt that he had himself seen most of the objects which he describes. That the Greek historians should be exact in what relates to the geography and productions of their own narrow soil, is nothing more than what must be expected. But when we find them accurate also in their descriptions of regions remote from Greece, and which were very imperfectly known to their countrymen in general, they furnish a proof of authenticity that may be extended to cases in which we are obliged to accept their testimony unsupported by other evidence.

A pertinent instance of this kind is furnished in the case of Arrian's history of Alexander's expedition—his Indian history, and his description of the shores of the Indian Ocean. The geographical details which occur in these works are, in general, so exact that modern travellers find little difficulty in identifying almost every spot he mentions. This proof of accuracy well supports the claim to the possession of authentic information which is advanced by the author at the commencement of his work, where he declares that his history has been compiled from the memoirs of Ptolemy and of Aristobulus—two of Alexander's generals; and that he had collated their assertions on all points, and had added from other sources, only such particulars as seemed to be the most worthy of credit.

Now when Arrian's history of Alexander's expedition is compared with that of Quintus Curtius, on points of geography, it will be found that the latter writer was either utterly ignorant on the subject, or that he was quite indifferent as to the correctness of his statements. This proof therefore of want of diligence, or want of information, detracts very greatly from the historian's authority on all points which rest on his sole testimony. We might say that it is fatal to his credit, in all such instances. Although an able and attractive writer, Curtius awakens the reader's suspicion by the very character of his style, which betrays his fondness for decoration and enlargement :—this suspicion is then not a little enhanced when we meet with direct evidence of his inaccuracy, in matters of fact.

The permanence of the names of places, under many modifications in the value of vowels or consonants, affords a very curious, as well as important means of authenticating the assertions of ancient historians. Innumerable instances might be adduced in which the names of obscure villages in Asia Minor, Armenia, Persia, Arabia, Palestine, Egypt, and Nubia, recall to every reader's recollection the names occurring in the ancient histories of the same countries. Those remote names could never have found their way into the pages of the Greek and Roman historians if they had not sought, or had not carefully employed, genuine documents in the composition of their works.

In many particulars the statements of the ancient geographers—Strabo, Ptolemy, Pliny, Stephen of Byzantium, and Pausanias, are at variance with each other, and with the narratives of contemporary historians; but in by far the greater number of instances there is nearly as much accordance as is usually found among modern travellers. And when the ancient geography, whether collected from geographers or historians, comes to be collated with the modern—whatever difficulties may here and there present themselves in the way of a perfect conciliation, no one can doubt that the former—taken as a whole—is a genuine account of facts, collected with industry, by actual observation.

4. A similar species of confirmation arises from a comparison of the descriptions given by ancient historians of the physical peculiarities, the manners, and the usages of nations, with facts known to attach to the modern occupants of the same countries. If national manners and usages are less permanent than the features of the country, or than the productions of the soil, they are much more so than might be supposed, when we recollect how many revolutions have swept across the surface of society in the course of ages. Though man is not absolutely the creature of the soil that supports him, and though he does not retain every peculiarity which descends to him from his progenitors, yet neither is he ever free from some permanent mark of tribe, of climate, or of locality. Or if, by the development of mind, and the advance of civilisation, his circumstances and his manners undergo, apparently, a thorough change, yet even then will there remain many lesser indications of his obsolete condition; and many habits and usages, that are too minute and trivial to have attracted attention—if they did not awaken his-

torical recollections, will continue to identify the
modern with the ancient race. Four conquests,
and eighteen centuries, have not wholly obliterated
from the English people all traces of their British
ancestors; and in some races, for example—the
Egyptian, the Arabian, the Jewish, and the
Scythian, a much more perceptible sameness has
been maintained throughout even a longer course
of ages.

Such living monuments of antiquity are not only
highly curious in themselves, but they are very
significant in illustration of ancient history. Yet
it must be acknowledged that the materials for
this kind of confirmatory comment are the most
abundant where they are of the least value; and
often the scantiest, where they would be the most
prized. For it is among half civilised nations,
that manners and modes of life are permanent;
while the advance of intelligence and refinement
produces changes so great as to leave only the
faintest traces of aboriginal characteristics. Thus,
in the plains of Asia, and in the deserts of Africa,
we find nations which, as to their physical peculiarities, their manners, and their usages, differ
little, if at all, from the descriptions given of their
predecessors on the same soil by Herodotus, or
Strabo. Meanwhile the successive occupants of
the European continent—active, intelligent, and
free, have passed under all forms of human life,
and therefore have retained few resemblances to
their remote ancestors.

One climate, indeed, necessities a much greater
degree of permanency in the habits of the people
than another. The fervours of the equatorial
regions, and the rigours of the north, subdue man

to a passive conformity with certain modes of life. These extremes of temperature avail much to vanquish his individual will, to forbid the caprices of his tastes, and to restrain his invention. But in temparate climates, almost every mode of life is found to be practicable, and almost all modes will therefore in turns be practised.

The permanency of manners, even where the most extensive revolutions have taken place, is strikingly displayed among the modern people of Greece. The successive generations of six-and-twenty centuries have passed away since the Iliad and Odyssey were composed; and yet, when the ancient race, as it is described by Homer, comes to be compared with the modern people, the points of sameness are very many. Not only is the language essentially the same; but the modes of thinking and feeling—the superstitions—the costumes—the habits of the inhabitants of particular spots have, in a large number of instances, been very little affected by the lapse of time. If the peculiarities of the race, as described by Homer, may still be recognised, it is no wonder if we find, in the present manners of the people, numerous illustrations of the pictures drawn by the historians of a later age. The descriptions given by Cæsar and Tacitus of the manners of the Gauls, Britons, and Germans, are capable of receiving a like authentication, though not in an equal degree, from usages still existing among the northern nations of Europe.

5. The existing remains of ancient art would very nearly supply the materials for a body of history, even if all books had perished. These relics sometimes serve to establish particular facts, and

sometimes they afford ground from which to deduce general inferences, relative to the wealth, the power, and the intelligence of the nations to whom they belonged. In either case the evidence they yield is of the most conclusive kind; for the solid material is actually in our hands, and it is before our eyes, and in most cases it can be liable to no misinterpretation.

So extensive are the inferences that may fairly be derived from these existing remains, that, as to some ancient nations, we know far more from *this* source, than is to be gathered from the entire evidence of written history: this, at least, is certain, that what is thus learned, if it be in some respects vague, possesses more of the substantial quality of knowledge, and much better deserves to be called *history* than do those bare catalogues of the names of kings, which are often dignified with the term. A name, or twenty names, unconnected with general facts—or a date, serving only to bring a mere name into its proper place in a chronological chart, may indeed impart the semblance of history, but it affords almost nothing of the substance. What we gather, for example, from written history, relative to the Assyrian empire, or to the early kingdoms of Greece, is much less significant than are the historical inferences relative to the people of Egypt, which are fairly deducible from the remains of their architecture.

The existing monuments of art, which are available as sources of historical information, are, 1, buildings and public works; 2, sculptures and gems; 3, inscriptions and coins; 4, paintings, mosaics, and vases; and 5, implements and arms.

For the purpose of confirming, or correcting, or

illustrating, the assertions of historians on particular points, recourse must most often be had to the evidence of inscriptions and coins; and every one knows that from these sources all the leading facts of Greek and Roman history may be authenticated. The latter are especially important, both on account of the information they convey, and of the mode of its transmission to modern times. No one could call in question the utility of inscriptions for the illustration of history: but the student who cannot devote his undivided attention to the subject, or who has not access to the fullest and best sources of information, may very probably waste his time upon documents that he will afterwards discover to be extremely fallacious. In no department of antiquarian learning have misrepresentations, deceptions, and errors of inadvertency more abounded. Authors who were long regarded as unexceptionable authorities are found to deserve little confidence, and on such points a writer who is not worthy of great confidence, is worthy of none.

Coins are concise public records. The device they bear is seldom devoid of some significant allusion to the peculiar pretensions of the realm or city; the image, corresponding in form and expression with sculptures or descriptions, fixes the identity of the personages; and the legend furnishes names, and other specific notices. Coins, therefore, concentrate several kinds of evidence; and, like books, by their multitude, by their wide diffusion, and by the mode of their conservation to modern times, they are, with very few and unimportant exceptions, placed far beyond the reach of fraud or deception. The cabinets of the opulent, in all countries, are filled with series of these historical records; and the spade is every day turning up counterparts to those already known. Statues and buildings have been discovered here and there; but coins are the produce of every soil which civilisation has at any time visited.

Sculptures are either historical or poetical; those of the first kind yield a confirmation to history which, though indefinite, is worthy of attention. That the principal personages whose names occur in history were represented by the artists of their times, is not only probable, but is a well-known fact. Statues or busts of the most distinguished public persons were given to the world by several artists, and they were placed in all the principal cities of the republic or the empire, that claimed any reflection of their glory. The principle of competition among artists would secure some tolerable uniformity—the uniformity of resemblance to the originals, among these statues and busts; nor do we at all pass the bounds of probability in supposing them to be, in general, real and good portraits. There is, besides, in most of them, an air of individuality, which at once convinces the practised eye of their authenticity.

So much as this being assumed, the congruity of these forms with the character of the men, as it is presented on the page of history, carries with it a proof of the truth of those records which few observers of the human physiognomy will feel disposed to question. In order to perceive the force of this kind of evidence it is not necessary to call for the aid of any system of physiognomical science (so called); every one's intuitive discernment will suffice for the purpose. Let the simplest observer of faces and forms, who has read the history of Greece and Rome, look round a gallery of antique statues and busts; and he will be in little danger of misnaming the heads of Themistocles and of Alexander, of Plato and of Cicero, of Phocion and of Alcibiades, of Demosthenes and of Euclid, of Julius Cæsar and of Nero. To those whose eye is exercised in the discrimination of forms, the best executed of these antique heads speak their own biography with a distinctness that gives irresistible attestation to the accounts of historians.

Mythological or poetical sculptures afford inferences of a more general kind; most of which are suggested also by an examination of the temples of which they were the furniture. The exquisite forms of the Grecian chisel declare that the superstition they embodied, although it was frivolous and licentious, was framed more for pleasure than for fear;—that it was rather poetical than metaphysical. They do indicate certainly that the religious system of the people was not sanguinary or ferocious; and that it was not fitted to be the engine of priestly despotism. One would imagine that the ministers of these deities were more the servants of the people's amusements, than the tyrants of their consciences, their property, and their persons.

The Grecian sculptures give proof that the superstition to which they belonged, however false or absurd it might be, was open to all the ameliorations and embellishments of a highly refined literature. In contrast with these are the sacred sculptures of India, which disgust us as undisguised and significant representatives of the horrid vices enjoined and practised by the priests. But the lettered taste of the Greeks taught their artists to invest each attribute of evil with some form of beauty. The hideousness of the vindictive passions must be hid beneath the character of tranquil power; and the loathsomeness of the sensual passions must be veiled by the perfect ideal of loveliness. Art, left to itself, does not adopt these corrections; nor do the authors of superstitious systems ask for them. There must be poetry, there must be philosophy at hand, to whisper cautions to the wantonness of art, and to confine its exuberances within the limits of propriety.

When the remains of ancient structures are examined for the purpose of collecting thence historical information, they must be viewed under three distinct aspects; namely—the resources that were required for their construction—the purposes to which they were devoted, and the taste which they display. A few instances will show the nature, and the extent of the inferences that may fairly be drawn from such an examination.

The remains of Egyptian architecture have long outlasted the fame of the men whose names they were charged to transmit to distant times. Or if some few names have been handed down by historians, or have been drawn from their hieroglyphical concealments by the genius of modern research, the whole amount of such discoveries may be comprised in a few lines, and it falls very far short of conveying anything like a history of the people. But some general facts relative to the wealth, the commerce, the industry, the institutions, the manners, and the superstitions of the Egyptians, have been reported by historians; and the descriptions of that country and of its people, given by Herodotus, Strabo, Diodorus, and Plutarch, confirmed as they are by incidental allusions in other writers, and especially by a few significant expressions occurring in the Jewish Scriptures, afford a tolerably complete idea of this, the most extraordinary of all nations—ancient or modern. Now this testimony of the historians is corroborated, with a peculiar distinctness, by those ruins which still lead hosts of travellers to the banks of the Nile.

These stupendous remains attest in the first place, the unbounded wealth that is affirmed by historians to have been at the command of the Egyptian monarchs;—a wealth derived chiefly from the extraordinary fertility of the country, which, like the plains of Babylon, yielded a three hundredfold return of grain. And as the revenues of a vast empire were added to the home resources of the Babylonian monarchs, so the products of a widely extended commerce came in to augment the treasures of the Egyptian kings. The mouths of the Nile were the centres of trade between the eastern and the western worlds; and that river, after depositing a teeming mud in one year, bore upon its bosom in the next, the harvest it had given, for the feeding of distant and less fertile regions. Nor was the industry of the people—numerous beyond example, wanting to improve every advantage of nature. But for whom was this unbounded wealth amassed, or under whose control was it expended? The testimony of historians coincides with that of the existing ruins in declaring that a despotism—political and religious—of unexampled perfection, and very unlike anything that has since been seen, disposed of the vast surplus products of agriculture and of commerce for the purposes of a gigantic egotism.

By what forms of exaction or of monopoly the Egyptian kings held at their command the property and the services of the people, cannot be certainly determined; but it seems as if one only centre of real possession was acknowledged, and that habits of thinking and acting—bound down to unalterable modes, by a thousand threads of superstitious observance, favoured the tranquil transfer of all rights to the head of the state. With such resources therefore at his disposal, and with a people much better fitted by their temperament and habits for labour than for war—the inhabitants of fertile plains have ever been less warlike than those of mountainous regions—the master of Egypt might find it easy to expend his means in realising monstrous architectural conceptions.

That degree of scientific skill in masonry which belongs to a middle stage of civilisation, in which the human faculties are but partially developed, is what the accounts of historians would lead us to expect; and it is just what these remains actually display. There is science—but there is much more of cost and of labour than of science. The works undertaken by the Egyptian builders were such as a calculable waste of human life would be certain to complete; but they were not such as involve a mastery of practical difficulties by means which mathematical genius must devise.

The Egyptian builders could rear pyramids, or excavate catacombs, or hew temples from out of solid rocks of granite; but they attempted no works like those that were executed by the artists of the middle ages. For to poise so high in air the fretted roof and slender spire of a Gothic Minster required a cost of mind greater far than appears to have been at the command of the Egyptian kings.

The purposes to which the structures of Egypt apparently were devoted, agree also with the accounts of historians. The established depotism was indeed such as to permit capricious sovereigns to indulge their personal vanity without restraint; nevertheless, better and more wise maxims of governments were acknowledged, and often followed; and so it is that the traces of public works of vast extent, and of great utility, everywhere attest the intelligence and the good dispositions of some of the Egyptian kings. Canals, piers, reservoirs, aqueducts, are not less abundant than temples and pyramids. Indeed, the temples of Egypt must not be placed altogether to the account either of the vanity of kings, or of the pride of priests; for as the Roman emperors expended a portion of the tribute of the world in the erection of theatres for the gratification of favoured provinces, so the Egyptian kings, for the pleasure of their subjects, reared, in all parts of the land, those sacred menageries of worshipful bulls, crocodiles, cows, apes, cats, dogs, onions, and other—the like august symbols of the common religion. It is recorded that the two kings whose names were held in execration by posterity on account of the cruel labours they exacted from their people, were not builders of temples—but of pyramids.

A mound of earth, one foot in height, satisfies that feeling of our nature which impels us to preserve from disturbance the recent remains of the dead; but a pyramid five hundred feet in height was not too tall a tomb for an Egyptian king! The varnished doll, hideous to look at, into which the art of the apothecary had converted the carcase of the deceased monarch, must needs rest in the deep bowels of a mountain of hewn stone! More complete proof of the utter subjugation of the popular will in ancient Egypt cannot be imagined than what is afforded by the fact, that so much masonry should have been piled, for such a purpose, almost to the clouds. The pyramids could never touch the general enthusiasm of the people, they could only gratify the crazy vanity of the man at whose command they were reared. These tapering quadrangles, as they were the product, so they may be viewed as the proper images of a pure despotism; vast in the surface it covers, and the materials it combines, the prodigious mass serves only to give towering altitude to—a point.

A literature like that of Greece would have protected the Egyptians from the toils of building pyramids :—for, had they possessed poets like Homer, historians like Thucydides, and philosophers like Aristotle, their kings would neither have dared, nor indeed have wished, to attach their fame to bulks of stone, displaying no trace of genius, either in the design, or the execution. The Egyptian kings consigned their names to the custody of pyramids, which have long since betrayed the trust.—The Greeks committed the renown of their chiefs to the frail papyrus of the Nile, and the record has shown itself to be imperishable.

The accordance of the taste displayed in the forms and embellishments of the Egyptian temples, with the temperament and the institutions of the people, as described by historians, deserves to be noticed; though, of course, no very positive conclusions ought to be drawn from facts of this class. It is the province of art, whatever may be the material upon which it works, to combine, in various proportions, the two elements of effect—sameness and difference—uniformity and variety—harmony and opposition. A work of art in which these principles should be wholly disjoined, or which should exhibit only one of them—if that were possible—might amaze the spectator, but could never produce pleasure. To combine them in exact accordance with the intended effect of the work, is the perfection of art. If the impression to be produced inclines to the side of grandeur and sublimity, the principle of sameness or uniformity must predominate; and every variety that is admitted in the embellishments must be quelled by constant repetitions in the same form.

But if the sentiment to be awakened is that of pleasure—gaiety, and voluptuousness, the second principle, or that of difference, variety, and opposition, must triumph over the first. Now a uniform preference of one of these styles in works of art, must be held to characterise the prevailing temper of the people whom they are intended to please.

But now the Egyptian architecture is distinguished, perhaps beyond that of any other people, by its subjection to the law of uniformity, and by the apparent aim of the artist to vanquish the imagination of the spectator by an aspect of sublimity; to kindle the sentiment of awe was the intention; and bulk and sameness were the means.

This character of Egyptian art, which prevails almost without exception among the existing remains of the more ancient structures, comports well with the idea of the subjugation of the people beneath a system of stern religious and civil despotism. And yet further, it has a remarkable significance when considered in its relation to the nature of the worship to which these temples were devoted. While we gaze with amazement and awe at the massy buttresses of these structures—at their towering obelisks—at their long ranges of columns, formed as if to support the weight of mountains, and at the colossal guards of the portico, we have to recollect that these temples were the consecrated palaces of crocodiles, of cows, of ichneumons, of dogs, cats, or apes. It seems as if, for the very purpose of effecting the most complete degradation of the popular mind, the national superstition had been framed from the vilest materials it was possible to find; while, to enhance and secure its influence, a nobly-imagined art combined every element of awful grandeur. The imagination was first seduced by a show of sublimity, in order that the moral sense might, the more effectually, be, in the end, trodden in the dust.

The mathematical ornaments, and the vegetable imitations of the Egyptian architecture might be noticed, which, besides being admirably imagined and executed, are in perfect harmony with the general taste of the buildings, and thus consist with what we suppose to have been its main intention. But the character of the human figures attached to many of the temples, demands attention.

Not a few of these figures exhibit the highest degree of excellence—within certain bounds; these bounds are—a strict adherence to the national contour and costume (neither of which could have been preferred by artists who had seen the people of Europe and Asia) and a rigid observance of architectural directness of position. In a very few examples the artists so far transgressed the rules thus imposed upon them, as to prove that they had the command of attitudes more varied than those which ordinarily they exhibited; indeed, it is contrary to all analogy to suppose, that so much executive talent should exist along with an incapacity to give more life and variety to the figure. The Chinese, who as artists are vastly inferior to the ancient Egyptian sculptors, ordinarily pass far beyond them as to the range of action and position which they give to their human figures. Even if a taste so rigid had belonged to the first stage of art, it must—unless otherwise restricted, have admitted amelioration in the course of time. The artists of a second age would no doubt have sought reputation by venturing beyond the limits within which their predecessors had been confined.

It seems then hardly possible to find a reason for that frozen uniformity which is exhibited in the Egyptian sculptures, unless we suppose that art—like everything else, was the slave of an omnipresent despotism. The human forms which support the porticos or roofs, stand and look as if they knew themselves to be in the presence of Superior Power. Freedom of position, or an attitude of force, or of agility, or even of inattentive repose, or any indication of individual will, would have broken in upon the idea of universal subjection. The master of Egypt must look upon no forms that do not speak submission.

And yet there is an air of serenity (though it be not such as springs from the consciousness of personal dignity) tending towards gaiety, in most of these sculptures: the look indeed is altogether servile; yet it is unrepining, and it seems to express entire acquiescence in that immutable order of things which transferred the rights of all to one.

That such a condition of the social system as this actually existed in the times when the Egyptian temples were reared, must not be positively affirmed, merely on the grounds above mentioned; but if, amidst the ill-founded encomiums bestowed upon the Egyptian institutions by ancient historians, there may clearly be traced the indications of a state of unexampled subjection to fixed modes of action in the social, the religious, and the political systems of the people, the existing monuments of their architecture and sculpture are to be acknowledged as according well with these indications. Yet if this accordance were thought to be fanciful, let it be attempted to associate our notions of the Grecian people, and their institutions, with the Egyptian architecture and sculpture.—It would be impossible to combine ideas so incongruous.

The Grecian architecture, although its elements were evidently derived from that of Egypt, is contrasted with it in almost every point. The people to whom these comparatively diminutive, and yet faultless structures belonged, manifestly, were not masters of boundless national wealth; but their intelligence so much exceeded their resources that they at once reached the highest point of art, which is to induce upon its materials a new value—a value so great, that the mere cost of the work is forgotten. In surveying the Egyptian temples we wonder at the wealth that could suffice to pay for them; in viewing those of Greece we only admire the genius of the architect who imagined them, and the taste of the people who admired them.

The plains of Greece are burdened by no huge monuments, the only intention of which is to crush the common feelings of a nation beneath the weight of one man's vanity; but its surface was thick set with temples which were the property of all— temples, free from gloom, and unstained with cruel rites.

A more striking point of contrast cannot be selected than that presented by a comparison of the human figures (above-mentioned) that are attached to the Egyptian temples, with those that decorate the Grecian architecture. The Grecian caryatides assume the attitude of as much liberty, ease, and variety of position as may comport with the burdensome duty of supporting the pediment: they give their heads to the mass of masonry above them—not with the passiveness of slaves, but as if with the alacrity of free persons. The Egyptian figures stand like the personifications of unchanging duration; but as to the Grecian caryatides, one might think that they had but just stepped up from the merry crowd, and were themselves the pleased spectators of the festivities that are passing before them.

The Roman architecture, as compared with that of India or of China, is only so far less barbarous, as it is more Grecian. In the arts the Romans were imitators, and they are hardly ever to be admired when they wandered from their pattern. Those structures in which they might best claim the praise of originality—namely—their vast amphitheatres, are rather monuments of wealth, luxury, and native ferocity of character, than of taste or intelligence.

The structures which shed the greatest lustre upon the Roman name, are those public works—roads, bridges, and aqueducts, which, in almost every country of Europe, mark the presence of their legions; and these attest that vigour of character—that unconquerable perseverance—that regard to utility, and especially, that steady pursuit of universal empire, which history declares to have characterised the Roman people and government.

The student of history, although he may not have access to museums, and although costly antiquarian publications should never come into his possession, may find, even in his seclusion, some visible and palpable proofs of the authenticity of the Roman historians; for the circuit of a few miles in many districts of the British Islands, will offer illustrations of the narratives of Cæsar, of Tacitus, and of Suetonius. Though the occupation of Britain by the Romans was of shorter continuance than that of almost any other country—included within the empire, and though their possession of the island was always partial and disturbed, they yet made themselves so much at home with our ancestors as that our soil teems with the relics of their sojourn of three hundred years. Roman camps, roads, walls, and baths;—mosaics, vases, weapons, utensils, and coins, are as abundant, almost, in England as in Italy; and they are quite abundant enough to substantiate the proud glories that are claimed for the Roman arms by their historians.

If then there were room to entertain a doubt of the authenticity of the body of ancient history—taken in the mass; or if the credibility of a single author comes to be questioned; or if a particular fact be opened to controversy, it is far from being the case that we are left to rely, alone, upon the validity of general arguments in proof of the apparent competency, veracity, and impartiality of the ancient historians; on the contrary, we may, in almost all cases, appeal to unquestioned facts, supporting the affirmative side of such questions. For instance, we may compare the testimony of the historians themselves—one with another; or with that of contemporary writers in other departments of literature, whose allusions to public events or persons are of an incidental kind; or we may compare the descriptions that are given by historians of natural objects, or of national peculiarities with the same objects or peculiarities—still existing; or, to take a method still more precise, and still more palpably certain, we may read upon the face of marble, or brass, or gold, or silver, or precious stones—long buried in the earth, explicit records of the very events, or memorials of the very persons, mentioned by historians. Or we may examine the remains of public works and buildings, described by historians, and find them accordant with their accounts of the power, tastes, and habits of the people that reared them.

Notwithstanding all these means of proof, various as they are, there may yet remain some points of history that are not satisfactorily attested, or that are liable to reasonable suspicion; yet as to the great mass of facts, these will be found to be so fully established as to render scepticism regarding them altogether absurd.

But now the proof which establishes the general authenticity of ancient historians, and which demonstrates that their writings are, in the main, what they profess to be—that is—genuine narratives of events, composed and published in the age to which they are usually assigned, carries with it, by implication, a proof of the genuineness of other remains of ancient literature. If, for example, we have under our touch, palpable evidence that the works of Tacitus are genuine and authentic, we can no longer deny that the raft on which ancient books floated down through so many ages was substantially secure; and we may safely conclude that whatever mists may seem to hang over some parts of the channel of transmission, the vessel and its cargo did actually pass, undamaged, through the gloom of ages.

Though this inference may be applicable to the remains of ancient literature more in the mass, than in detail; it nevertheless possesses a conclusive force when brought to bear upon vague and sweeping attacks upon the genuineness and integrity of ancient writings, as if they were incapable of any certain proof. Those who profess to entertain doubts of this sort, do not ordinarily apply themselves with care to the examination of any one instance, nor attempt patiently to refute particular proofs; but rather they fling about broad assertions, tending to destroy all confidence in the process and medium through which the records of antiquity have been conveyed to modern times. Now to such vague insinuations, a full and sufficient reply is given, when we adduce demonstrative proof of the authenticity of historical works which could not have contained consistent and circumstantial truth unless they had actually been written in the age to which they are attributed. If then *some* books have descended—entire, through eighteen or twenty centuries, others may have done so; and if so, then no objection can be maintained against ancient books, *à priori;* nor can any suspicion rest upon particular works—except such as may be justified by specific proofs of spuriousness.

CHAPTER XIII.

GENERAL PRINCIPLES, APPLICABLE TO QUESTIONS OF THE GENUINENESS AND AUTHENTICITY OF ANCIENT RECORDS.

CIVILISATION has not ordinarily, if indeed it has ever done so, sprung up spontaneously in any land. A germ of the arts, and of literature, transmitted from people to people, and passed down from age to age, has taken root and become prolific, in a degree, proportioned generally to the amount and variety of those elements of social and intellectual improvement that may have been received from distant sources.

These germs of civilisation may have been transported, and scattered by colonisation, by trade, or by conquest; but they are never so fully expanded as when they are cherished by an imported literature. It is not by comparing themselves with themselves, that individuals, or that nations, become wise; and though there are fruits of genius which seem to owe nothing to extraneous sources, the general perfectionment of reason and of taste can be attained only by an extended knowledge of what has been thought and performed by men of other nations, and of other times.

Among all the inestimable advantages which have raised the inhabitants of England and of France and of Germany, above those of Turkey or of China, very few can be named that have not—directly or indirectly—sprung from a knowledge of the civilisation, the arts, and the literature of ancient nations. What is it that would be left to the people of Europe, if all this knowledge, and all its remote consequences, could at once be subtracted from their religious, their political, and their intellectual condition? But it must be remembered that it has chiefly been by *the transmission of books*, from age to age, that this yeast of civilisation is now possessed and enjoyed. If those works which we believe to be genuine are not so in fact, we may be said to hold all the blessings of social and intellectual advancement by a forged title. For on such a supposition the first stock, or the rudiment of our advantages has sprung from a mass of fabrications. No one entertains such a supposition; and yet it must be admitted if any *general* objections are to be allowed to disparage the mode in which ancient literature has been transmitted to modern times.

If we except the almost forgotten enterprise of the Jesuit, Harduin, no such general objections are ever formally made, or insinuated, in relation to the remains of classic literature, and this for two reasons;—first, because an attempt to support a sceptical doctrine of this sort would be treated by the *learned* with contempt, as proceeding from a whimsical love of paradox, or from an inane ambition to attract attention; and secondly, because the *unlearned* could never be induced to take so much interest in a controversy of this kind, as might reward the pains of those who attempted to delude them.

But it is otherwise in relation to the Holy Scriptures; for while some few of the learned are, from sinister motives, willing to aid an attempt to bring the authority of these books into suspicion, there are always thousands of the community who may easily be engaged to listen to objectors, and who, from their want of information, and their incapacity to reason correctly, are easily made the dupes of any plausible sophistry.

Nor is it merely the uneducated classes that are exposed to the artifices of sophists; for persons whose acquirements in general literature are respectable, seem sometimes to be perplexed by objections of a kind which, if levelled at the remains of classic authors, they would deem undeserving of any serious regard.

This strange and often fatal inconsistency, may sometimes arise from the influence of moral causes, which it does not fall within the design of this volume to notice; but it is often attributable to a want of attention to some common principles of evidence which, though they are so obvious that it may seem almost frivolous to insist upon them, are never respected by objectors, and are seldom remembered by the victims of sophistry. The most prominent of these principles may be classed under the five following heads.

I. Facts remote from our personal observation may be as certainly proved by evidence that is fallible *in its kind*, as by that which is not open to the possibility of error.

By *certain* proof is here meant, not merely such as may be presented to the senses, or such as cannot be rendered obscure, even for a moment, by a perverse disputant;—but such as when once understood, *leaves no room for doubt in a sound mind.*

And this degree of certainty is every day obtained, in the common occasions of life, by means of evidence that is fallible in its nature, and which may be questionable in all its parts, *separately* considered. Let us take such an instance as this. —A person receives letters from several of his friends in a neighbouring town, informing him that an extensive fire has happened the night before, in that place, in consequence of which many of the inhabitants have been driven from their homes:—presently afterwards, a crowd of the sufferers, bringing with them the few remains of of their furniture, passes his door:—his friends arrive among them, and ask shelter for their families;—the next day the papers contain a full description of the calamity. Does this person entertain any doubt as to the alleged fact? He cannot do so; and yet he admits that human testimony is fallacious:—he knows that men lie much oftener, than that towns are burned down:— perhaps there is not one of all those who have reported the fact whose veracity ought to be considered as absolutely unimpeachable;—some of them deserve no confidence:—and as for the public prints, they every day admit narratives that are altogether unfounded.

Scepticism of this sort, on such an occasion, if it be supposable, could only arise from a degree of mental perversity, not much differing from insanity. In other words, this amount of evidence is such as leaves absolutely no room for doubt in a sound mind; nevertheless, the material of which it is composed—if we may so speak—is in itself fallible, and as to all the parts of it, if *separately taken*, they might be rejected.

Or we may take an example or two of another kind.—It has been long affirmed by voyagers, and on their authority it has been assumed as certain by the compilers of geographical works, and by the framers of charts, that, midway in the Pacific Ocean, there are several groups of inhabited islands. And the people of England, generally, think these affirmations as certain, as that two and two are four. And yet who does not know that voyagers are too fond of bringing home tales, invented to amuse the weariness of a long voyage, and published to win the wonder of the vulgar, or turn a penny? Now it may be imagined that some question of national importance—some argument for the remission of taxes—depended upon proving that such islands do not exist; and then let it be supposed that certain interested disputants are permitted to win the ear of the common people, and to keep it to themselves: in such a case the proof of this fact—certain as it is, might easily be made to appear very questionable, or to be altogether unworthy of belief—in a word, a trick of the Government, contrived to wring money from the people!

Or again:—It has been affirmed by historians that some two hundred years ago the Parliament of England quarrelled with their king—levied war against him—vanquished, and beheaded him, and set up a republican form of government, in the place of the monarchy. But in proof of facts so improbable as these we have no better evidence than the testimony of prejudiced political writers: the whole story rests on the credit of old books or manuscripts; nor is there one of the writers who have repeated the narrative that may not be con-

victed of some misrepresentation; and some of
them are plainly chargeable with many direct
and wilful untruths. Notwithstanding this array
of objections, yet the principal events of the
civil war are, in the estimation of all persons of
sound mind, as certainly established as any
mathematical proposition. The same may be
said of innumerable facts—much more remote,
or apparently obscure, than those above mentioned;
and yet they are so proved, that they
cannot be questioned without doing violence to
common sense.

The difference between the proof obtained by
mathematical demonstration, and that which results
from an accumulation of oral or written testimony,
is not—that the latter must always, and *from its
nature*, be less certain than the former; but that
the certainty of the former may be *exhibited* more
readily, and by a simpler and more compact
process, than that of the other. If it were denied
that the three angles of every triangle are equal
to two right angles, an actual measurement of
lines, or the placing of two pieces of card one
over the other, would end the dispute in a moment:
or even if the problem were of a more complicated
kind, belonging to the higher branches of mathematical
science, and therefore if it were such as
could not be made plain to an uninstructed person,
by any means, or to any one by a very brief
process, yet whoever will choose to bestow time
enough and is capable of giving attention enough
to the demonstration, will not fail, at length, to be
convinced of its truth; for all the parts of which
it consists are certain, and their connection, one
with another, is also certain. But the certainty

that is obtained from a mass of testimony, oral or written, does not result from the solidity of the separate parts, or the firmness of the cement which connects them; but from the irresistable pressure of the multifarious mass. The strength of mathematical demonstration is like that of a pier;—the strength of accumulated testimony is like that of the swelling ocean when its tides are mantling upon the shore.

II. Facts, remote from our personal knowledge, are not necessarily more or less certain in proportion to the length of time that has elapsed since they took place.

An illusion of the imagination, taking its rise, naturally, from the indistinctness of our individual recollections of infancy, and from the entire obliteration of many of the records of memory, leads us, involuntarily, to attach an idea of obscurity, and of uncertainty, to whatever is remote in time. And besides; if the knowledge of remote facts has been imperfectly, or suspiciously, transmitted, and if there be a want of direct evidence on any point of ancient history, then the distance of time does really decrease the chances of collecting any *new* evidence; and therefore such facts must always be shrouded in uncertainty.

But whatever has been well and sufficiently proved in one age, remains not less certainly proved in the next, so long as all the evidences continue in the same state. Indeed—as we have before remarked, historical evidence often greatly increases in clearness and certainty by the lapse of time. If in the time of Leo X. it was certain that Augustus ruled the Roman world sixteen hundred years before that period, we have no need to deduct anything from our persuasion of the truth of the fact, on account of the four centuries which have since elapsed. On the contrary, the proof of it has become much greater, both in its amount, and in its clearness, now, than it was then.

The proof of the genuineness of books, even if it should not gather particles of evidence, yet remains, from age to age, unimpaired. Nor is the proof of the genuineness of modern works more satisfactory, although it may be more abundant, than that of ancient books. We could not be persuaded that the Paradise Lost was written in the last century by some obscure scribbler; nor would it be a whit less absurd to suppose that the Æneid was composed in the tenth century, or the Iliad at any time subsequent to the invasion of Greece by Xerxes.

The degree of certainty that is attainable on any point of ancient history, or literature, is regulated —not by distance of time, but by the state of the world at the period in question; especially by the contraction, or the diffusion of general knowledge at that time. This certainty therefore rises and falls—it becomes bright or obscure, alternately, from age to age, and it does so quite irrespectively of distance of years. In sailing up the stream of time, mists and darkness rest upon the landscape at a comparatively early stage of our progress; but as we ascend, light breaks upon the scene in the full splendour of a noonday sun; scarcely an object rests in obscurity, and whatever is most prominent and important, may be discerned in its minutest parts.

III. The validity of evidence in proof of remote facts is not affected, either for the better or the

worse, by the weight of the consequences that may
happen to depend upon them.

No principle can be much more obviously true
than this; and if the reader chooses to call it a
truism, he is welcome to do so: and yet none is
more often disregarded. With the same sort of
inconsistency which impels us to measure the
punishment of an offence—not by its turpitude,
but by the amount of injury it may have occasioned,
we are instinctively inclined to think the most
slender evidence *good enough* in proof of a point
which is of no importance; while we distrust the
best evidence as if it were feeble, on any occasion
when the fact in question involves great and
pressing interests. We are apt to think of evidence
as if it were a cord or a wire, which, though it
may sustain a certain weight, must needs snap
with a greater. And yet the slightest reflection
will dissipate a prejudice that is so groundless and
absurd.

It is very true that the degree of care, of diligence, and of attention, with which we examine
evidence, may well be proportioned to the importance of the consequences that are involved in the
decision. A juryman ought indeed to give his
utmost attention to testimony that may sentence a
prisoner to a month's confinement; but if he be
open to the common feelings of humanity, he will
exercise a tenfold caution when life or death is
to be the issue of his verdict. This is very
proper; but no one who is capable of reasoning
justly would think that, if the proof of guilt in
the former case has been thoroughly examined,
and is quite conclusive, it can become a jot
less convincing, if it should be found that some

new interpretation of the law makes the offence capital.

The genuineness of the satires and epistles of Horace is allowed by all scholars to be unquestionable; and any one who has examined the evidence in this instance, must call him a mere sophist who should attempt to raise a controversy on the subject. Would the case be otherwise than it is, even though the proof of the genuineness of these writings should overthrow the British constitution; or should make it the duty of every man to resign his property to his servant?

The evidence of the genuineness and authenticity of the Jewish and Christian Scriptures has, for no other reason than a thought of the consequences that are involved in an admission of their truth, been treated with an unwarrantable disregard of logical equity—and even of the dictates of common sense. The poems of Anacreon, the tragedies of Sophocles, the plays of Terence, the epistles of Pliny, are adjudged to be safe from the imputation of spuriousness, or of material corruption; and yet evidence ten times greater as to its quantity, variety, and force, supports the genuineness of the poems of Isaiah, and the epistles of Paul.

This violation of argumentative equity, in relation to the Scriptures, has been favoured by the mere circumstance of their having to be so continually defended. It matters little how impudently false an imputation may be; the reply, though, in the most absolute sense, conclusive, is apt to beget almost as much suspicion as it dissipates. Herein consists the strength of infidel writings;—they call for a defence of that which is attacked, and this defence seems to imply that

there is a question which may fairly be argued,
and that it is in some degree doubtful. Let the
genuineness of the most indubitable of the classics
be boldly questioned in a popular style, and let it
be defended in a form level to the mode of attack
—and level also to the ignorance of the middle
and lower orders, and the result would produce
quite as many cases of doubt, as of conviction.

What course ought to be pursued, or which
alternative should be adopted, if a case should arise
wherein evidence, intrinsically good, seems to
support a narrative that is palpably incredible,
and contradictory to common sense, is a question
that may well be left undecided until such a case
actually presents itself. No such incongruity
weighs against our acceptance of the Jewish and
Christian Scriptures; for the miracles they report,
wrought for purposes so wise and benign, accord
with every notion we can antecedently form of the
Divine character and government.

IV. A calculation of actual instances, taken
from almost any class of facts, will prove that a
mass of evidence which carries the convictions of
sound minds, is incomparably more often true than
false.

Evidence may be spoken of as *good* if it be such
that, after an ordinary amount of examination, it
does not appear to be liable to suspicion. However
much of falsification and of error there may be in
the world, there is yet so great a predominance of
truth, that any one who believes indiscriminately
will be in the right a thousand times to one,
oftener, than any one who doubts indiscriminately.
Habitual scepticism will render a man the victim
of almost perpetual error. Indeed, either to

believe by habit, or to doubt by habit, must be regarded as the symptom of a feeble or diseased mind. And yet the former is vastly more congruous to the actual condition of mankind, and to the ordinary course of human affairs, and is more safe, and is more reasonable, than the latter.

No man, unless his mind is verging towards insanity, acts in the daily occasions of common life on the principles of scepticism; for with such a rule of action in his head, he must retreat from human society, and take up his abode in a cavern. Not only is the sceptic an anomalous being among his fellows, but his scepticism itself is an anomaly in his own ordinary conduct; it is an insanity on single points, which of all kinds is the least hopeful of cure.

Adherence to truth is an element of human nature, just as is the love of kindred: and although the operation of both principles is liable to interruption, such deviations from the impulses of nature must always be held to arise from the influence of some specific inducement. Wilful, difficult, and hazardous falsifications, prompted by no assignable motive of interest or ambition, if indeed such are ever attempted, need not be included in a calculation of probabilities. If, therefore, in listening to a professed narrative of facts, we have reason to feel secure against the ordinary motives of deliberate falsehood; and if, on the contrary, the veracity of the narrator is guaranteed by the circumstances in which he is placed; if, moreover, his testimony is confirmed by a measure of independent evidence; and if it is uncontradicted by testimony of equal value; and if the whole case has been again and again scrupulously examined by persons of every cast of mind—then, and in such a case, if indeed a remaining possibility of delusion exists, it is so incalculably small, that to take it up *in preference* to the positive evidence, must be accounted an infatuation arising from folly or perversity.

Let then the rule above mentioned be applied to the existing remains of ancient literature. Among the works that were brought to light and printed in the fifteenth and sixteenth centuries, there were not a few—though few in comparison with the whole—which were very soon discovered to be spurious productions—imitations of the style of ancient authors. Although at first sight they seemed to possess a claim to genuineness, they were soon found to be destitute of that external evidence which may be collected from the quotations of subsequent writers; or there was a manifest failure in the attempted imitation of style; or there were oversights, in phrases or allusions, such as served fully to expose the deception. All these cases stand excluded, therefore, from the intention of our proposition; for they do not possess evidence of authenticity that could be spoken of as *seemingly good*.

Besides works obviously spurious, there were a few of which the claim to genuineness was good enough to justify controversy, and which yet find a few advocates among scholars; although the majority of critics has returned a verdict against them. Now these doubtful works, inasmuch as their genuineness is not generally acknowledged, may also be excluded from our proposition; for the evidence in their favour can barely be called—seemingly good.

Now after exclusions of this kind have been made, no one acquainted with the evidence that supports the genuineness of the unquestioned portion of ancient literature, and who has given attention to the controversies which have been carried on relative to doubtful works, and who is aware of the assiduity, the acuteness, the learning, the eager pertinacity of research, that have been brought to bear upon such questions, will affirm that there are ancient works, generally supposed by scholars to be genuine, which are in fact spurious. Every one who is competent to form an opinion on the subject grants, that even if there be a chance that a few of the classic authors, the genuineness of which has never been doubted, are after all spurious, such a chance is incalculably small—it is so small, as to leave nothing but paradoxes and absurdities in the hands of those who, on such ground, should attempt to bring them under suspicion.

V. The strength of evidence is not proportioned to its simplicity, or to the ease with which it may be apprehended by all persons; on the contrary, the most conclusive kind of proof is often that which is the most intricate and complicated.

In the mathematical sciences there are many propositions, so simple and so readily demonstrated, that all to whom they are explained may be supposed to carry away an equally clear apprehension of their truth; but the higher departments of these sciences abound with theorems which, though not in any degree less certain than the simplest axioms, are shown to be true by means of a process which may require hours, or even days to work it out. Among those who actually attend to all the parts of such a process, there will be wide differences in the kind and degree of conviction that is obtained of the truth of such propositions. Some, though they may firmly believe the demonstration to be perfect, as well because they have examined —one by one—the links of which it consists, as because they know it is assented to by calculators more competent than themselves, are yet unable, either from the want of habit, or of capacity, to *comprehend* the method of proof; or to perceive distinctly the connection of the parts, and the real *oneness* of the whole. They have walked in the dark over the ground—groping their way from step to step;—they are satisfied that they have arrived, by a right path, at a certain point, though they cannot survey the route.

But another calculator, long practised in the refined modes of abstract reasoning—expert in leaping with certainty over intervals which others must slowly pace, and capable, by the vigour and comprehension of his mind, of retaining his hold of a multitude of particulars, sees the certainty of such operose demonstrations with as much ease as another finds in comprehending an elementary proposition. Yet the conclusion which perhaps not fifty men in Europe can, with full intelligence, know to be true, is actually as true as the axiom which the schoolboy comprehends at a glance.

Now all evidence on questions of antiquity, whether the facts be historical or literary, thus far resembles an operose demonstration in mathematical science, that it is remote from the intellectual habits, and extraneous to the usual acquirements, even of well-educated persons: very far remote, therefore, must it be from the mental range of the uninstructed classes. The strength of our convictions, as to matters of fact, remote in time or place, must bear proportion to the extent and the exactness of our knowledge, and to the consequent fulness and vividness of our conceptions of that class of objects to which the question relates. By long and intimate familiarity with ancient authors, and by an extensive acquaintance with the relics of antiquity, of all kinds, the imagination of the scholar bears him back to distant ages, with a full and distinct consciousness of the reality of those scenes and persons. Nor is this ideal converse with remote objects like that which is produced by fictitious narratives; for such excursions of the the fancy through unreal regions, are disconnected with the rest of our ideas and convictions: on the contrary, the ideal presence of an accomplished mind in the scenes of ancient history is firmly, and by innumerable ties, combined with the knowledge of present realities. The imagination does not flit on the wing of a fantasy, from the real, to an unreal world; but it tracks its way, with a steady step, on solid ground, from times present, to times past; the intelligent conviction of truth travels up to the farthest point of its progress.

To those who are thus conversant with history, all facts or events—literary or historical—if they be satisfactorily attested, are held in the mind with a firmness of persuasion which cannot, by any statements, or any reasonings, however conclusive or perspicuous, be imparted to other minds; because, neither its own powers of comprehension, nor its variety of knowledge, can be so imparted.

CHAPTER XIV.

RELATIVE STRENGTH OF THE EVIDENCE WHICH SUPPORTS THE GENUINENESS AND AUTHENTICITY OF THE HOLY SCRIPTURES.

SOME copies of Quintilian's Institutions of Oratory, very much corrupted and mutilated by the ignorance or presumption of copyists, were known in Italy before the fifteenth century. But in 1414, while the Counsel of Constance was sitting, Poggio, a learned Italian, was commissioned by the promoters of learning to proceed to that place, in search of ancient manuscripts, which were believed to be preserved in the monasteries of the city and its vicinity. His researches were rewarded by discovering in the morastery of St. Gall, beneath a heap of long-neglected lumber, a perfect copy of the Institutions.

The manuscript thus discovered, was soon subjected to the examination of critics; it was collated with existing copies, it was compared with the references of ancient authors, and thus was ascertained to be genuine, and, in the main, uncorrupted. And yet the substance of the evidence on which this decision rests might be comprised in a page.

The abridged history of Rome, by Paterculus, has come down to our times only in a single manuscript, and that one is so much corrupted, that critics have despaired of restoring the text to its purity. It happens, also, that this history is quoted by one ancient author only—Priscian, a grammarian of the sixth century. Yet, notwithstanding this scantiness of the evidence, and this corruption of the single existing copy, the genuineness of the work is fully admitted by scholars. The style, the allusions, the coincidences, are such as to satisfy those who are competent to estimate the value of this sort of proof. But now if this proof were formally set before us, and even if it were as much expanded as it would bear, it must look exceedingly meagre; and, to uninformed readers, it must appear slender as a thread, and insufficient to sustain any weighty consequence. But scholars, in reading the book, feel that sort of conviction of its genuineness which is experienced by a traveller, who has spent his life in passing from country to country, conversing with men of all nations: when this travelled person meets foreigners in the streets of London, he does not need to look at passports before he can know whether these strangers, whom individually he has never before seen, are Swedes, or Hungarians, or Armenians, or Hindoos, or West Indians; the commonest observer scarcely hesitates on such occasions; but the old traveller feels a conviction which mocks at the demand for formal proof.

After we have excepted a few doubtful cases, the genuineness of classic authors is perceived by scholars, with a vividness and distinctness that is not dependent upon the quantity of assignable evidence which must be adduced in reply to objectors. On this ground it may be affirmed, that, if only a single manuscript, containing certain of St. Paul's Epistles, had been preserved, and even if no quotations from these writings were to be found, competent scholars (no practical consequences being implied in the question) would doubt that these writings are in fact what they profess to be. Those minute and indescribable characters of genuineness which meet the instructed eye in every line of these Epistles would be enough, apart from that argument which has been derived from the internal accordances of the history and the letters, as exhibited by Paley in the Horæ Paulinæ.

But although the external proof of the genuineness of ancient books might, in a large proportion of instances, be dispensed with as superfluous, it ought not to be disregarded; especially as it is the kind of evidence which may best be made intelligible to readers. Yet even this, when adduced in its particulars, is not often duly appreciated; nor is it likely to produce its due impression, unless it be viewed in its place among facts of the same class. We propose, therefore, without troubling the reader with details which are to be found, at large, in many well-known works, and which he may be supposed to have in recollection—or within his reach—to direct him to a few principal points of the comparison which may be instituted between the classical and the sacred writings, in relation to the proof of the genuineness and authenticity of each kind.

The Jewish and Christian Scriptures may then be brought into comparison with the works of the Greek and Roman authors, in the following particulars:—

1. The number of manuscripts which passed down through the middle ages, in the modes which have been described in the preceding chapters.

About fifteen manuscripts of the history of Herodotus are known to critics: and of these, several are not of higher antiquity than the middle of the fifteenth century. One copy, in the French king's library (there are in that collection five or six), appears to belong to the twelfth century; there is one in the Vatican, and one in the Florentine library, attributed to the tenth century: one in the library of Emmanuel College, Cambridge, formerly the property of Archbishop Sancroft, which is believed to be very ancient: the libraries of Oxford and of Vienna contain also manuscripts of this author. This amount of copies may be taken as more than the average number of *ancient* manuscripts of the classic authors; for although a few have many more, many have fewer.

To mention any number as that of the existing *ancient* manuscripts, either of the Hebrew or Greek Scriptures, would be difficult. It may suffice to say that, on the revival of learning, copies of the Scriptures, in whole or in part, were found wherever any books had been preserved. In examining the catalogues of conventual libraries—such as they were in the fifteenth century, the larger proportion is usually found to consist of the works of the Fathers, or of the ecclesiastical writers of the middle ages; next in amount are the Scriptures—sometimes entire;

more often the Gospels, the Acts, the Epistles, or the Psalms, separately; and last and fewest are the classics, of which, seldom more than three or four, are found in a list of one or two hundred volumes. The number of *ancient* manuscripts of the Greek New Testament, or parts of it, which hitherto have been examined by editors, is nearly five hundred.

If in the case of a classic author, twenty manuscripts, or even five, are deemed amply sufficient (and sometimes one, as we have seen, is relied upon), it is evident that many hundreds are redundant for the purposes of argument. The importance of so great a number of copies consists in the amplitude of the means which are thereby afforded of restoring the text to its pristine purity; for the various readings collected from so many sources, if they do not always place the true reading beyond doubt, afford an absolute security against extensive corruptions.

2. The high antiquity of some existing manuscripts.

A Virgil (already mentioned) in the Vatican, claims an antiquity as high as the fourth century: there are a few similar instances; but generally the existing copies of the classics are attributed to periods between the tenth and fifteenth centuries. In this respect the Scriptures are by no means inferior to the classics. There are extant copies of the Pentateuch, which, on no slight grounds, are supposed to have been written in the second, or third century: and there are copies of the Gospels belonging to the third, or the fourth, and several of the entire New Testament, which unquestionably were made before the eighth. But the actual age of existing manuscripts is a matter of more curiosity than importance; since proof of another kind carries us with certainty some way beyond the date of any existing parchments.

3. The extent of surface over which copies were diffused, at an early date.

The works of the most celebrated of the Greek authors always found a place in the libraries of opulent persons, in all parts of Greece, and in many of the colonies, soon after their first publication; and a century or two later they were read, wherever the language was spoken. But a contraction of this sphere of diffusion took place at the time when the eastern empire was being driven in upon its centre; and during a long period these works were found only in the countries and islands within a short distance of Constantinople. As for the Latin classics, how widely soever they might have been diffused during three or four centuries, the incursions of the northern nations, and the consequent decline of learning in the West, went near to produce their utter annihilation. Many of these authors were actually lost sight of during several centuries.

It is a matter of unquestioned history that the Jews, always carrying with them their books, had spread themselves throughout most countries of Asia, of southern Europe, and of northern Africa, before the commencement of the Christian era; nor is it less certain that, wherever Judaism existed, Christianity rapidly followed it. Carried forward by their own zeal, or driven on by persecutions, the Christian teachers of the first and second centuries passed beyond the limits of the Roman empire, and founded churches among

nations that were scarcely known to the masters
of the world. Nor were the Christian Scriptures
merely carried to great distances in different
directions;—they were scattered through the mass
of society, in every nation, to an extent greatly
exceeding the ordinary circulation of books in
those ages: these books were not in the hands of
the opulent, and of the studious merely; for they
were possessed by innumerable individuals, who,
with an ardour beyond the range of secular motives,
valued, preserved, and reproduced them. And
while many copies were hoarded and hidden by
private persons, others were the property of
societies, and by continual repetition in public, the
contents of them were imprinted on the memories
of their members.

The wide, and—if the expression may be used
—the *deep* circulation of the Scriptures, preserved
them, not merely from extinction, but, to a great
extent, from corruption also. These books were
at no time included within the sphere of any one
centre of power—civil or ecclesiastical. They
were secreted, and they were expanded far beyond
the utmost reach of tyranny or of fraud.

4. The importance attached to the books by
their possessors.

In a certain sense, the religion of the Greeks
and Romans was embodied in the works of their
poets; but the religious fervour of the people had
never linked itself with those works, as if they
were the depositories of their faith: books were
the possession of the opulent and the educated
classes;—they were prized by the few as the means
of intellectual enjoyment. But Judaism first, and
Christianity not less, were religions of historical

fact: the doctrines and the laws of these religions were inferences, arising naturally from the belief of certain memorable events, and from the expectation of other events, that were yet to take place; the record of the past had become at once the rule of duty, and the charter of hope. To the dispersed and hated Jew his books were the solace of his wounded national pride: to the persecuted Christian his books were his title to "a better country," and his support under present privations and sufferings. If the canonical books are valued by the Christian of modern times who believes them to be divine, they were valued with a far deeper sense by the early Christians, who, on the ground of undoubted miracles, received them as the word of Him who is omnipotent.

The veneration felt by the Jews for their sacred books was of a kind that is altogether without parallel: the reverence of the Christians for theirs, if it was not more profound, was much more impassioned, and this feeling gave intensity to a sentiment wholly unlike any with which one might seek to compare it: the fondness of a learned Greek or Roman for his books, was but in comparison as the delight of a child with his toys.

To this deep feeling towards the sacred writings, in the minds of Christians, was owing, not only the concealment and the preservation of copies in times of active prosecution; but the assiduous reproduction of them by persons of all ranks who found leisure to occupy themselves in a work which they deemed to be so meritorious, and which they found to be so consoling.

5. The respect paid to them by copyists of later ages.

We have seen that, throughout the middle ages, though nothing like a widely diffused taste for the classic authors existed, yet at all times, there were, here and there, individuals by whom they were read and valued, and by whose agency and influence so much care was bestowed upon their preservation as served to insure a safe transmission of them to modern times. But that the Latin authors, at any time after the decline of the western empire, received the benefit of a careful and competent collation of copies there is little reason to believe. Of the Greek authors there were issued new *recensions* from Alexandria, while that city continued to be the seat of learning; and some measure of the same care was exercised by the scholars of Constantinople; yet even there the celebrated works of antiquity suffered a great degree of neglect during the last four centuries of the eastern empire.

But in this respect, as well as in those already mentioned, the text of the Scriptures—Jewish and Christian—possesses an incomparable advantage over that of the classic authors. The scrupulosity and the servile minuteness of the Jewish copyists in transcribing the Hebrew Scriptures are well known; in a literal sense of the phrase, "not a tittle of the law" was slighted: not only—as with the Greeks—was the number of *verses* in each book noted, but the number of words and of letters; and the central letter of each book being distinguished, it became, as a point of calculation, the key-stone of that portion of the volume. This unexampled exactness affords security enough for the safe transmission of the text; and if there were any grounds for the suspicion that the Rabbis, to weaken the evidence adduced against them by the Christians, wilfully corrupted some particular passages, we have other security, as we shall see, against the consequences of such an attempt.

The flame of true piety was, at no time, extinguished in the Christian community; nor can any century or half century of the middle ages be named, in relation to which it may not be proved that there were individuals by whom the books of the New Testament were known and regarded with a heartfelt reverence and affection. There were, besides, multitudes in the religious houses who, influenced perhaps by superstitious notions, thought it a work of superlative merit to execute a fair copy of the Scriptures, or any part of them, and all the adornments which the arts of the times afforded, were lavished to express the veneration of the scribe for the subject of his labours.

And more than this;—the Scriptures, especially in the first eight centuries, underwent several careful and skilful revisions in the hands of learned and able men, who, collating all the copies they could procure, restored the text wherever, as they thought, errors had been admitted. The prodigious labours of Origen in restoring the text of the Septuagint version have often been spoken of. The fathers of the Western, the African, and the Asiatic Churches—especially Jerome, Eusebius, and Augustine, with such means as they severally possessed, did what they could to stop the progress of accidental corruption in the sacred text, by instituting new comparisons of existing copies.

6. The wide local separation, or the open hostility of those in whose custody these books were preserved.

This is a circumstance of the utmost significance, and if it be not *peculiar* to the Jewish and Christian Scriptures, yet it belongs to them in a degree which places their uncorrupted preservation on a basis immeasurably more extended and substantial than that of any other ancient writings. The Latin authors were scantily dispersed over the Roman world, and never were they in the keeping of distant nations, or hostile parties. The Greek classics had indeed, to some extent, come into the hands of the western nations, as well as of the Greeks, in earlier times, and during the middle ages. And, if any weight can be attached to the fact, some of these works were also in the keeping of the Arabians: but they were never the subject of mutual appeal by rival communities.

The Hebrew nation has, almost throughout the entire period of its history, been divided, both by local separation, and by schisms. Probably the Israelites of India, and certainly the Samaritans, have been the keepers of the books of Moses—*apart from the Jews*, during a period that reaches beyond the date of authentic profane history. Throughout times somewhat less remote the Jews have not only been separated by distance, but divided by at least one complete schism—that on the subject of the Rabbinical traditions, which has distinguished the sect of the Karaites from the mass of the nation.

The reproach of the Christian Church—its sects and divisions—has been in part at least, redeemed by the security thence arising, for the uncorrupted transmission of its records. Almost the earliest of the Christian apologists avail themselves of this argument in proof of the integrity of the sacred text. Augustine especially urged it against those who endeavoured to impeach its authority: nor was there ever a time when an attempt, on any extensive scale—even if otherwise it might have been practicable—to alter the text would not have raised an outcry in some quarter. From the earliest times the common Rule of Faith was held up for the purposes of defence or of aggression by the Church, and by some dissentient party. Afterwards the partition of the Christian community into two hostile bodies, of which Rome and Constantinople were the heads, afforded security against any general consent to effect alterations of the text. And in still later ages a few uncorrupted communities, existing within the bounds of the Romish Church, became the guardians of the sacred volume.

7. *The visible effects of these books from age to age.*

On this point also the history of the Greek and Latin classics affords only the faintest semblance of that evidence by means of which the existence and influence of the Scriptures may be traced from the earliest times after their publication, through all successive ages. The Greek and Latin authors indicated their continued existence scarcely at all beyond the walls of schools and halls of learning. During a full thousand years the world saw them not—governments did not embody them in their laws or institutions;—the people had no consciousness of them. They were less known, and less thought of abroad, than were the ashes of the dead—than the bones, teeth, blood, tears, and tatters of the Greek and Romish martyrs.

How different are the facts that present themselves on the side of the Jewish and Christian Scriptures! The Jews—in the sight of all nations—have, through a well-known and uncontested period of two thousand five hundred years, exhibited a living model of the venerable volume which was so long ago delivered to them, and which still they fondly cherish. And though long since debarred from the enjoyment of all that was splendid or cheering in their institutions, and though rent away from their land as well as their worship, and though too often blind to the moral grandeur of their law, and mistaken in the meaning of their prophets, they hold unbroken the shell of the religious system which is described in their books. Whatever in their religion was of less value—whatever served only to cover and protect the vital parts—whatever was the most peculiar, and the least important, whatever might have been laid aside without damage or essential change, has been retained by these wanderers, while that which was precious—the sacred books excepted—has been lost.

The Christian Scriptures have marked their path through the field of time, not in the regions of religion only, or of learning, or of politics; but in the entire condition—moral, intellectual, and political—of the European nations. The history of no period since the first publication of these writings can be intelligible apart from the supposition of their existence and diffusion. If we look back along the eighteen centuries past, we watch the progress of an influence, sometimes indeed marking its presence in streams of blood—sometimes in fires, sometimes by the fall of idol temples, sometimes by the rearing of edifices decked with new symbols; nor can the distant and mighty movement be explained otherwise than by knowing that the books we now hold and venerate were then achieving the overthrow of the old and obstinate evils of idolatry. It is needless to say that the history of Europe in all subsequent periods has implied, by a thousand forms of false profession, and by the constancy of the few, the continued existence of the Christian Scriptures.

8. The body of references and quotations.

The successive references of the Greek authors, one to another, though they are amply sufficient, in most instances, to establish the antiquity of the works quoted, furnish a very imperfect aid in ascertaining the purity of the existing text, or in amending it where apparently it is faulty. A large number of these references are merely allusive, consisting only of the mention of an author's name, with some vague citation of his meaning. And even in those authors who make copious and verbal quotations, such as Strabo, Plutarch, Hesychius, Aulus Gellius, Stobæus, Marcellinus, Photius, Suidas, and Eustathius, a lax method of quotation, in many instances, robs such quotations of much of their value for purposes of criticism. And yet, after every deduction of this kind has been made, the reader of the classics feels an irresistible conviction that this network of mutual or successive references could not have resulted from machination, contrivance, or from anything but reality; it affords a proof, never to be refuted, of the genuineness of the great mass of ancient literature.

But as to the Jewish and Christian Scriptures, this kind of evidence, reaching far beyond the mere proof of antiquity and genuineness, is ample and precise enough to establish the integrity of nearly the *entire text* of the books in question. These writings were not simply succeeded by a literature of a similar cast; but they actually created a vast body of literature altogether devoted to their elucidation; and this elucidation took every imaginable form of occasional comment upon single passages—of argument upon certain topics, requiring numerous scattered quotations, and of complete annotation, in which nearly the whole of the original author is repeated. From the Rabbinical paraphrases, and and from the works of the Christian writers of the first seven centuries (to come later is unnecessary) the whole text of the Scriptures might have been recovered if the original had since perished.

If any one is so uninformed as to suppose that this kind of evidence is open to uncertainty, or that it admits of refutation, let him, if he has access to an ordinary English library, open the volumes of writers of all classes since the days of Elizabeth, and see how many allusions to Shakespeare, and how many verbal quotations from his plays, and how many commentaries upon portions, or upon the whole of them he can find;

and then let him ask himself if there remains the possibility of doubting that these dramas—such in the main as they now are, were in existence at the accession of James I. If these quotations and allusions were not more than a fifth or a tenth part of what they actually are, the proof would not, in fact, be less conclusive than it is.

9. Early versions.

For the purpose of establishing the antiquity, genuineness and integrity of the Scriptures, no other proof need be adduced than that which is afforded by the ancient versions now extant. When accordant translations of the same writings, in several unconnected languages, and in languages which have long ceased to be vernacular, are in existence, every other kind of evidence may be regarded as superfluous.

In this respect a comparison between the classic authors and the Scriptures can barely be instituted; for scarcely anything that deserves to be called a translation of those writers—executed at a very early period after their first publication, is extant. But, on the other side, the high importance attached by the Jews to the Old Testament, and by the early Christians to the New, and the earnest desire of the poor and unlearned to possess, in their own tongue, the words of eternal life, suggested the idea, and introduced the practice, of making complete and faithful translations of both.

Thus it is that, independently of the original text, the Old Testament exists in the Chaldee paraphrases or Targums; in the Septuagint, or Greek version; in the translations of Aquila, of

Symmachus, and of Theodosian; in the Syriac and the Latin, or Vulgate versions; in the Arabic and in the Ethiopic; not to mention others of later date.

The New Testament has been conveyed to modern times, in whole or in part, in the Peshito or Syriac translation, in the Coptic, in several Arabic versions, in the Ethiopic, the Armenian, the Persian, the Gothic, and in the old Latin versions.

10. The vernacular extinction of the languages, or of the idioms, in which these books were written.

To write Attic Greek was the ambition and the affectation of the Constantinopolitan writers of the third and fourth centuries; and thus also, to acquire a pure Latinity, was assiduously aimed at by writers of the middle ages; and, in fact, a few of them so far succeeded in this sort of imitation that they executed some forgeries, on a small scale, which would hardly have been detected, if they had not wanted external proof.

But now the pure Hebrew—such as it had been spoken and written before the Babylonish captivity, had so entirely ceased to be vernacular during the removal of the Jews from their land, that immediately after their return the original Scriptures needed to be interpreted to the people by their Rabbis; nor is there any evidence that the power of writing the primitive language was affected by these Rabbis, whose commentaries are composed in the dialect that was vernacular in their times.

As to the Hellenistic Greek of the New Testament, differing as it does, from the style of the classic authors, and even from that of the Septuagint, to which it is the most nearly allied, it very soon passed out of use; for the later Christian writers, in the Greek language, had, in most instances, formed their style before the time of their conversion; or at least they aimed at a style, widely differing from that of the apostles and evangelists. The idiom of the New Testament, in which phrases or forms of speech borrowed from the surrounding languages occur, resulted from the very peculiar education and circumstances of the writers, which were such as to make their dialect, in many particulars, unlike any other style; and such as could not fail soon to become extinct.

11. The means of comparison with spurious works; or with works intended to share the reputation that had been acquired by others.

Imitations—whether good or bad—are useful in serving to set originals in a more advantageous light. Good imitations, calling into activity, as they do, all the acumen and the utmost diligence of critics, enable them to place genuine writings out of the reach of suspicion. Bad imitations, by serving as a foil or contrast, exhibit more satisfactorily, the dignity, the consistency, and the simplicity of what is genuine.

Several good imitations of the style of Cicero have appeared in different ages, and they have called for so much acuteness on the part of critics as have materially strengthened the evidence of the genuineness of his acknowledged works. In like manner the celebrated epistles of Phalaris excited a learned and active controversy, the beneficial result of which was not so much the settling of the particular question in debate, as the concentration of powerful and accomplished minds upon the general subject of the genuineness of ancient books, by means of which other questionable remains of antiquity received the implicit sanction of retaining their claims, after they had been brought within the reach of so fiery an ordeal.

Many bad imitations of classic authors have been offered to the world, and some such are still extant; and sometimes these are appended to the author's genuine works. No one can read these spurious pieces immediately after he has made himself familiar with such as are genuine, without receiving, from the contrast, a forcible impression of the truth and reality of the latter. The life of Homer, for example, which is usually appended to the history of Herodotus, and which claims his name, and which has something of his manner, yet presents a contrast which few readers can fail to observe.

No *good* imitations, either of the Jewish or Christian Scriptures, have ever appeared; but in the place of that elaborate investigation which the existence of such productions would have called forth, other motives of the strongest kind have prompted a fuller and more laborious examination of the Scriptures than any other writings have endured.

Bad imitations of the style of the Scriptures— some of the Old Testament, and many of the New—have been attempted, and are still in existence; and they are such as to afford the most striking illustration that can be imagined of the difference in simplicity, dignity, and consistency, which one should expect to find, severally, in the genuine and the spurious. The apocryphal books (which however are not, most of them, properly termed *spurious*) afford an advantageous contrast in this way, to the genuine or canonical writings of the Old Testament; and as to the spurious gospels—passing under the names of Peter, Judas, Nicodemus, Thomas, Barnabas—a very cursory examination of them is enough to enhance, immeasurably, the confidence we feel in the genuineness of the true Gospels and Epistles.

The preservation of these latter worthless productions to modern times, is an extraordinary fact, and it affords proof of a state of things, the knowledge of which is important in questions of literary antiquity—namely, that there were many copyists in the middle ages who wrote, and went on writing, mechanically, whatever came in their way, without exercising any discrimination. Now there is more satisfaction in knowing that ancient books have come down through a blind and unthinking medium of this sort, than there would be in believing that we possess only such things as the copyists, in the exercise of an assumed censorship, deemed worthy to be handed down to posterity. It is far better that we should—by accident and ignorance, have lost some valuable works, and that, by the same means, some worthless ones have been preserved, than that the results of accident and ignorance should have been excluded by the constant exercise of a power of selection governed by, we know not what rule or influence. Nothing more pernicious can be imagined than the existence, from age to age, of a synod of copyists sagely determining what works should be perpetuated, and what should be suffered to fall into oblivion. Happily for literature and religion, there were, in the monasteries, numbers of unthinking labourers, who, in selecting the subject of their mindless toils, seemed to have followed the easy rule of taking—the next book on the shelf!

12. The strength of the inference that may be drawn from the genuineness of the books to the credibility of their contents.

Nothing can be more simple or certain than the inference derived from the acknowledged antiquity and genuineness of an historical work, in proof of the general credibility of the narrative it contains. If it be proved that Cicero's Orations against Catiline, and that Sallust's History of the Catiline War, were written by the persons whose names they bear; or if it were only proved that these compositions were extant and well known as early as the age of Augustus; that they were then universally attributed to those authors, and were universally admitted to be authentic records of matters of fact; and if the same facts are, with more or less explicitness, alluded to by the writers of the same, and of the following age, there remains no reasonable supposition, except that of the truth of the story—in its principal circumstances, by aid of which the existence and the acceptance of these narratives, these orations, and these allusions, so near to the time of the conspiracy, can be accounted for.

In Sallust's History some facts may be erroneously stated; or the principal facts may be represented under the colouring of prejudice. In the Orations of Cicero there may be (or we might for argument sake suppose there to be) exaggeration, and an undue severity of censure; but after any such deductions have been made, or any others which reason will allow, it remains incontestably certain that, *if these writings be genuine, the story, in the main, is true.* The sophisms of a college of sceptics, in labouring to show the improbability of the facts, or the suspiciousness of the evidence, would not avail to shake our belief if we are convinced that the books are not spurious.

Nor is this inference less direct, or less valid in the case above mentioned, than in any similar instance of more recent occurrence. It is as inevitable to believe that Catiline conspired against the Roman state, and failed in the attempt, as that the descendants of James II. excited rebellions in Scotland, or that a French General was for a short time king of Naples. In the one case, as in the others, unless the documents—all of them, have been forged, the facts must be true.

The principle upon which such an inference is founded, scarcely admits of an exception. Narratives of alleged, but unreal facts, may have been suddenly promulgated, and for a moment credited; or false narratives of events—concealed by place or circumstances from the public eye, may have gained temporary credit. Or narratives, true in their outline, may have been falsified in all those points concerning which the public could not fairly judge; and thus the false, having been slipped in along with the true, has passed, by oversight, upon the general faith. But no such suppositions meet the case of various public transactions, taking place through some length of time, and in different localities, and which were witnessed by persons of all classes, interests, and dispositions, and which were uncontradicted by any parties at the time, and which were particularly recorded, and incidentally alluded to, by several writers whose works were widely circulated —generally accepted, and unanswered, in the age when thousands of persons were competent to judge of their truth.

No one—to recur to the example mentioned above, is at liberty merely to say that he withholds his faith from Sallust, and from Cicero, as he might, on many points, withhold it from Herodotus, or Diodorus, or from Plutarch. Yet even in that case, he ought to show cause of doubt, if he would not be charged with the frivolous affectation of possessing more sagacity than his neighbours pretend to. But in the other case, while in professing to doubt the facts, he is not able to impugn the antiquity of the records, he only gives evidence of some want of coherence in his modes of thinking. He who professes not to believe the narrative, should be required to give an intelligible account of the existence of the writings, on the supposition that the events never took place.

When historical facts which, in their nature, are fairly open to direct proof, are called in question, it is an irksome species of trifling to make a halt upon twenty indirect arguments, while the *centre proof*—that which a clear mind fastens upon intuitively, remains undisposed of. In an investigation that is purely historical, and which is as simple as any that the page of history

presents, it boots nothing to say that the books of
the New Testament contain doctrines which do
not accord with our notions of the great system of
things; or that they enjoin duties which are
grievous and impracticable; or that they favour
despotism, or engender strifes. It avails nothing
to say that some professors of Christianity are
hypocrites, and that therefore the religion is not
true. No objections of this sort weaken in any
way that evidence upon which we believe that our
island was once possessed by the Romans. But
yet they have as much weight in counterpoising
that evidence, as they have in balancing the proof
of the facts that are affirmed in the New Testament. If such objections were ten-fold more
valid than sophistry can make them, they would
not remove, or alter, or impair, one grain of the
proper proof, belonging to the historical proposition under inquiry.

The question is not whether we admire and
approve of Christianity, or not; or whether we
wish to submit our conduct to its precepts, and
to abide by the hope it offers; or intend to risk
the hazards of it being true. The question is
not whether, in our opinion, these books have
been a blessing to the world, or the contrary;
but simply this—whether the religion was promulgated and its documents were extant, and
were well known throughout the Roman empire,
in the reign of Nero.

There are evasions enough, by means of which
we may remove from our view the inference
which follows from an admission of the antiquity
and genuineness of the Christian Scriptures.
But contradiction may be challenged when it is

affirmed that, if the Gospels, the Acts of the Apostles, the Epistles of Paul, of Peter, of John, and of James, were written in the age claimed for them, and were immediately diffused throughout Palestine, Asia Minor, Africa, Greece, and Italy, then this fact carries with it inevitably the truth of the Christian system.

Remote historical facts, though incapable of that kind of palpable proof which overrules contradiction, are yet open to a kind of proof which no one who really understands it can doubt. Just on this ground stand all the main facts of ancient history;—they are inevitably admitted as true by all into whose minds the whole of the evidence enters; and they are believed or doubted, in every degree between blind faith and blind scepticism, by those whose apprehension of the facts is defective, or obscure, or perverted.

When it is said that the events recorded in the four Gospels are presented to us in a form that has been purposely adapted to exercise our faith, it should be added, by way of illustrating the exact meaning of the words—that the events recorded by Thucydides and Tacitus are also presented to us in a form that is adapted to exercise our faith. Yet it would be more exactly proper to say—that this sort of evidence is adapted to give exercise to *reason;* for *faith* has no part in things which come within the known boundaries of the system in the midst of which we are called to act our parts. And here it should be understood that facts (intelligible in themselves) may, in the fullest sense, be supernatural, and yet when they are duly attested, in conformity with the ordinary principles of evidence, they as much belong to the system with which we are every day concerned, as do the most familiar transactions of common life.

The Scriptures do indeed make a demand upon our faith; but this is exclusively in relation to facts which belong to a world above and beyond that with which we are conversant, and of which facts we could know nothing by any ordinary means of information. Our assent to miraculous events, when properly attested, is demanded on the ground of common sense: the facts themselves are as comprehensible as the most ordinary occurrences; and the evidence upon which they are attested implies nothing beyond the well-known principles of human nature. If then we reject this evidence, we exhibit, not a want of faith, for that is not called for; but a want of reason. To one who affected to question the received account of the death of Julius Cæsar, we should not say "you want faith," but "you want sense." It is the very nature of a miracle to appeal to the evidence of universal experience, in order that, *afterwards*, a demand may be made upon faith, in relation to extra-mundane facts.

CHAPTER XV.

ILLUSTRATIONS OF THE PRECEDING STATEMENTS:— A MORNING AT THE BRITISH MUSEUM.

AND now, at this stage of our progress, let the reader indulge the author to the extent of a page of metaphor or allegory.—Imagine then that we are standing on the margin of a mighty river, the opposite shore of which is scarcely visible; and as to the origin of this world of water, it is far remote and is unknown:—as to the ocean into which it shall at length empty itself and its treasures—this is distant also, nor do we find it anywhere laid down in our maps. The flow of this river is tranquil—its surface is glassy; but upon this surface there float samples and fragments innumerable, of the products of each of the countries which it has watered in its course:—here come rafts, laden with well-packed bales, and there, confusedly mingled, are things more than can be counted—torn away—rent—shattered—coated with rust—wrapped around with weeds. Moving onward, we see the symbols and the devices of nations long ago extinct, and the utensils of a forgotten civilisation, and the products of lands—thousands of miles up the stream; and these entangled with the symbols, the devices, the rare and curious products of some country next above us. On the bosom of this mighty river there floats samples of all things, and these commingled in all imaginable modes.

This is our day-dream :—now for the interpretation of it. We have imagined ourselves to be stationed in any one of the saloons of the British Museum; or that we are passing up and down, from one of these halls to another: and at length are coming to a rest in the centre of the New Reading-room. The countless collections of antiquities—marbles—coins—gems—utensils—weapons—costumes—the manuscripts—the illuminations, and the printed books—what are all these things, but so many relics of remote ages which, favoured by various chances, have floated down to this, our own era, upon the broad surface of the River of Time?

But are these tens of thousands—these hundreds of thousands of individual objects, are they so many disjointed and disconnected particles?—this is far from being the fact. It is a very small number of things, in this vast collection, concerning which an instructed Curator would acknowledge his ignorance, as to what it is, and to what age it belongs, and of what country or people it is a relic. As to a thousand to one of all the single contents of the British Museum, each of them links itself, either nearly, or remotely, with the nine hundred, ninety, and nine, of its neighbours—right and left; or perhaps with some articles that are exhibited in the opposite wing of the building: as for instance—here is a coin, the legend upon which we should have failed to read, or to understand, had it not been that a Greek writer, of whose works a sole manuscript has come down to modern times, incidentally mentions a fact concerning some obscure town of Asia Minor, and its history, under the Roman emperors, of which otherwise we should have been ignorant.

Let us avail ourselves of another supposition, remote as it may be from the fact; and it is this—That the author, and the reader, of this book, whom we imagine to be now pacing together the saloons of the Museum, are possessed of that universality of learning, and that vastness of antiquarian accomplishment, which enables the gentleman at the centre table of the Reading-room to answer all inquirers, and to aid and guide them all in carrying forward their various researches. If, then, the author and the reader were gifted in any such manner as this, we might then, with a sort of second sight, or a veritable *clairvoyance,* look upon the countless stores around us as if they were all falling into an appointed order, or were obeying some natural law of mutual attraction and cohesion: as thus—there goes an almost illegible manuscript, attaching itself to a colossal sculpture—much as feathers stick themselves on to an electric conductor:—there are coins, arranging themselves spontaneously, like a crown of laurel leaves, around the brows of busts:—there are weapons and fragments of armour, edging themselves on to a copy of Polybius:—there are bits of a pediment, or the chippings of a column, claiming a standing-place upon the Greek text of Procopius—and why? it is because these fragments belong to an edifice of the times of Justinian, which he has described. And now, as to the printed books, and the manuscripts, whence many of the printed books drew their existence, if we will give way to the ideal for a few moments, we shall see them floating out from their shelves, in this vast circus, and knowingly arranging themselves, in a sort of pyramidal form, as if to exhibit their real relationship of quotation, and of reference, in the order of time—the more recent to the more ancient—the many to the few;—until the pile—made up of a million of books, is surmounted by the two or three that quote none older than themselves, and that are quoted by all.

What then is our inference? It is this: that as to the persons and the events—the doings and the notions—the thoughts and the ways—the customs and the manners—the philosophy—the literature—the religion—the politics—the civilisation of the nations of all those ages which are comprehended within the limits of what is called the historic period—these innumerable matters are assuredly known to us, at this time;—and they have become known to us with this degree of certainty (in the main) not by the precarious and insulated testimony of a few writers, whose works have reached modern times — we know not how; but very much otherwise than thus; for it is by means of the inter-related, and the mutually attestative evidence of thousands of witnesses—witnesses in stone and marble, in metallic substances, coins and brass plates, in membranous records, and in writings upon every other material, and in every imaginable fashion; and all these things are so netted together and so welded and dovetailed, and linked, and glued, and sealed, into a vast conglomerate, as that the combined testimony thence accruing in support of our voluminous historic beliefs is not less solid than are the granitic ribs of a continent; and is as various and as rich, as all the products of its surface—its faunas and its flora.

So much for a momentary glance at the treasures, the vast accumulations of the British Museum; but now we might usefully take the SYNOPSIS in hand, and give attention to some few of the articles that are named in it. What we are in search of are those attestations of ancient *written* evidences, touching the persons, the events, the manners, the religions, of ancient nations, which come upon us—we might say, by surprise, and which are derived from sources altogether and in every sense independent, and unconnected, one with another.

Take with you, in one hand, your Tacitus, Sallust, Dion Cassius;—and in the other hand, your Virgil, Horace, Juvenal, and Ovid. These writers—the one set as historians, the other set as poets, build up to our view the throne, and its personages, of the Imperial Times—say, of two centuries, reckoned back from the life-time of the last of them. But through what channels have *the books* come into our hands? The editors of the printed copies assure us that there had come into their possession, in each instance, one, two, three manuscripts, that had been raked out of the forgotten heaps of this or that monastery, or other conservatory of curious articles. As to the greater number of these manuscripts, they could not be assigned to an age much beyond the ninth century; therefore, on the supposition that they are genuine works—the products of a time seven hundred, or a thousand years earlier, what the editor had under his eye must have been nothing better than a copy—from a copy—or, perhaps, from several in succession! Is not this line of proof somewhat precarious? Ought we to trust ourselves to it?

Advance toward the left hand, from the entrance hall, and by the time you have moved on a dozen steps, the volumes in your hands, if they were gifted with consciousness, would begin to twitch and to jerk themselves about, as if uneasy in being held away from their old friends, right and left, whom they recognise, perched on the pedestals, and fixed to the walls. Whence is it that these solid antiquities have been brought hither? Not from those same lumber-vaults in the monasteries, or the royal libraries of Europe, whence we have received the aforesaid manuscripts;—not so, but from deep underground—from cavities—from underneath pavements, sixty feet or more lower than the present surface: they have been picked up in cornfields; they have been sifted from out of heaps of rubbish; they have been taken from the recesses of the houses of a city, buried by a volcanic eruption, many centuries ago. These manifold samples of an ancient civilisation have been fished up from the beds of rivers and the bottoms of lakes; and these recoveries have been effected in all these and many other modes over the extent of Europe, and of Southern and Western Asia, and of North Africa. There is no possibility therefore of calling in question this million-tongued testimony; we must not gainsay what is affirmed by these tongues of stone and of brass, of silver and of gold.

And the more, in any instance, the coincidence is slender and remote, or as one might say, frivolous or unimportant, so much the surer, and the more to be relied upon is it, in what it does affirm: as thus—Look to your Synopsis, page 87, Compartment III.:—"A pig of lead, inscribed with the name of the Emperor Domitian, when he was consul for the eighth year, A.D. 82, weighing 154 lbs. It was discovered in 1731 underground, on Hayshaw Moor, in the West Riding of Yorkshire, half-way between an ancient lead-mine, north of Pately Bridge, and the Roman road from Ilkley *(Olicana)* to Aldborough *(Isurium)*." This pig had slept where he was dropped about 1,650 years.

"A pig of lead, inscribed with the name of the Emperor Hadrian, weighing 191 lbs.; found in 1796 or '97, at Snailbeach Farm, parish of Westbury, 10 miles south-west of Shrewsbury." Then follow some other pigs, whose slumbers underground have been more or less prolonged and profound.

"A pig of lead, inscribed with the name of L. Aruconius Verecundus, and the letters METAL. LVTVD., probably the mine of *Lutudæ*. Found near Matlock Bank, in Derbyshire."

"A pig of lead, inscribed CL. TR. LVT. BR. EX. ARG.; found with three other pigs and some broken Roman pottery, at Broomer's Hill, in the parish of Pulborough, Sussex, January 31, 1824, close to the Roman Road, Stone Street, from London to Chichester."

"A pig of lead, inscribed with the name of Britannicus, the son of the Emperor Claudius, found on the Mendip Hills, Somersetshire."

So much for these pigs. What is it which they might say, if we were to bring them into court? Something of this sort: At this time, in the streets of the stannary towns in Cornwall, there are to be seen blocks—pigs of tin, stamped in a manner similar to the lettering of these pigs of lead in the British Museum. This stamping is effected for the purpose of securing the dues of the Duchy of Cornwall, and the symbols and the letters indicate the political fact that the Prince of Wales, as Duke of Cornwall, lays a hand upon every pound of tin that is smelted in the county; and thus, too, the stamping of the produce of the lead-mines of Britain gives evidence of the fact that the Romans were not merely resident in Britain at the time, but were masters also of the island, and the lords of its mineral products. Then the lettering itself finds its interpretation in the Roman imperial history, and this history comes into our hands, partly as it has been narrated by the Roman historians above mentioned; partly in the form of sculptures, statues, busts, and bas-reliefs; and partly, and very copiously, in the unquestionable form of the coins of the same emperors, which alone would suffice for putting us in possession of the series of events, greater and smaller, through a course of many centuries. But what the reader should here keep in view is this: that as our present thesis is—the safe and sure transmission of ancient books, by the means of often-repeated copyings, through the lapse of ages, an evidence to this effect—and it is the most conclusive that can be imagined or desired, is afforded us when, in passing through collections, such as those treasured in the British Museum, THE BOOKS in question are found to furnish a coherent, and a continuous, and an exact interpretation of these palpable and ponderous antiquities. Yet, it is manifest that, unless the books were in the main genuine, they could not have supplied any interpretations, such as are those which we find in them.

Go on now to the historical sculptures—the statues, and the busts of the imperial times. These, for the most part, are susceptible of authentication by means of the coins of the same emperors, which may be seen—by "order"—in another department of the Museum; the likenesses are indisputable, and the historic reality of the two samples of Roman art is thus far made good. But beyond this we may safely go. From the Roman writers—specially Tacitus, Suetonius, and Dion Cassius—we acquire what we need not doubt to be a true idea of the individual character, the temperament, the education, the public and private behaviour, and the style of the series of imperial persons, from Julius Cæsar, onward, to the times of each of these writers. What then is the verdict of our physiognomical instincts, when we compare the busts or statues, for instance, of Augustus and of Tiberius, of Nero, and of Trajan? We could no more take these, one for the other, than we could misname the portraits of Philip of Spain, or the Duke of Alva, put by the side of George Washington, or John Howard; or misjudge those of Oliver Cromwell, and John Milton; or of Admiral Blake, and Alexander Pope. We need not wait until a science of physiognomy has been concocted before we may risk a guess in writing the names under portraits of Lord Chatham, Dr. Johnson, and Oliver Goldsmith. Mistakes, in single instances, may be made, but not in the long run; and when, on the one hand, we take the entire series of royal portraits, eastern and western, from the first of the Ptolemies to Charlemagne, and, on the other hand, the *books* of the series of contemporary historians, we shall receive, from this large collation of independent evidences, an irresistible conviction of the general authenticity of the latter; and therefore we must cease to entertain doubts on this question of the secure transmission of ancient books to modern times.

It would be of little avail here to cite a few single instances of the agreement of Roman coins with written history, for such instances are countless. The reader who would wish to inform himself, in whole, or in part, on this extensive subject, should take in hand a Medallic History of Imperial Rome, which, as compared with the medallic treasures of the British Museum, will give him aid in following the train of public events through five or six centuries, exhibited and verified by the double line of testimonies—the metallic and the literary. Or he may be content to take, as a sufficient sample of this species of proof, the facts he will find brought together in a small volume, "Akerman on the Coins of the Romans relating to Britain."

There is another field upon which a gleaning, and more than a gleaning, may easily be made by help of the Roman poets as our guides. These writers—and we need name only Ovid, Horace, Virgil, and Propertius—are undoubtedly believed to have lived and flourished as the contemporaries of Julius Cæsar, Augustus, Tiberius. Their writings, as we have them now in our hands, are accepted as genuine; for the criticism which demonstrates the general integrity of the text (exceptions allowed for) is too erudite and careful to be called in question. Consequently, these writings have safely traversed a period of fifteen hundred years, ending with the date of the earliest printed editions: but this transit has been made by no other means than that of the copyists; and therefore, if, as we shall see, a superabundance of various and independent evidences removes the possibility of our doubting the fact, then this mode of transmission, precarious as it may seem, is found to be trustworthy, and our main point is established—namely, that ancient books have indeed come down to modern times—whole and entire. Let us look, for a moment, to this corroborative evidence—such as we find it offered to the eye, in passing through the saloons of the British Museum.

The Roman poets, were not, perhaps, themselves very firm believers in the Grecian mythology —considered religiously or historically; nevertheless, they took it up—such as it had come into their hands—and it was a splendid inheritance— a boundless treasury of bright conceptions of superhuman power, beauty, grace; a scheme of elegant sensuousness, with a touch of sublimity. Its fables, far more available for poetic purposes than any system of serious truths could have been, opened before the Roman poets a broad meadow land, in roaming through which the imitative, more than originative turn of the Roman mind, might gather fruits and flowers, ripe and gay, and which asked only to be taken and enjoyed. So it is, therefore, that in every imaginable mode of lengthened poetic narrative, and of transient allusion, and of direct and of allusive reference, the gods and the goddesses, and the demi-gods, and the heroes of Greece come up upon the stage of the Roman poetry. These repetitions—these borrowings or plagiarisms, and these flashing glances, are countless:—sometimes they are formal; sometimes they are informal:—they are broad daylight views in some places, and in places innumerable they are as sparks only—visible for an instant.

Now with what objects is it that these mythologic passages are in harmony?—with what is it that they correspond? Our answer is—With tens of thousands of relics of ancient art which, through channels altogether independent of those through which the books have reached us, have come, at this time, to fill, and to overfill the cabinets and museums of Europe—and thus, also, our British Museum.

But then this mass of ponderable and visible evidences is inter-related in a very peculiar manner, which should be borne in mind. We have just now referred to the correspondence which connects the historic sculptures—the statues and the busts of Roman personages, male and female, and the likenesses of the same men and women which are so copiously supplied in collections of the Roman imperial mintage. But now we pass on to the Græco-Roman Saloons—the first, the second, and the third, as well as the basement room. These are filled with mythologic sculptures —recovered from the soil of Italy and Greece:— they show us in inimitable marbles, those same divinities, the principle and the subordinate, which the mind of Greece had imagined, and which the Roman artists adopted: these beautiful creations we at once recognise as the celestial *personæ* with whom we have made acquaintance in the pages of the Roman poets: the conception of superhuman grace and power is the very same; and the attendant symbols are the same. And now furnish yourself with the requisite order for inspecting the collection of antique gems—precious (often) as to their material—precious, incalculaly more so, by means of that exquisite taste and that inimitable executive skill which have made them what they are.

These microscopic sculptures, in consequence of the value of the material, and the costliness of the work, and from their smallness, and the facility of preservation, were eagerly sought after by the opulent at the very time of their production; and they have been most carefully hoarded in every age, by the same class of persons; and they have suffered far less injury in the lapse of time than antiquities of any other kind. Especially the *intaglios*—the indented sculptures, are, for the most part, as perfect and sharp now as they were eighteen hundred years ago. What is it, then, that these gems of art bring under our modern eyes?—it is the very same ideal personages of the same mythology;—and the symbols are the same, and the air, and the grace, and the attributes of beauty and power are the same;—there is the same sensuousness—there are the same ambiguous adventures;—there is the same poetry and the same art—poetry and art, admirable, indeed, how much soever it may be open to censure as to its moral quality.

Here then we have in view three independent, but perfectly concurrent and *mutually interpretative* evidences—namely, *first,* the sculptures; *secondly,* the gems; and then the books—the poetry. If, in examining one of these classes of antiquities, we find ourselves at a loss in attempting to decipher its symbols or its allusions, any such difficulty vanishes—in most instances—when we betake ourselves to another class:—as thus—the gem expounds the statue; or the poet, in a single verse, sheds his beam of light upon both. Thus it is that—with the *three* at our command—ANTIQUITY, throughout the rich and splendid region of its mythologies, stands unveiled before us! Must we not grant that so many coherences, and so many correspondences, and so many interpretative agreements—countless as they are—can have had their source in nothing but the realities of the age whence we believe them to have descended to modern times? But if it be so, then it is true that ancient books—to wit, the Roman poets—have been securely sent forward—thanks to the copyists!—from age to age, through all the intervening years of so many centuries.

If it were a volume that was now to be filled, instead of the few pages of this chapter, and if, instead of a morning at the British Museum, an entire season were to be diligently spent there, we should still want space and leisure for specifying a sample only of those articles which might properly be referred to in illustration of our present argument. Instead of doing so, we must move forward through the Elgin Saloon, only stopping to make this one observation—that these sculptures, and these bas-reliefs, and these inscriptions, would be to us, at this time, nothing better than a vast confusion—a mass of insoluble enigmas, if we did not carry with us the written remains of the Greek and Roman literature—the works of the historians, and the poets, and the dramatists, and the orators, which were the creations of that same age of refined intelligence, and exquisite taste, and artistic skill: but so it is, that the written memorials of that brief period are found to be available for interpreting the solid memorials of the same times, and these again for illustrating those. It was indeed a brief period. —it was a blossoming and a fruit-bearing summer month of the world's dull millennial year; and during the long period that followed it—the autumn months, and the winter—there were none among the living who could either have written these books, or who could have chiselled these marbles; but the books in one manner, and the marbles in another, have separately floated down upon the billows of time; and here we have them, confronted under one roof—ten thousand witnesses, attesting the reality of ancient history.

From the classic antiquities we now advance, and enter the Assyrian Galleries. Everybody knows, or may easily know, in what way the sculptures, buried so many centuries, have now come to fill these long apartments, and how they thus find a resting-place under the roof of the

British Museum. The places whence they have come, and the circumstances of their disinterment, are (as we must suppose) known and familiar to the visitor in whose company we are spending this morning in its saloons. This being so, and if, moreover, we may believe that he has become, in some degree, conversant with the literature of ancient Greece—especially with its historians—Herodotus, Thucydides, Xenophon, Diodorus, and also Strabo—he will be qualified to understand what we mean in speaking of that *broad confirmation* of the authenticity of ancient history which it receives from a glance at the contents of the "Assyrian Galleries."

The above-named Greek writers, and these illustrated as they are by the contemporary literature, give us a distinct image of Greece, and of its people, with their intellectuality, and their religion, and their taste; and this portraiture is quite homogeneous in itself, and, as we have already said, it is corroborated and exhibited, in ten thousand instances, by the sculptures, and other objects found in the saloons we have just now visited. But now these same writers open up to us also—sometimes formally, and sometimes incidentally—a prospect, eastward, far over the regions outstretched beyond the limits of the Greek civilisation. In those illimitable expanses there existed a civilisation; but it was quite of another aspect; there was government, and social order; but these were wholly unlike the institutions of Greece. There were religions; but they breathed another spirit: they uttered other voices; they spoke of a different national economy. There was the same human nature; but it had been developed as if under conditions proper to another world.

Now I will ask my companion to tell me with what sort of feeling it is, that, in passing from the monuments of Grecian life, and the remains of its arts, he enters these Assyrian galleries. Does there not take place an involuntary impression to this effect—as if we were here setting foot upon the soil of another world? We have crossed the threshold that divides one phase or mode of human existence from another mode of it; there are here displayed before us the indications of a different climate, a different terrestrial surface; and the vegetation that covers it is of another class, nor are the animals that roam over it the same; and the human forms, and the visages, and the costumes, and the attitudes, and the occupations, and the rites, are of another mould. In these galleries we are surrounded with the symbols and the appendages of a sombre and remorseless despotism. Greece had its warriors and its heroes, and its many orders of mind, and each freely developed; but *here* the one master of prostrate millions of men is the solitary being: all things follow, or precede, or revolve around him: there is one will, and it carried its purposes unchecked, alike by reason or humanity.

Here then are the monuments of a world, such as that outlying and distant eastern world whereof we find scattered notices in the extant remains of the Greek literature. These notices serve as the interpretation, so far as they go, of these ponderous remains. The historians, the orators, the poets, flourishing under a refined civilisation, look over their inclosures, and they sketch, at points, the far-off barbaric civilisation of Asia, and we recognise, in the *written* memorials of that ruder social life, the features and characteristics of its sculptured memorials—as they are now in view.

These coincidences are, we say, *an evidence at large* of the authenticity of that portion of ancient history which might seem to stand most in need of corroboration. It is a broad witnessing to the truth. We might, however, descend to the particulars, and then might verify this proof in very many of its details; but we must go on, and only fix attention, for a moment, upon a single line of these confirmatory coincidences; and it is one which carries with it a momentous inference.

There is one body of extant writings which is not only of much earlier date than the Greek literature—earlier even than its traditions, but which sprung up within the circle of the Asiatic world; it is not Grecian—it possesses not the same merits, the same graces, or merits of a kindred order; it has its own. Asiatic it is; and yet it was so much insulated, and it was so decisively national, that the report it makes of the surrounding social economies, is, in a great degree, an independent report; it looks on, as from a distance. We may expect, therefore, to find in the Hebrew literature—in its historians, poets, and prophets—a *reflection* of Asiatic life, rather than a native or home-made exhibition of it; and such is the fact. The monster despotisms that had their seats by the side of the Tigris and the Euphrates, appear like phantoms of destructive power, as seen from the heights of Palestine. Now, what we affirm is this; that the idea we obtain in perusing the Hebrew literature, of the Asiatic military despotisms, and of their horrific superstitions, is conspicuously realised—it is held out to our view with a vivid force and distinctness, as we walk up and down, gazing in awe upon these monstrous sculptures. The Hebrew writers denounce these destroyers of the nations; and now let us confess that they have pictured them truly; they have not calumniated those remorseless tyrants—even the men of these colossal busts and these bas-reliefs, when they recount their deeds of blood, their spoliations, and their oppressions.

Besides and beyond this—which we have called a broad confirmation of ancient history, and which arises spontaneously from the aspect of these Assyrian antiquities—it is well known, and we are supposing our companion to be aware of the fact, that, since the disinterment of these Assyrian sculptures, great progress has been made in the work of deciphering the inscriptions which appear upon many of them. At this time it may safely be affirmed that these records, inscrutable as they were thought to be, have spoken out their meaning. It is true also that these utterances from a long unknown world have fallen in with the testimony of written history—Grecian and Biblical, and that in relation, especially, to the latter, many highly significant coincidences have presented themselves, rewarding the patient intelligence of those who have laboured on this field. But to this subject we shall have occasion to return in a following chapter.

The marvels of the Egyptian galleries might lead us away even into yet another world; but we have already touched upon the subject (pp. 138, *and following*), and therefore hasten forward, making a momentary stop at one object only, namely, the celebrated "Rosetta stone," thus described in the Synopsis:—

"The Rosetta stone, containing three inscriptions of the same import, namely, one in hieroglyphics, another in a written character, called demotic or enchorial, and a third in the Greek language. These inscriptions record the services which Ptolemy the Fifth had rendered his country, and were engraved by order of the Synod of Priests, when they were assembled at Memphis for the purpose of investing him with the royal prerogative. It is the key to the decipherment of the hieroglyphical and demotic characters of Egypt. This stone was found near Rosetta, and it appears to have been placed in a temple dedicated to Atum by the monarch Nechao, of the twenty-sixth dynasty: it is of basalt."

The industry and the sagacity of a succession of learned men have so far availed (greatly by aid of the threefold inscriptions of the Rosetta stone) as that the history of Egypt, up to a very remote age, has been recovered, and has been carried to its place, so as to synchronise with that of the surrounding nations. Every such conquest, or, as we may call it, inroad upon the dark regions of bygone ages, gives a further confidence to our belief in the general trustworthiness of ancient written history. The ancient historians were indeed sometimes misinformed, or perhaps negligent in putting together their materials; nevertheless, on the whole, they have acquitted themselves as honest and intelligent witnesses.

In ascending the north-west staircase, we must not fail to notice several framed and glazed specimens of Egyptian writing, which enliven the walls. These manuscripts are on the Egyptian papyrus, the texture of the material in several instances being quite discernible. These should be looked at as furnishing the best possible illustration of the statements already made in general terms (Chapter V.) What we have there spoken of may here be (not handled indeed, but) seen.

It will now be time to bring our visit to the Museum to a close, lest we should be allured by its multifarious treasures—the memorials of all ages, to wander too far from our proper subject. Yet a glance must be had at the manuscripts that are exposed to view in cases in the saloons on the eastern side of the Museum. These manuscripts, to some of which we must hereafter make a reference, bring under the eye all those varieties of material, of decoration, and of character as to the writing, which already have been briefly mentioned. Among them we may find samples of the writer's art, and of the art of the writer's brother—the decorator, as seen in the illuminations; some of them are in the highest degree sumptuous and magnificent; others are more business-like :—a few that have held their integrity as books through sixteen hundred years, and many during a thousand years. The summers and the winters—times of war and devastation—times of peace :—years of narrow risks from spoliation, conflagration, barbarian recklessness;

and centuries, perhaps, when throughout noiseless days and nights not a breath, not a hand, moved the dust that was always coming to its long rest upon the cover! So it has been that a safe transmission of the inestimable records of mind has had place, notwithstanding the mischances, the storms, the violences, the ignorance, and the neglects, of so many years.

CHAPTER XVI.

FACTS RELATING TO THE CONSERVATION, AND LATE RECOVERY, OF SOME ANCIENT MANUSCRIPTS.

SOME of the most ancient, and the most valuable of the manuscripts which at present enrich the British Museum, have been very lately acquired, being the product of the researches of learned travellers in Egypt, and in the islands of the Ægæan Sea, and the countries bordering upon it. These researches and these journeys have been undertaken expressly for the purpose, and with the hope of discovering, and of bringing away, some of those literary treasures which were known, or believed, to lie neglected, and almost forgotten, in the now dilapidated monasteries of Egypt and Greece. This hope has, to some extent, been realized, and these labours rewarded; as we may now briefly mention.

The desolate region which stretches away far to the west on the parallel of the Delta of the Nile, bears the marks of having been, at some remote period, and to a great extent, covered with water. The remains of this dried-up sea still appear, as small lakes, filling the cavities among the rugged hills that skirt the desert toward the valley of the Nile. Upon the margins of these lakes is found the Natron, which may be called natural salt-soap, and whence, also, large quantities of pure nitre are obtained. These lakes have received their designation from this natural product.

The district, NITRIA, is frequently mentioned by ancient authors; as by Strabo (Book xvii.) and by Pliny (Book xxxi. 46), and again by the Church writers of the fourth and following centuries; especially by those of them who speak of the monastic institutions of their own times. Around these dreary waters the monks of that time established themselves in great numbers;— so many, indeed, that the emperor Valens, thinking that he could find a more useful employment for them than that of reciting the Psalter, enlisted as many as five thousand of them in his legions. But here, notwithstanding disturbances of this kind, these recluses continued to find a refuge from the world, and its temptations—or so they thought; and here, by the aid of grants from some of the better-minded of the emperors, or of opulent and religious persons, many religious houses were constructed; some of them being of ample dimensions, and so built as to be capable of resisting the attacks of the marauders of the desert; and as their precincts included spacious gardens, they might, for lengths of time, support the frugal life of their inmates, even if besieged.

As to these establishments,* we find incidental notices of them sufficient to assure us that, in some, if not in all of them, the copying of books afforded occupation to a class of their inmates; and that this was the fact, we now have evidence in the results of the researches above referred to. In some instances there has been enough of con-

* I have lately brought forward some facts of this kind, relating to an abbot of a Nitrian monastery. ESSAYS, &c.; NILUS.

tinuous life in a decaying monastery, even though the building may seem to be little better than a huge ruin, to maintain the "Copying-room" in some activity. In others, where a score of monks, or even fewer, have slumbered away their term of years, they have yet retained a vague traditionary belief in the value of the manuscripts which they knew to lie, in heaps, in some cell or vault, never visited, by themselves. In some cases the books, which had been huddled away from the library in a moment of danger, when an enemy was under the walls, have remained—safe and forgotten, in their concealment—perhaps for centuries. Thus it has been that—by the intellectual activity of one age, by the slumbering or the inert industry of the next period, and at length, by the utter mindlessness of centuries—the precious products of the ancient world have been conserved for our use in this age. May we not well notice and admire that providential interposition which, in these varying and precarious modes, has made us the inheritors of the wealth of the remotest times!

Among those modern travellers who have prosecuted these researches, one of the most eminent is the learned Tischendorff, whose labours in the field of Biblical criticism have become known to all readers in that line. This accomplished traveller directed his attention especially to the monasteries of the Natron Lakes. He visited them by joining himself to a caravan proceeding from Cairo to the Italian settlement, Castello Cibara.—"Shortly after daybreak," he says, "we saw in the distance upon the left, in the middle of the Desert, a lofty stone wall, and still further on, a second. These were two of the Coptic monasteries. Presently afterwards one of the salt lakes glittered in the distance, with its obscure reddish blue waters, and a flock of flamingoes sprung out of its reeds. Upon the right was the Castello Cibara; in the background the low Libyan hills formed a dark-red border to the whole scene. About nine in the morning we reached our destination, and I found in the midst of the Desert a hospitable hearth." What follows, although not closely related to our immediate subject, is not very remotely connected with it; and a few sentences further may be cited.

"In the afternoon we made an excursion to the fields and lakes of nitre. What a singular scene! In the midst of this sandy waste, where uniformity is rarely interrupted by grass or shrubs, there are extensive districts where nitre springs from the earth like crystallised fruits. One thinks he sees a wild, overgrown with moss, weeds, and shrubs, thickly covered with hoar frost. And to imagine this winter scene beneath the fervid heat of an Egyptian sun, will give some idea of the strangeness of its aspect.

"The existence of this nitre upon the sandy surface is caused by the evaporation of the lakes. . . . The nitre lakes themselves, six in number, situated in a spacious valley, between two rows of low sandhills, presented a pleasing contrast, in their dark blue and red colours, to the dull hues of the sand. . . . There are four Coptic monasteries at the distance of a few leagues apart. Ruins and monasteries, and heaps of rubbish, I observed scattered in great numbers throughout the district. I was told that there were formerly

about three hundred Coptic monasteries in this
desert. . . . Both externally and internally,
these monasteries closely resemble one another.
Sometimes square, at others in the form of a
parallelogram, they are inclosed by walls tolerably
high, and usually about one hundred feet long.
From their centre a few palms frequently peer
forth, for every monastery has a small garden
within its circuit, and is also furnished with a
tower, slightly elevated above the walls, and
containing a small bell. . . . Within the walls
are seen nothing but old and dilapidated ruins,
amongst which the monks find a habitation. The
tower I have just described is insulated from the
body of the monastery, and approachable only by
means of a drawbridge supported on chains, offering thus an asylum against enemies, who may
have mastered the monastery. This tower com-
mands the entrance. The interior consists of a
chapel, a well, a mill, an oven, and a store-room,
all required in the event of a long siege, and the
apartment assigned to the library. . . . Here
and there, in the mural structure of the entrances
to the cells and chapelries, we obtain a glimpse of
the fragment of a marble pillar, or of a frieze, or
some similar decoration. Thus has the sordid
present been built out of the splendour and
grandeur of the past."

The scattered fragmentary remains of the architectural magnificence of a remote age may properly be regarded as so many attestations of those
incidental notices of these same establishments
which occur in the writers of that age; and thus
it is that the literary evidence, touching the
decaying and almost forgotten ancient manuscripts

that have been dragged forth from their concealments, is found to consist well with the visible history of the structure wherein they have been so long conserved.

The learned traveller from whose journal the above citations have been made, had been anticipated in his search for manuscripts by several European scholars; and therefore it was little that he found available for his immediate purpose—the collation of manuscripts of the New Testament. What we are just now concerned with are those characteristics of Oriental stagnation and motionless decay, and of monastic persistence, which have been the very means of ensuring an undisturbed custody of literary treasures through the stormy passage of many centuries. The decrepit inmates of these ruins cherish the traditions of a more stirring time, and they are aided in doing so by the pictures of the saints and founders of those times. Some of these pictures are manifestly of great antiquity, and they have been conserved, with reverential regard, by each successive series of abbots and monks. Thus says Tischendorff:—

"The chief pictorial representations, in all the four monasteries (those visited by him), were those of St. Macarius, and St. George. In the third, which bears the name of the Syrian, or the Virgin of the Syrians, St. Ephraim (Ephrem Syrus, whose voluminous writings are extant) is held in high honour. A tamarind-tree was there shown me, which had miraculously sprouted forth from the staff of St. Ephraim, who, upon entering the chapel, had stuck it into the ground outside. In the second, St. Ambeschun was represented as the patron. In the fourth, besides St. George, St. Theodore was represented on horseback, with the vanquished dragon beneath his feet."

In speaking of the main object of his journey, the author says :—

"The special locality set apart for the library (in these buildings) is the tower chamber, which is accessible only by means of the drawbridge. No spot in the monastery could be safer from the visits of the fraternity than this. Here are seen (I speak of the first monastery) the manuscripts heaped indiscriminately together. Lying on the ground, or thrown into large baskets, beneath masses of dust, are found innumerable fragments of old, torn, and destroyed manuscripts. I saw nothing Greek; all was either Coptic, or Arabic; and in the third monastery I found some Syriac, together with a couple of leaves of Ethiopic. The majority of the MSS. are liturgical, though many are Biblical. From the fourth monastery (presently to be mentioned) the English have recently acquired an important collection of several hundred manuscripts for the British Museum, and that at a very small cost. The other monasteries contain certainly nothing of much consequence; yet much might be found to reward the labour of the search. The monks themselves understand extremely little about the matter. Not one among them, probably, is acquainted with Coptic, and they merely read mechanically the lessons of their ritual. The Arabic of the olden MSS. but few can read. Indeed, it is not easy to say what these monks know beyond the routine of their ordinary church service. Still their excessive suspicion renders it extremely difficult to induce them to produce their manuscripts, in spite of the extreme penury which surrounds them. Possibly they are controlled by the mandate of their patriarch. For my own part, I made a most lucky discovery of a multitude of Coptic parchment sheets of the sixth and seventh centuries, already half destroyed, and completely buried beneath a mass of dust. These were given to me without hesitation; but I paid for the discovery by severe pains in the throat, produced by the dust I had raised in the excessive heat. . . . The monks (taught at length to think much of the value of their literary treasures) are too much accustomed to the visits and to the gold of the English."

Among these "English" whose visits and whose gold have spoiled the good monks of the Egyptian desert, one of the most noted is the Hon. Robert Curzon, jun., whose entertaining volume, published about ten years ago, has brought his amusing adventures to the knowledge of most people who read at all. Notwithstanding the notoriety of this distinguished traveller's discoveries and his successes in the desert, it would be an omission of what is very pertinent to our argument, not to cite a few paragraphs from his accounts of his "Visits to Monasteries in the Levant."

Preserved—a contradiction, as it may seem—by the very means of the neglect and ignorance, the stupidity and the recklessness, of those in whose custody they have been—the most valuable manuscripts have often been converted to the meanest purposes. A learned traveller mentioned by Mr. Curzon, in inquiring for manuscripts, was told that there were none in the monastery; but when he entered the choir to be present at the service, he saw a double row of long-bearded holy fathers, shouting the Kyrie eleison, and each of them standing, to save his bare legs from the damp of the marble floor, upon a great folio volume, which had been removed from the conventual library, and applied to purposes of practical utility in the way here mentioned. These volumes, some of them highly valuable, this traveller was allowed to carry away with him, in exchange for some footstools or hassocks, which he presented to the monks.

Mr. Curzon visited the Levant in 1833, and the following years: his description of the monasteries near the Natron Lakes differs little from that of the traveller already cited; but he was fortunate in his researches, not merely as a first comer, but as more amply provided with the means of purchase, and also perhaps better skilled in the sort of diplomacy which the business in hand required. The Coptic manuscripts which he found in one of these monasteries were most of them lying on the floor, but some were in niches in the stone wall; all except three were on paper. One on parchment was a superb manuscript of the Gospels, with commentaries by the early fathers of the Church: two others were doing duty as coverings to a couple of large open pots or jars, which had contained preserves, long since evaporated. "I was allowed to purchase these vellum manuscripts, as they were considered to be useless by the monks; principally, I believe, because there were no more preserves in the jars."

On the floor was a fine Coptic and Arabic dictionary, which the monks would not then sell; but some years afterwards their reluctance was overcome by a more liberal offer. He prevailed, by aid of a tempting bottle, to get access to a long-forgotten cellar or vault, crammed with manuscripts in all stages of decay, but from which some were rescued and brought away.

The description given by this traveller, first of the desert, and then of the contrast presented by the interior of one of these monasteries, will enable us to understand the attractions of this secluded mode of life to many who had retired to it from the troubles of the open world. To men of sedentary and literary habits, especially, it would be peculiarly attractive; and these would find their happiness through the round of long years, in the occupation of copying books. Mr. Curzon thus presents to us the contrast above mentioned. He says:—

"To those who are not familiar with the aspect of such a region as this, it may be well to explain that a desert, such as that which now surrounded me, resembles more than anything else, a dusty turnpike road in England, on a hot summer's day, extended interminably, both as to length and breadth. A country of low rounded hills, the surface of which is composed entirely of gravel, dust, and stones, will give a good idea of the general aspect of a desert. Yet, although parched and dreary in the extreme from their vastness and openness, there is something grand and sublime in the silence and loneliness of these burning plains; and the wandering tribes of Bedouins who inhabit them are seldom content to remain long in the narrow inclosed confines of cultivated land. There is always a fresh breeze in the desert, except when the terrible hot wind blows; and the air is more elastic and pure than where vegetation produces exhalations, which, in all hot climates, are more or less heavy and deleterious. The air of the desert is always healthy, and no race of men enjoy a greater exemption from weakness, sickness, and disease, than the children of the desert, who pass their lives in wandering to and fro, in search of the scanty herbage on which their flocks are fed, far from the cares and troubles of busy cities, and free from the oppression which grinds down the half-starved cultivators of the fertile soil of Egypt.

"Whilst from my elevated position, I looked out on my left, upon the mighty desert, on my right how different was the scene! There, below my feet, lay the convent garden, in all the fresh luxuriance of tropical vegetation. Tufts upon tufts, of waving palms overshadowed the immense succulent leaves of the banana, which in their turn rose out of thickets of the pomegranate, rich with its bright green leaves and its blossoms of that beautiful and vivid red which is excelled by few even of the most brilliant flowers of the East. These were contrasted with the deep dark green of the caroub or locust-tree; and the yellow apples of the lotus vied with the clusters of green limes with their sweet white flowers which luxuriated in a climate too hot and sultry for the golden fruit of the orange, which is not to be met with in the valley of the Nile. Flowers and fair branches exhaling rich perfume, and bearing freshness in their very aspect, became more beautiful from their contrast to the dreary arid plains outside the convent walls, and this great difference was owing solely to there being a well of water in this spot, from which a horse or mule was constantly employed to draw the fertilising streams which nourished the teeming vegetation of this monastic garden."

If we carry this picture back to those times when these Nitrian monasteries were entire in their structure, and were complete in all things proper to a well-appointed religious establishment —when imperial favour, and the patronage of the wealthy were at the command of the community —we may be inclined to think that the conventual life might seem enviable to many in those times, who were beating about in the storms of the open world. No doubt this tranquil existence had its charms, even for such as relinquished much when they buried themselves in a monastery. How attractive must it have been to those who lost nothing in making the exchange, and to whom the vow of poverty brought with it, in fact, an exemption from want, turmoil, labour, misery! It was thus that these establishments kept their cells ever full, and their refectory halls always furnished with guests.

The lively writer from whom we have cited the passages just above, appears to have received his idea of the founders of these religious houses from the absurd legendary literature of a later time. If he had only taken the pains to acquaint himself with the extant writings of some of these good men, he might perhaps have come to think of them more worthily, and then he would have abridged a little the ridicule he heaps upon them. As for instance,—the Great Saint of the Egyptian monks—St. Marcarius, concerning whom, and his austerities, there is abundance of childish absurdity in the "Lausiac Memoirs," and in other books of that class, is, on sufficient evidence, believed to be the author of Homilies and Treatises which indicate a sincere and sober-minded piety, far remote from the extravagance and the foolish ostentation with which his later biographers have encumbered his better fame.

It is pertinent to our present argument to say, that the existence, in the fourth and following centuries, of works so substantially good as are those of this Marcarius, and others, is indicative of a far higher condition of the Christian community, in those times, than we should imagine in looking into the monkish literature of later ages. In truth, it was the substantial merits of many of the early Christian writers that gave an impulse to the zeal and assiduity of the copyists. We have evidence of this in the frequent occurrence of the works of the principal writers of the fourth century, among the now neglected heaps of the Egyptian, and other monasteries.

From the same writer—Mr. Curzon, we may cite a description of an Abyssinian copying apparatus, and library, and the writers there employed—illustrative, as it is, of what has been affirmed in the preceding chapters.

The library, or consistory, of some Abyssinian monks was their refectory also:—

"On my remarking the number of books which I saw around me, the monks seemed proud of their collection, and told me that there were not many such libraries as this in their country. There were perhaps nearly fifty volumes; and as the entire literature of Abyssinia does not include more than double that number of works, I could easily imagine that what I saw around me formed a very considerable accumulation of manuscripts, considering the barbarous state of the country from which they came. The disposition of the manuscripts in this library was very original . . . The room was about twenty-six feet long, twenty wide, and twelve high; the roof was formed of the trunks of palm-trees, across which reeds were laid, which supported the mass of earth and plaster, of which the terrace-roof was composed. The interior of the walls was plastered white with lime; the windows, at a good height from the ground, were unglazed, but were defended with bars of iron-wood, or some other hard wood; the door opened into the garden, and its lock, which was of wood also, was of that peculiar construction which has been used in Egypt from time immemorial. A wooden shelf was carried in the Egyptian style round the walls, at the height of the top of the door; and on this shelf stood sundry platters, bottles, and dishes for the use of the community. Underneath the shelf various long wooden pegs projected from the wall; they were each about a foot and a half long, and on them hung the Abyssinian manuscripts, of which this curious library was entirely composed.

"The books of Abyssinia are bound in the usual way, sometimes in red leather, and sometimes in wooden boards, which are occasionally elaborately carved in rude and coarse devices: they are then inclosed in a case, tied up with leather thongs; to this case is attached a strap for the convenience of carrying the volume over the shoulders, and by these straps the books were hung to the wooden pegs, three or four on a peg, or more if the books were small: their usual size was that of a small, very thick quarto."

The labour required to write an Abyssinian book, it is said, is "immense, and sometimes many years are consumed in the preparation of a single volume. They are almost all written upon skins; the only one not written upon vellum that I have met with is in my possession; it is on charta bombycina. The ink which they use is composed of gum, lamp-black, and water. It is jet black, and keeps its colour for ever. Indeed, in this respect, all oriental inks are infinitely superior to ours, and they have the additional advantage of not being corrosive or injurious either to the pen or paper. Their pen is the reed commonly used in the East, only the nib is made sharper than that which is required to write the Arabic character. The ink-horn is usually the small end of a cow's horn, which is stuck into the ground at the feet of the scribe . . . seated upon the ground, the square piece of thick greasy vellum is held upon the knee, or on the palm of the left hand. The Abyssinian alphabet consists of eight times twenty-six letters, two hundred and eight characters in all; and these are each written distinctly and separately, like the letters of a European printed book. They have no cursive writing; each letter is therefore painted, as it were, with the reed-pen, and as the scribe finishes each, he usually makes a horrible face, and gives a triumphant flourish with his pen. Thus he goes on letter by letter, and before he gets to the end of the first line he is probably in a perspiration, from his nervous apprehension of the importance of his undertaking. One page is a good day's work; and when he has done it, he generally, if he is not too stiff, follows the custom of all little Arab boys, and swings his head or his body from side to side, keeping time in a sort of nasal recitative, without the help of which it would seem that few can read even a chapter of the Koran, although they may know it by heart."

The habitudes of Eastern nations undergo so little change in the lapse of ages that, probably, these descriptions of things as they are now, would differ little from a similarly graphic account of the same operations, dated a thousand years back. Where the arts of life remain in their rude state, all those operations which depend upon them continue nearly the same. We may infer this from the identity of many implements and tools, such as are now seen in Museums, with those at present in use in the same countries; and the same inference is warranted by what we meet with in the illuminations of ancient manuscripts, which often exhibit the usages and methods of common life; just as we see those of China displayed in the decorations of its potteries, and its screens.

"The paint-brush used by the illuminators of Egypt is made by chewing the end of a reed till it is reduced to filaments, and then nibbling it into a proper form the paint-brushes of the ancient Egyptians were made in the same way; and excellent brooms for common purposes are made at Cairo by beating the thick end of a palm-branch till the fibres are separated from the pith; the part above which is not beaten, becoming the handle of the broom. The Abyssinian having nibbled and chewed his reed till he thinks it will do, proceeds to fill up the spaces between the inked outlines with his colours; . . . the colours are mixed up with the yolk of an egg, and the numerous mistakes and slips of the brush are corrected by a wipe from a wet finger or thumb, which is generally kept ready in the artist's mouth during the operation; and it is lucky if he does not give it a bite in the agony of composition when, with an unsteady hand, the eye of some famous saint is smeared all over the nose by an unfortunate swerve of the nibbled reed."

These descriptions of the oriental literary craft, may perhaps fail to bring before us what might have been witnessed in the copying-room of a *Greek* monastery a thousand years ago; but as to the technical part of the operation it was not even then in a much higher state of efficiency. For it appears that copies executed in what, to Europeans, seems the rudest manner—as to apparatus, and implements, and accommodation—are often of great beauty—the patient skill and adroitness of the scribe and artist, who is never hurried in his work, making up for the deficiences of his appointments

Mr. Curzon's explorations in these Nitrian monasteries, although not the first that had been made by European travellers and scholars, had the effect of drawing the attention of learned persons afresh towards them; and the result has been to bring to light very many literary treasures which otherwise must soon have fallen into a state of irrecoverable decay. Of these restored treasures, a very remarkable example has just now come before the world; and the reader may inspect it, if he has the opportunity to take in hand a sumptuous quarto, entitled, "Remains of a very ancient Recension of the Four Gospels in Syriac, hitherto unknown in Europe; discovered, edited, and translated by William Cureton, D.D., &c., 1858."

The account which the learned editor gives of this volume agrees well with that idea of the course of things in the Nitrian monasteries which has been brought before us in Mr. Curzon's descriptions of what he found there. From his Preface we learn that—

"The manuscript from which the text of the Fragments of the Gospels contained in this volume has been printed, was one of those obtained in the year 1842, by Archdeacon Tattam, from the Syrian monastery, dedicated to St. Mary Deipara, Mother of God, in the valley of the Natron lakes. It consisted of portions of three ancient copies, bound together to form a volume of the Four Gospels, with a few leaves in a more recent hand, added to make up the deficiencies."

A note added to the last leaf of the volume is such as is commonly found at the end of similar manuscripts. In it the copyist dedicates his labour to the glory of the Holy Trinity, and commends himself to the prayers of those who may read it— these rendered efficacious through the prayers of "the Mother of God, and of all the saints continually." This note bears date in the year 1533 of the Greek reckoning, which corresponds with the year 1221 A.D. The leaf upon which this note occurs, and which contains some verses of St. Luke's Gospel, is a palimpsest vellum, "which was formerly a part of a manuscript of the sixth or seventh century, and originally contained a portion of the first chapter of St. Luke, in Syriac."

On the first leaf of the same volume, there is a note in a more ancient hand; to this effect:—

"This book belonged to the monk Habibai, who presented it to the holy convent of the Church of Deipara, belonging to the Syrians in the Desert of Scete. May God, abounding in mercies and compassion, for the sake of whose glorious name he set apart and gave this spiritual treasure, forgive his sins, and pardon his deficiencies, and number him among His own elect in the day of the resurrection of his friends, through the prayers of all the circle of the saints! Amen, Amen.—Son of the living God, at the hour of Thy judgment, spare the sinner who wrote this!"

The way in which this volume was put together is characteristic of the times in which it was done, and of that union of religious feeling and of literary (not heedlessness but) inobservance, which attach to the monastic mode of life after it has subsided into its inert and mindless condition. Dr. Cureton says that "the volumes containing the fragments that are now published, were taken, as it would appear, almost by hazard, without any other consideration than that of their being of the same size, and then arranged so as to form a complete copy of the Four Gospels. There were several other volumes in the Nitrian Library made up in this manner. The person who arranged them seems to have had no idea of selecting the scattered parts of the same original volume, which had fallen to pieces, but merely to have taken the first leaves which came to his hand, which would serve to complete a copy of the Gospels, and then to have bound them together. In this way it came to pass, that parts of three or four manuscripts were found mixed up with three or four others, written at different times, and by different scribes; and sometimes, indeed, not even of the same exact size, apparently without regard to any other circumstance than merely to render the context perfect."

So far as could be done, this intermixture of leaves has been remedied, by bringing the corresponding portions of the same copy again into their original juxtaposition, so as to constitute continuous copies of several different manuscripts. Within the one volume, such as it had been obtained from the Nitrian monastery, there were included some leaves of thick vellum, apparently transcribed in the sixth or seventh century, and written in a very large, bold hand, with divisions of sections—some of very thin and white vellum, in a large hand, in two columns, similar to the former; but apparently rather older; and some in a different style and of other dates.

Dr. Cureton expresses his belief (as to portions at least) of what has thus been recovered, that they were transcribed in or about the middle of the fifth century; and that they represent a text —especially so far as concerns the recovered portions of the Gospel of St. Matthew—which has been unknown to European scholars; and is, therefore, "of the highest importance for the critical arrangement of the text of the Gospels."

The use to be made of this ancient copy is not a subject properly belonging to this volume; but it will be well that the reader should bring into his own view the highly significant facts that are, as we may say, linked together in an instance of this sort. Let us then recount them: and we may do so with the more satisfaction, inasmuch as they are now so recently made public; and because, also, the instance, taken in all its circumstances, may stand as fairly representative of very many of those which constitute the evidence adducible in proof of the same transmission of ancient books to modern times.

The Church writers of the fourth and fifth centuries make frequent references to the monastic establishments of the Scetic desert.* In these religious houses, well-ordered and amply furnished as they were in those times, the business of copying books was a principal occupation of such of the recluses as were inclined by their habits and tastes to pursue it. There are notices of these establishments from time to time, down to the Mahometan era; when, although some of the monasteries were dismantled or plundered, more of them were treated indulgently, or even reverentially, by the Arabian conquerors. Several Saracenic writers mention the Nitrian monasteries in a style of oriental encomium. With varying fortunes, the principal of them—that especially of St. Mary Deipara—maintained their existence, and were, at times, even in a flourishing condition, during what are called the Dark Ages. Great additions were made to the libraries, and particularly in the class of Syriac and Aramaic books, which had been brought from similar establish-

* These are, Palladius, Eusebius, Socrates, Jerome, Rufinus, Evagrius Cassian; and others incidentally.

ments in Mesopotamia and the remoter East. Incidental notices in evidence of the continuance, and, to some extent, of what we may call the vitality, of four or five of these Nitrian religious houses, may be collected from the writers, in succession, who refer to Egypt, and to its ecclesiastical affairs—down to modern times—or, as we should say, to the revival of learning in Europe. An Arabian author of the fifteenth century affirms that the monasteries, formerly a hundred in number, were, in his time, seven only; but he specifies that of St. Macarius, and speaks of it as a fine building, though its occupants were few.

From about this time, therefore—namely, from the fifteenth century, and until our own times—these ancient structures, with their dosing inhabitants, the mindless guardians of whatever they might contain—have remained as sepulchres, subjected to no other invasions or spoliations than those of Time. The dust of one year has settled down upon the dust of preceding years, in these oven-like vaults, through the tranquil lapse of four centuries. Some peculiar circumstances have contributed to ensure the preservation of the manuscripts hoarded in these tombs, and these ought to be kept in view. Among these are, *first*, the slumbering ignorance of the monks, together with the unknowing superstition with which they guard their libraries: along with this is the jealousy of the monks toward their abbots; the brethren always suspecting their superiors of an intention to purloin, and to make a commerce with, the books which were held to be the property of the community. Again, there is to be noticed a usage of the copyists, and of the owners of costly manuscripts—namely, that of subjoining a note to the last page of a book, imprecating curses upon any one who should dare, at any distant time, to dispose of, or to alienate the book for his private advantage. Not the least effective of these conservative circumstances has been this—that, in some instances, the entire contents of a monastic library have—in some moment of danger, while an enemy was thundering at the gate—been huddled into a cellar or a vault, and there covered with rubbish—safe for a hundred years or more. It was just in this condition that a large portion of the manuscripts which are now carefully preserved in the British Museum, was discovered by those who have lately succeeded in bringing them off.

In the lapse of these last four centuries, the monasteries of the Egyptian desert have frequently been visited by European travellers and men of learning. Among these was Robert Huntington, afterwards bishop of Raphoe, whose collection of Oriental manuscripts has found its home in the Bodleian Library: this visit was in the year 1678 or 1679. The celebrated Joseph Simon Asseman, in the year 1715, who had been preceded by his cousin Elias, examined these collections and brought away, to enrich the Vatican, a small number of books—Arabic, Coptic, and Syriac. About the same time the Jesuit Claude Sicard visited those of the monasteries that were still inhabited, and found the books packed in chests, covered with dust, and in a neglected condition; they were stowed away in the tower or keep (above mentioned).

In illustration of what we have said concerning the persistence of the monks in refusing to part with their books, we may cite the evidence of a traveller—the Sieur Granger, who visited the Natron monasteries in the year 1730. He says, that the buildings at that time were falling into decay, and the dust destroying the books and manuscripts, of which the monks made no use whatever. Their own patriarch had represented to them that the sum which the books would produce would be sufficient to enable them to restore their churches and to rebuild their cells: but they declared they would rather be buried in the ruins. Lord Prudhoe visited the monasteries in 1828. After much difficulty he got access to a chamber in which was a trap-door, through which he "descended, candle in hand, to examine the manuscripts, where books and parts of books, and scattered leaves, in Coptic, Ethiopic, Syriac, and Arabic, were lying in a mass on which," he says, "I stood. . . . To appearance it seemed as if, on some sudden emergency, the whole library had been thrown for security down this trap-door, and that they had remained undisturbed in their dust and neglect for some centuries."*

In this manner it is that we feel our way from century to century, keeping an eye all the way upon those remains of a distant time, the safe transmission of which is our immediate theme. In this transit we are now reaching the shore of the times we live in. Those fragments of the Gospels which already we have mentioned, and

* An account in full of these researches appeared in No. CLIII. of the Quarterly Review (1845), and afterwards in the Edinburgh Review.

many other highly important manuscripts, which are now in the British Museum, were obtained at different times by Dr. Tattam (Archdeacon of Bedford), who twice visited Egypt expressly for this purpose. In one of these monasteries, in a vault, the manuscripts and fragments of books covered the floor, eight inches deep, where they had laid, apparently many years. As many as 317 books, entire or in part, were then purchased, and they safely reached their destination: most of them are on vellum; some on paper—all in Syriac, Aramaic, or Coptic; and these, with those before obtained, made 360 volumes of manuscripts. Some of these volumes contain two, three, or four distinct works, written at different periods, but bound up together:—altogether perhaps containing not fewer than a thousand manuscripts—derived from Mesopotamia, Syria, and Egypt, and belonging to different times, from the fifth to the thirteenth century. In fact, it now appears that a few of them are of a much higher antiquity than the fifth century.

In the course of time, as the Mahometan influence extended itself throughout the East, and became more and more exclusive and intolerant, the Christian recluses of Mesopotamia, Syria, and Arabia gradually retired, or were driven westward, bringing with them, when they could do so, their books. Thus it was that the monasteries of the Egyptian desert became stored with these manuscripts in the languages of the East, and especially of Syria and Arabia.

The separate books of the Old and New Testaments, or fragments of them, abound in these recovered stores. Liturgies, and Lives of the

Saints, the spurious Gospels also, and the works of the early Christian writers, together with the canons of Councils, are also largely present among them; and altogether, many additions to religious literature, and some few to classic literature, have hence accrued. Among these recoveries, in the department of Christian literature, we should name the three Epistles of St. Ignatius—believed to be the only genuine epistles of this father. Fragments also of what are termed the Festal Epistles of St. Athanasius, in Syriac, have been found in the same manner; and the circumstances attaching to this one instance, as narrated by the learned editor, are so characteristic of the times and places which we have now in view, that they may properly be reported in this place; the more so because the publications in which these accounts first appeared, are of a kind rarely coming under the eye of general readers.

It was the custom of the patriarchs—and thus of Athanasius, during the forty years of his official life—to address a circular-letter each year to his clergy, informing them of the day in which the Easter solemnities were to be observed. Nothing more than some fragments of these Epistles, in the Greek original, had reached modern times. But it is now a Syriac version of many of them that has come to light.

The treasures of Syriac literature obtained by Dr. Tattam, in Egypt, as we have already mentioned, were deposited in the British Museum: it was a vast mass—a chaos of manuscripts and fragments; there were volumes and parts of volumes, and single sheets, and torn fragments of sheets, large and small. This mass of commingled materials was consigned to the care of Dr. Cureton, as belonging to his department; and it became his duty to examine, and to report concerning the whole—a task which seemed to defy human skill and industry. This labour, which at first appeared to need no addition, was, however, afterwards doubled by the arrival of another mass, almost equal to the first; for the fact had transpired that the monks, who received payment as for their entire library, had contrived to hold back a large portion of the whole; which, however, was afterwards obtained by means of a further payment.

A laborious adjustment of these materials—part to part—resulted in bringing to light several Syriac versions of treatises of which the titles were known, but of which the Greek originals have been lost. Among these, and claiming to be noticed, are some of the writings of Eusebius, the ecclesiastical historian; and with them the Theophania, or "Manifestation of Christ," of which an English translation has been published, by the late Dr. Lee. The manuscript of this Syriac work appears, by dates attached to it, to be not less than fifteen hundred years old, and in fact to have been written a few years only later than the time of the publication of the original treatise.

A curious circumstance connected with one of these ancient manuscripts is mentioned by Dr. Cureton. To one of the leaves of this manuscript —midway in the volume, there is attached a note to this effect: "Behold, my brethren, if it should happen that the end of this ancient book should

OF ANCIENT MANUSCRIPTS.   243

be torn off and lost, together with the writer's subscription and termination, it was written at the end of it thus: viz., that this book was written at Orrhoa, a city of Mesopotamia (Edessa), by the hands of a man named Jacob, in the year seven hundred and twenty-three, in the month Tishrin the latter it was completed; and agreeably to what was written there, I have written also here, without addition, and which I wrote in the year one thousand and three hundred and ninety-eight of the era of the Greeks."

These dates, according to our era, correspond with the years A.D. 411, for the time of the transcription of the volume, and A.D. 1086 for that of the note. What this writer anticipated as probable did actually take place; for the end of the sheet containing the original note of the copyist had been torn off and lost; how small then appeared the probability that the actual fragment should have escaped so many risks of utter destruction, and that it should be recovered. Yet so it was! In the mass of fragments which were afterwards obtained, and brought to England, there were several bundles, promiscuously made up, and consisting of separate leaves or parts of leaves, which were in fact the gatherings and sweepings from the floor, after the principal volumes had been taken up.

"One by one," says Dr. Cureton, "I untied the bundles (there were about twenty) and diligently and eagerly examined their contents. As I opened the fourth I was delighted at recognising two pieces belonging to one of the leaves of this precious book; in the next I found a third: and now, reader, if thou hast any love for the records of antiquity; if thou feelest any kindred enthusiasm in such pursuits as these; if thou hast ever known the satisfaction of having a dim expectation gradually brightened into reality, and an anxious research rewarded with success,—things that but rarely happen to us in this world of disappointment—I leave it to thine own imagination to paint the sensations which I experienced at that moment, when the loosing of the cord of the seventh bundle disclosed to my sight a small fragment of beautiful vellum, in a well-known hand, upon which I read the following words." . . .

These words were those of the original copyist, which had been copied as above mentioned, and attached to another part of the volume, and which fixed its date to the time above stated. This note had itself been torn, yet enough of it remained entire to verify the facts that have been reported. The first sentence of this note is written in red, the second in yellow, and the third in black. Dr. Cureton thus presents to view the series of facts connected with this manuscript; and the statement of them, which we abridge, is quite pertinent to our present purpose. It was written in the country which was the birth-place of Abraham, the Father of the Faithful, and the city whose king was the first sovereign who embraced Christianity; it was written in the year of our Lord 411. It was subsequently transported to the valley of the Ascetics, in Egypt, probably in A.D. 931, and presented to the monastery of St. Mary Deipara. In A.D. 1086, some person with careful foresight, fearing lest the memorial of the transcription of so valuable a book should be lost, took the precaution to copy it into the body of the volume. At what time in the lapse of centuries this fear was realised is not known ; but when the volume came to light in 1839, this had taken place; and in that year it was transferred from the solitude of the African desert to London. Three years later two fragments of it followed it to England; and in 1847, other portions were found and restored to their places in it; and then also the transcriber's own notification of the date of his labours were found in a heap of fragments, and was attached to the leaf whence it had been torn. Through so many chances, and in traversing countries of Asia, Africa, and Europe, it has held its way through a period of one thousand four hundred and thirty-six years. Here then is an instance in point, establishing the fact of the safe transmission of ancient books to modern times.

Other instances, not less striking than this, are reported in the pamphlet whence we have derived the one here brought forward. One of these is that of a palimpsest, upon which was discovered the traces of a very ancient copy of the Iliad— legible beneath a Syriac version of an obscure author.

The subscriptions of the monastic copyists are characteristic of the times, and of the feelings of the men to whose assiduity we are indebted for whatever we possess of acquaintance with antiquity. The following may be cited as an instance, and it is one among many of a similar kind :—

"This book belongs to Daniel, a secular presbyter and visitor of the province of Amida, who gave diligence and procured it for the benefit of himself and of those who, possessed with the same object of love of divine instruction, may approach it, and desire to profit their lives by the truth that is in it. But the poor Simeon, presbyter and a recluse, who is in the holy convent of my Lord Simeon of Cartamin, transcribed it. May every one therefore, who asks for it, that he may read in it, or write from it, for the sake of the love of God, pray for him who gave diligence and obtained it, and for the scribe, that he may find mercy in the day of judgment, like the thief who was on the right hand (of the cross), through the prayers of all the saints, and more particularly of the holy and glorious and perpetual Virgin, the Mother of God, Mary. Amen, and Amen, and Amen."

Another of these subscriptions ends thus :—

"Whosoever removeth this volume from this same mentioned convent, may the anger of the Lord overtake him, in this world, and in the next, to all eternity. Amen."

These imprecations were not impotent forms; for they took great hold of the minds and consciences of those who had the custody of the literary treasures of each monastery; and the instances are frequent in which a religious (we should not call it a superstitious) fear, availed to counterbalance the sordid motive to which collectors of MSS. made their appeal. Shall we either blame or contemn the needy brethren who professed their readiness to be buried under the ruins of their monasteries rather than violate their consciences by accepting gold for their books? These scruples—if such a word should be used in this instance—have at length given way, and Europe—or the learned throughout it—will turn to good account the spoils that have been thus obtained.

Just above (p. 243), we have brought forward an instance in which we are able, with certainty, to track our path from the Printing Press of this very year, in following upward the history of a Manuscript to the remote age of the copyist by whom it was executed. Another instance, varying from this in its circumstances, has just now made its long-desired appearance. What we refer to is Cardinal Mai's edition—in five quarto volumes—of the celebrated Vatican Manuscript of the Old and New Testament (the former is, of course, the Greek of the Septuagint). It has long been known that the Vatican Library contained a manuscript of high antiquity, and great value; but which was guarded with so much jealousy that a glimpse of it—or, at most, a brief examination of a few places in it, was the utmost favour that could be obtained from the papal authorities. Several Biblical scholars had visited Rome for the express purpose of inspecting, or examining, these precious remains; but with little success. One of the last of these—Dr. Tregelles—thus describes it:—

"This MS. is on very thin vellum; the letters are small, regularly formed uncials; three columns are on each page (with some exceptions): the original writer placed neither accents nor breathings, but these have been added by a later hand; they are, however, so delicately written, and with ink which has so much faded in colour (if indeed it ever were thoroughly black), that some who have carefully examined the MS. have thought that the accents and breathings were not additions to what was originally written. It is, however, an established fact, that they did proceed from a later corrector: this is proved by microscopic examination, and also from their omission in places in which the later hand introduced a correction; and also it may be remarked, that if the original copyist had written these fine strokes with the same ink as the letters, they would, of course, have faded in the same proportion, and thus would now be discernible only with difficulty.

"The appearance of this MS. now is peculiar; for after the older ink had considerably faded, some one took the trouble of retouching the letters throughout; this was probably done to make them more legible for actual use. When, however, this *restorer* differed from the original copyist in orthography, he left letters untouched; and sometimes, he appears to have corrected the readings, or, at least, they are corrected in ink of a similar colour; and in cursive letters.

"This MS. is void of interpunction; and the only resemblance to it is found in a small space being left between the letters where a new section begins. The initial letters, as left by the first copyist, are not larger than the rest; but a later hand has added a large initial letter in the margin, and has erased (wholly or partially) the original initial."

It is affirmed of this Vatican Manuscript, that "its antiquity is shown by its palæographic peculiarities, the letters even resembling, in many respects, those found in the Herculanean Rolls; the form of the book, the six columns at each opening resembling, in appearance, not a little a portion of a *rolled* book; the uniformity of the letters, and the absence of all punctuation:" all these points are regarded as indicative of a high antiquity. Dr. Tregelles adds that he had just received a single skin of an Hebrew roll; and the general effect of that portion of a book of the rolled form, when looked at by itself, singularly resembles one page of the Codex Vaticanus . . . the history of this Hebrew fragment is peculiar, for it was found in a dry shaft beneath the Mosque of Omar, at Jerusalem—the ancient site of the Temple. The three columns contain Genesis xxii. 1—xxiv. 26. The material is a red skin, prepared for writing on one side only.

A faithful edition of this noted manuscript had long been looked for by those engaged in the criticism of the Scriptures; and this has at length been given to the world. During many years, the late Cardinal Mai had been engaged in accomplishing this task; and though he did not live to see it actually published, he had made provisions for its appearance. With what relates to the exactness of this edition we have nothing to do in this place:—it is said to be not altogether faultless; but perhaps it is as little chargeable with errors as ought to be expected, the immensity of the labour in carrying it through the press being duly considered.

The faultiness of the *manuscript*—the mischances, and the oversights of the original scribe, are matters immediately connected with our subject; and it may be proper briefly to refer to them:[*] in truth, a knowledge of the usual extent

[*] The reader who is a *student* in Biblical criticism will know where to look for precise information on this ground.

of such errors, and of the sources of them, tends decisively to strengthen a reasonable confidence in the general trustworthiness of the literary remains of remote times. So much of human frailty attaches to these, as to all other labours of the human head and hand, as should exclude a fond or superstitious regard to them;—yet the amount of error is far from being enough to shake our confidence in the genuineness and integrity of these precious relics of antiquity—taken as a whole.

Some considerable portions of the original copy have, in the lapse of ages, been torn away, or lost from it;—or in some way they have perished:—as to the deficiency at the end, the wanting books may perhaps never have been added:—these are the concluding portions of the Epistle to the Hebrews, the three Pastoral epistles, and the Apocalypse. These chasms have, however, been supplied by copyists of a later age. The errors of the original copyist are such as must attach to labours of this kind, in which the writer either trusts to his eye, in looking to his exemplar; or to his ear, in listening to a reader. Each mode has its disadvantages; in the one case, words of similar appearance are easily taken, the one for the other, even when the substitution may have been productive of an absurd reading;—for the mind of the writer may have gone for a moment —like the fool's eyes—to the ends of the earth. In this mode also a clause may easily have been omitted, or even an entire line dropped out of its place. In the latter mode—when a reader dictates, word by word—to the writer, the same mischances may have had place; and in addition to these, there will be the *mishearings* of the scribe, and the faulty enunciations of the reader. On the whole, the errors are such as indicate, what man at the best is liable to—momentary lapses of attention, notwithstanding even a high rate of habitual accuracy, and of conscientious care; they are not more than may thus be accounted for; and as to the damage thence arising, it is quite inconsiderable; for while one copyist nods, another is awake; and as to the Scriptures, the abundance of manuscripts, and of quotations, and of ancient versions, is such as to reduce the instances of really ambiguous and important readings to a very small number; and of these—few as they are—very few affect at all any article of our belief, or any moral precept. The general inference is this—that, while the aids of erudite criticism are indispensable, for securing to us the possession of a text—the best that may now be possible—no text which it is possible at this time to obtain, can deserve that sort of superstitious regard with which some religious persons would fain look at the Bible in their hand. The most faulty text in existence may safely be regarded as a true and trustworthy conveyance of the message of eternal life; and also as a true and a trustworthy expression of that moral code according to which all actions will be judged. Souls will not perish, nor even be endangered, through erroneous readings; nor in any single instance will it appear that the conduct and temper that are becoming to a Christian will have been tarnished, or in any manner made less ornamental, because an ancient transcriber of the Gospels or Epistles has written $\hat{\eta}\mu\epsilon\hat{\iota}s$, where he ought to have written $\hat{\upsilon}\mu\epsilon\hat{\iota}s$.

The history and description of several noted ancient manuscripts of the Scriptures, similar to that of the Vatican Manuscript, might here be brought forward, if it were useful to do so; but, in regard to our present purpose, it may be more serviceable to fix the reader's attention upon this one instance, and to insist, for a moment, upon the value of the facts, of which it is a sample.

We have then before us—let us suppose it—now on our table—five bulky quarto volumes, printed at Rome about fourteen years ago, but just now brought forward. These volumes contain the Greek version of the Old Testament—the Septuagint—and the Greek of the New Testament—and the editor informs us that they are printed from a manuscript which has long been stored in the Vatican library. This manuscript has in fact been seen, and in part examined, by a succession of European scholars, during the course of three centuries past; and a portion of it was long ago given to the world in a printed edition. At what time, or in what manner, this manuscript came to be where now it is found, is not known, nor are these facts of much consequence; for when it is examined by those whose studies and habits have made them familiar with literary antiquarian relics—those who "by reason of use have their senses exercised" to judge of things that differ, such persons, in narrowly inspecting the material—the vellum—the ink—the form and disposition of the colours—the character of the letters—the juxtaposition of words—the *species* of sectional division, as compared with the sectional divisions prevalent at different times:—these and other minute characteristics being considered—these skilled persons differ little in their judgment as to the date of the manuscript, and agree in fixing a time about the middle of the fourth century, when it passed from under the hand of an assiduous, and on the whole, a careful copyist. We are landed, therefore, let us say—in the mid years of that century when Christianity had everywhere got the ascendancy; or some time during the reigns of Constans and Constantius.

Now the possession of so large a quantity of very costly material—the finest vellum, and the command of so much time as must have been employed in executing a careful and uniform copy, in uncial letters, of the Old and New Testament, are evidence of the fact that the copyist was in a position favourable for accomplishing his task in an efficient manner; nor can it be doubted that he would take proportionate care to select a manuscript—as his exemplar—the best he could find. Probably he would provide himself with *several* such manuscripts for purposes of collation, in doubtful instances; he would seek for the oldest manuscripts that might be then obtainable. In supposing so much as this, we assume only what it is reasonable to assume. But a manuscript which, in the middle of the fourth century, would be accounted ancient—we are now thinking of the New Testament—must have been, at the least— a hundred and fifty, or two hundred years old. We have now in our hands a great number of MSS. that are undoubtedly more than a thousand years old—two hundred years therefore comes far within the range of the ordinary longevity of books on vellum.

Take it as probable that the copyist whose labours are before us in the Vatican Manuscript, had on his table manuscripts that were two hundred years old, and then these will have been executed during the reign of Antoninus Pius, and in Egypt probably. But now I have on *my* table what may enable me to form an opinion of the value of the manuscripts which the transcriber of the Vatican Manuscript had then on *his* table; for I have before me the voluminous works of the Christian writers of that very time—such as Justin Martyr, Tatian, Athenagoras, Irenæus, Clement of Alexandria, Hermias, Origen, and others:—not to come down to a later time. These works have reached modern times through various and independent channels; they have come abroad, drawn forth from hiding-places, widely apart. But now these various writings abound with quotations from the canonical books; and although these quotations are not always exact in the wording, they are mainly identical with the text of the Vatican Manuscript. I turn to one of the above-named writers—Clemens Alexandrinus. The passages in the Old Testament which he either refers to explicitly, or quotes *verbatim*, are so many, that they make a list which fills not fewer than twelve folio pages, double columns. Now, in turning to the places where these citations occur, and in comparing them with the Vatican Septuagint, I find them to correspond, word for word, in a large proportion of instances. Clement, it is evident, had before him a Greek version of the Old Testament, which was mainly the same as the manuscript from which the Vatican MS. was derived. But now,

if it might be imagined that a modern editor of
Clement had made alterations in the text, with
the view of bringing these quotations into conformity with the Vatican Septuagint, any such
supposition as this is excluded by the fact that,
in frequent instances, there are variations in the
wording of quotations; it hence appears that the
editor has *not* done what I might conjecture that
he would do. Besides, it is not one ancient
writer, but very many that quote the Old Testament freely, and frequently; sometimes they do
so with perfect accuracy, sometimes with less
care; but yet they do it so as to furnish over-
abundant evidence of the fact that the Greek
version of the Old Testament, such as we now
find it in the Vatican Manuscript was familiarly
known to, and was in the hands of, the Christian
community at that early time;—as it had been
for centuries before that time.

We have thus adduced a few instances in which
the history of particular manuscripts may be
traced up from the present time to a remote age
—some a thousand—some fourteen hundred years.
Many similar instances might be brought forward,
if it were thought necessary, or even useful, so to
do; but the reader, if indeed he wishes to acquaint
himself more fully with facts of this class, may
easily do so by looking into the catalogues that
have been published of the manuscripts contained
in the principal libraries of Europe; or, not to
travel far—the Bodleian, Oxford; or that of the
British Museum. The manuscripts in the Museum
are the Cottonian, the Harleian, those of the
King's Library, Ayscough's, Hargrave's, and the
Lansdowne MSS., of all which collections separate

catalogues have been published. There are, besides, in the Museum, several collections of Oriental manuscripts, and many recent additions, such, for instance, as those that have lately been obtained from the Nitrian monasteries, and which have been mentioned above.

CHAPTER XVII.

THE PROCESS OF HISTORIC EVIDENCE EXEMPLIFIED IN THE INSTANCE OF HERODOTUS.

WE have now seen in what way, and liable to what conditions, the mass of ancient literature, including the Holy Scriptures, has been sent forward through the long track of centuries intervening between the times of its production and the revival of learning, and the employment of the printing-press, in these modern times.

What I now propose to do is to place before the reader—in a single and a very signal instance, the entire historic process; or that method of proceeding by means of which we, at this time, may find our way retrogressively upwards, along the high road of history from this, our nineteenth century, to the times—four and five hundred years before the Christian era. This journey is not of less extent than two thousand five hundred years, and it brings us to the time of the last of the Hebrew prophets.

A very frequent phrase in historical writings of any sort relating to antiquity is this, "Herodotus informs us, so and so." Now my questions in hearing this, are these:—"This Herodotus, who was he? When did he live? What did he write? and how do I know that the books which bear his name on the title-page were written by any such person, or at the time to which they are usually assigned? And then, supposing these questions to be answered to my satisfaction, What reason have I for believing that the narratives which I find in these books are, in the main, true? How does it appear that what I read is *history*, and is not *fiction*?

We select Herodotus as a sample of this process, or this method of historic proof, for several reasons:—such as these. This Greek writer stands forward as the "Father of history;" he is the earliest of all extant writers of this class, excepting those of the Old Testament; his writings embrace a great compass of subjects—in fact, they give us, in outline or in detail, almost all we know of the nations of a remote antiquity. Then there is this peculiar circumstance attaching to the writings of this author, that, after having been much disparaged in modern times, and his credit greatly lowered, he has, within a few years, been restored to his place of authority by the greater intelligence of recent writers; and by an extension of our knowledge of the countries spoken of by him, as to their natural productions, their arts, their works, and their history. Of late —and almost every year has done something to bring about this result—Herodotus has returned to his position; and his assailants and critics have, in consequence, fallen out of repute. These writings, therefore, are samples at once of the authenticity of ancient history, and of what may be called the immortality of historic truth—its resurrection to a new life, after a period of entombment.

To begin at the beginning;—I will now suppose that I have before me several works in English, French, German, Italian, Latin, each of them purporting to be—"The History of Herodotus, translated from the Greek." In collating these books it becomes evident that they are all derived from some one source. But it may be well to give attention to some facts at this stage of our progress.

We affirm that the Greek text of Herodotus, such as it now appears, was extant some time before the publication of the earliest printed editions. Ostensible and tangible proof of what we here allege, is afforded by the existence, at the present time, as we shall presently state, in several public libraries, of many manuscript copies of the Greek text, which, by the date affixed to them, by the character of the writing, by the appearance of the ink, and material, and by the traditionary history of some of them, are clearly attributable to different ages, from the tenth century to the fifteenth. But now if it were possible to suppose that all these copies were derived from one MS., and that one a forgery of a late date, an examination and comparison of them, and a comparison of the manuscripts with the printed editions, will furnish several special demonstrations of the point affirmed. In 1474, twenty-eight years *before* the appearance of the first printed edition of the Greek text, Laurentius Valla, an Italian scholar, published at Venice a Latin translation of Herodotus, purporting to have been made from the Greek. Now if, in comparing this translation with the Greek manuscripts that are still extant, it were asked which

is the *original*, the Latin or the Greek? no one
acquainted with the structure of language could
hesitate in declaring for the latter; for in the
Latin (as in every translation) ellipses are supplied, exegetical and connective phrases are
introduced; and what is still more decisive, there
are many passages in the Greek where an obvious
and consistent sense is evidently misunderstood in
the Latin; for Valla seems, from all his translations, to have been but imperfectly acquainted
with the Greek language. In such instances the
occasion of the translator's error may often be
detected; by which means incontestable proof is
afforded of the fact now supposed to be questioned,
namely—that the Greek is the *original*, and the
Latin the translation. Again: The Latin, as
compared with the Greek, is deficient in many
entire paragraphs, and in many single sentences.
In the Greek these passages are one with the
context; but in the Latin, the hiatus is either
abrupt and apparent, or it is concealed by a connective sentence, evidently inserted as a link
between the disjoined portions of the text. Now,
when evidence like this is presented, we need not
lay stress upon the traditional history of particular manuscripts, nor upon their apparent antiquity, nor upon the genuineness of the dates
affixed to them; for from the facts actually before
us, we can draw only one inference. Without
going further, therefore, we may conclude with
certainty, that several Greek manuscripts of
Herodotus were in existence some time before
the publication of the printed editions; and by
consequence, the averments of the first editors
are confirmed, who declare that they derived

their text from manuscripts—already known to the learned.

The Greek text of Herodotus was, for the first time, printed by Minutius Aldus, at Venice, September, 1502. Copies of this beautiful and correct edition, "corrected by a collation of many manuscripts," are still extant:—it is distinguished by its retention of the forms of the Ionic dialect—a proof that the editor followed a pure and ancient manuscript, for the Ionic forms are generally lost in those copies, the text of which has passed through many transcriptions. This edition, with corrections and notes, was reprinted at Basil, in 1541, and again in 1557, by Joachim Camerarius. In 1570 the Aldine text of Herodotus was printed at Paris, by Henry Stephens, who does not profess himself to have collated manuscripts. The titlepage declares that the books were "ex vetustis exemplaribus recogniti:" but in his second edition, Stephens confesses that up to that time he had not been able to procure an ancient copy by which to correct the text; he must, therefore, in the phrase just quoted, be understood to refer to the manuscripts that were consulted by Aldus. G. Jungerman, assuming the edition just mentioned as the basis of his own, in which however he made, without specification, many conjectural emendations, printed the Greek text, at Frankfort, in 1608. This was the first edition in which the text was divided into sections, as it now appears. The London edition, dated 1679, and published under favour of the name of the learned Thomas Gale, was derived, without acknowledgment, from that of Jungerman. Hitherto the editions were only successive reprints of the

Aldine text; and came, therefore, all from a
single source; but in 1715, an edition of Herodotus was published at Leyden, under the care
of Gronovius, who collated the former editions
with some manuscripts before unknown, or not
examined. A Glasgow edition appeared in 1761;
and two years later that of Wesseling, printed
at Amsterdam. Some quotations from this editor's
preface will give the general reader a good idea
of the method of conducting these literary labours,
and of the security afforded for the purity of
the text of ancient authors. Several German
and Dutch editions have appeared since that of
Wesseling; the most esteemed are those of Bor-
heck, Reiz, Schaefer, and Schweighæuser. Of
the laborious care bestowed by the learned
editors upon these editions, the following citations from their prefaces will give evidence.
Wesseling says:—

"The forms and proprieties of the Ionic dialect
I have restored, wherever they could be gathered
clearly *from the ancient codices,* and have replaced
some readings which, without cause, had been
rejected. Innumerable passages I have relieved
from errors, yet *very rarely on mere conjecture,*
and only in those words which the genius of the
language would not admit; and in many instances
have thought it enough just to point out the
means of amending the text, where it is evidently
corrupted." In quoting this passage from Wesseling, Schweighæuser says, "Neither have we,
except in a very few places, admitted conjectural
emendations into the text; and these only where
it was evident that all the readings of all the
existing copies were corrupted, and where an

emendation presented itself which not merely seemed probable, but which was so clear and certain as to need no argument in its favour." Very judiciously, this editor refuses to impute to the temerity or ignorance of copyists *all* the variations from the Ionic forms; since it is evident that Greek writers who adopted *one* of the dialects, allowed themselves the liberty of occasionally using the common forms of the language: he therefore restores the ionicisms only when he has the authority of MSS. for so doing. Of Wesseling's extreme caution, Schweighæuser thus expresses his opinion:—" In this edition, excepting a few errors, easily corrected, or some cases which may be open to disputation, the learned have nothing to complain of; unless it be, that, in adopting better readings, warranted by MSS., as well as in correcting, on probable conjecture, some places manifestly faulty in all copies, the Editor was too timid—so much so, indeed, that many approved readings which he might well have admitted into the text, he ventured not to adopt. And often he preferred to leave, untouched, manifest and gross corruptions, rather than to put in their place his own emendations, or those of others, though decidedly approved by himself. As to conjectural emendations, even in those places where all the MSS. are plainly in fault, we have seen him, in his preface, ingenuously confess that he had rather be thought too cautious, than too bold: and who would not esteem,—yes, and admire,—rather than condemn, this illustrious man, blaming his own timidity in this sort:—" In attempting to restore the language of Herodotus, I have been restrained often by more than a due timidity; but such is my nature." This editor, in his preface, states that, having been applied to, to superintend a reprint of Wesseling's Herodotus, he had declined doing so, unless he should be able to obtain, from the French king's library, the loan of the MSS. of Herodotus, there preserved:—the troubles of the times preventing this, he sought for some one, residing at Paris, who would freely undertake the irksome and painful toil of collating Wesseling's text with all those codices; and at length, by means of a learned friend, he met with a young man, a native of Greece, who executed the task of comparing the text—word by word—with the five principal manuscripts in the library, and making a *separate* list of the various readings in each.

From the mass of variations brought before him, the office of the editor is to select that one which most recommends itself, either by the superior authority of the codex in which it appears, or by its particular probability, or seeming accordance with the author's style or meaning, or with the proprieties of the language. And not seldom it happens that the most inferior copies have chanced to preserve an evidently genuine reading, where the best have, as plainly, erred.—"No MS.," an eminent critic has said, "ought to be thought unworthy of being consulted." Yet in cases of importance, where there may be room for doubt among the existing variations, the canon must be obeyed which enjoins that, "Codices should rather be *weighed* than numbered." Although discussions on subjects of this kind cannot but seem uninteresting, and even trivial to general readers—and perhaps absurd, when the gravity and strenuousness with which, sometimes, the most minute points are argued, is observed; yet it ought never to be forgotten that *the credit, the purity*, and *the consistency* of ancient literature, are very greatly promoted by the indefatigable zeal of those who devote their lives to these learned and unattractive labours.

But I now look into some of the printed editions. For instance, here is a small folio volume, in excellent style, as to type, and paper, and execution, printed in Paris, MDLXX., and edited by Henry Stephens. I have also in hand the edition edited by J. Schweighæuser, in four volumes octavo, reprinted in London, 1822; and also a more recent edition, namely—that of Professor Gaisford, in two volumes octavo. Besides these there are ten other editions of the Greek text—German, Dutch, and English. I open these several editions, at hazard—say at the beginning of the third book—THALIA: I find that they correspond, word for word, for some way on; but in the fifth line I find an unimportant variation—one form of a word is used instead of another; and further on the order of the words is a little different, but the sense is the same. Sometimes one particle or expletive is used instead of another; sometimes those expletives that barely affect the sense in any way, are omitted. Frequently the orthography of proper names is differently given in the different editions. Very rarely are these variations of so much importance as would affect the sense in a translation. But now, from the fact of the verbal identity of these editions throughout by far the larger part of them, and also from the occurrence of not infrequent, and yet inconsiderable differences, I infer, first—that they have all had a common source in some one original exemplar; and, secondly—that there have been many copyings from that first copy; and that it has been in the course of these repetitions, in which the ear, the eye, and the hand of many writers have done their part, that these departures from the author's first copy have taken place. In a word, the *printed* editions have followed *manuscripts;* and these have undergone those chances, and those mischances which, in the ordinary course of things, must attach to a process like this, notwithstanding the care and the fidelity of those who practise it.

The next step, then, is to make search for those ancient manuscripts, or for some of them, whence these printed editions have been derived. About fifteen such manuscripts are now known, and may be inspected in public or private libraries. One of the purest of these is preserved in the French King's library (now the Imperial) and it is thus described:—It is a parchment in folio, purchased in 1688, containing the nine books of Herodotus. This codex is by far the best of all, and appears to have been executed in the 12th century. It is distinguished by its uniform retention of the forms of the Ionic dialect—an indication of the antiquity and purity of the copy from which it was derived. The same library contains also several other MSS. of this author, which are thus described:—A codex on paper, formerly belonging to the Colbertine library, containing the nine books of Herodotus: in the margin are notes of some value This MS. was executed in 1372. A

copy on paper, written in the year 1447. The
negligence of the copyist is, in this instance, much
to be complained of, for sometimes entire phrases
are wanting. Yet it contains some readings that
deserve attention. A MS. on paper, dated 1474.
Besides the nine books of Herodotus, this codex
contains parts of the works of Isocrates, and
Plutarch, together with a lexicon of words peculiar to Herodotus. A MS., which along with
extracts from several Greek authors, contains part
of the first book of Herodotus, as far as c. 87.
Although this codex is of late date, the extract
from Clio appears to have been made from a very
ancient copy. Some other codices in the same
library afford also parts of our author's work.
There is a codex formerly in the Florentine
library, which from the condition of the parchment, and the antique style of the writing, is
manifestly of great antiquity. Montfaucon assigns
it to the tenth century. This codex belongs to
the same family as that of Askew, and the Medicean. Yet neither was it copied from the latter,
with which, indeed, it might dispute the palm of
excellence; but being derived from a more ancient
source, it offers many approved readings, differing
from the Medicean, where that is in fault, or
where it offers no emendation of the common text.
This Medicean codex is thus described in the
Catalogue of the Florentine library: "Herodotus:—a very ancient codex, valuable beyond all
praise. It is on paper, in quarto, well preserved:
executed in the tenth century. The titles of the
books are in uncial letters of gold; it contains 374
pages." This copy was followed with a too superstitious reverence by Gronovius; yet being com-

pelled to consult it in the public library, and under the eye of the librarian, he has not seldom mistaken its readings. A MS. of Herodotus, formerly in the library of Archbishop Sancroft, and afterwards in that of Emmanuel College, Cambridge, has been deemed of high antiquity, and great value. The libraries of Oxford contain also some codices of our author, and several are known to be in the possession of private persons. "These manuscript copies," says Wesseling, "brought to light from various places, have not, it is manifest, originated all from one source (in modern times). Where the copy followed by Valla is torn or defective, there also the Vienna, the Vatican, and the Oxford MSS. are wanting. And in what these are remarkable, so is the Florentine. But the Medicean MS., that of Cardinal Passio, and of Askew, for the most part agree. The three first mentioned, seem to have been derived all from some one more ancient parchment, the writer of which, offended perhaps at the frequent digressions of the first book, very daringly cut them all off; and lest the hiatus should seem harsh, he skilfully fitted the parts, so as to preserve the continuity of the style. The three last, on the contrary, were derived from the copy of a transcriber better informed, who scrupled to make any needless alterations. A great number of the various readings which distinguish these MSS. are attributable to the copyists who have substituted the common forms of the language, and words better known, in the place of the Ionic forms and of obsolete words."

All that is of any importance in proof of the genuineness and integrity of ancient books, is to know that there are *now* in existence *several* copies, evidently of older date than the first printed edition of the author; and that these copies, by their general agreement, and, not less so, by their smaller diversities, prove, at once, their derivation from the same original, and their long distance from that original; since many of these diversities are such as could have arisen only from many successive transcriptions. Beyond these simple facts, the knowledge of codices, and of various readings, is interesting to none but editors and critics.

We may now fairly assume as certain, so much as this—that the work before us—mainly such as we now have it in our hands, is *an ancient work*, and that it has come down to modern times in that mode of which, in the preceding chapters, we have given some account, and have adduced several instances. Our next question is this—To what age this work ought to be attributed? Or this—When did the author live and write? In obtaining an answer to this question, or to these two questions—considered as one, we must look to that succession of writers, retrogressively examined, who mention Herodotus, and his History, who describe it, and make quotations from it, or who give summaries of its contents. The proper and the most complete proof of the antiquity and genuineness of ancient books, is that which is thus derived from their mutual references and quotations. There is an independence in this kind of evidence which renders it, when it is precise and copious, quite conclusive. It is not the evidence of witnesses, who first have been schooled and cautioned, and then brought into court to do their best for the party by whom they are summoned; but it is the purely incidental testimony of unconnected persons, who, in the pursuit of their particular objects, gather up, and present to us, the facts which we were in search of. Besides—these facts have a peculiarity, which renders them eminently capable of furnishing precise and conclusive proof. A book is an aggregate of many thousand separable parts, each of which, both by the thought it contains, and by the choice and arrangement of the words, possesses a perfect individuality, such as fits it for the purpose of defining or identifying the whole to which it belongs; and if several of these definite parts are adduced, the identification is rendered the more complete. This kind of definition is moreover capable of being multiplied, almost without end; for each writer who quotes a book, having probably a different object in view, selects a different set of quotations, yet all of them meeting in the same work. We are thus furnished with a complicated system of concentric lines, which intersect nowhere—but in the book in question.

Then it is to be remembered that each of these quoting writers stands himself as the centre of a similar system of references, so that the complication of proof becomes infinitely intricate, and therefore it is so much the more conclusive. It is again involved, and so is rendered secure, by the occurrence of double or triple quotations; for example —Photius quotes Ctesias—quoting Herodotus. The proof of genuineness in the instance of a standard author, is by such means as these extended, attenuated, and involved in a degree to which no other species of evidence makes any approach.

It hardly needs to be said, that this high degree of certainty, resulting from the complication, as well as the number of testimonies, belongs only to works that are explicitly and frequently quoted by succeeding writers. And yet this sort of proof is deemed to be in its nature so valid and satisfactory, that a very small portion of it is ordinarily admitted as quite sufficient. If, for instance, a book is explicitly mentioned only by one or two writers of the next age, the evidence is allowed to decide the question of genuineness; unless when there appears some positive reasons to justify suspicion. But with *questionable* matters we have not now to do.

It cannot be thought necessary to adduce separately any proof of the genuineness of the works that are about to be cited; since they all possess an established character, resting upon evidence of the same kind as that which is here displayed in the case of Herodotus. To bring forward all this proof, in each instance, would fill volumes.

We have seen that many manuscript copies of Herodotus, of which several are still preserved, were extant before the first printed editions appeared; and from a comparison of these manuscripts, as well as from the date which some of them bear, and from their seeming antiquity, it is evident that the work had then been in existence much longer than three hundred years; for these several manuscripts exhibit, as we have said, in their various readings, those minute diversities which are found to arise from repeated transcriptions, made by copyists in different ages and

countries—some of these copyists being exact
and skilful, while others were careless and ignorant. This proof of antiquity is more conclusive
than that which arises from a mere traditionary
history of a single manuscript, or from a date
affixed to a copy; for the date may be spurious,
or the tradition may be unauthentic; but in the
various readings we have before our eyes a species
of decay, which time alone could produce.

It is thus that we have assumed it as certain,
that the text of this author was extant at least as
early as the twelfth century. And if it were
supposed that we could not trace the history of
these manuscripts higher than that time, then we
should turn to this other species of evidence,
namely—that arising from the quotations of a
series of writers, extending upwards from the age
in which the history of the manuscripts merges
in obscurity, to the very age of the author.

The evidence which we adduce for this purpose
we divide into two portions;—in the first portion proving—that the history of Herodotus was
known to the learned during a period of a thousand years, from A.D. 1150 to A.D. 150.

Eustathius, archbishop of Thessalonica, flourished in the latter part of the twelfth century.
His Commentaries upon the Iliad and Odyssey of
Homer, contain many references to Herodotus,
that are more or less full and precise. Among
these, the following afford sufficient proof of the
point we have to establish; for they leave no
room to doubt that the History of Herodotus, as
now extant, was in the hands of this learned
prelate. In the course of these commentaries he
says, " But Herodotus seems to resemble Phere-

cydes and Hecatæus, who (in writing history) threw aside the adornments of the poetic style." Again, "Herodotus (Erato 74) says that Nonacris is a city of Arcadia where the waters of Styx arise." Again, "Herodotus, that sweet writer of the Ionic." Eustathius cites our author to illustrate the meaning of the word *mitra*—girdle or turban. On the word *phalanx* he quotes from the fourth book a sentence in which Herodotus calls Pythagoras "a man eminent among the Greeks for his intelligence." He quotes a passage relative to the Egyptian bread from the second book. Again, "Menelaus certainly visited those other Ethiopians whom Herodotus describes as bordering upon the Egyptians:" he alludes to the account given by our author of the sheep sacred to the sun in Apollonia. Eustathius quotes Herodotus, in proof that the Athenians were of Pelasgian origin.

Suidas, a learned Byzantine monk, is believed to have flourished at the close of the eleventh century. His Lexicon contains a brief Life of Herodotus; besides which, there occur under other words, not fewer than two hundred incidental references to different parts of the history. They are for the most part verbal citations of a very exact kind, adduced in illustration of the meaning, or the orthography of words.

Photius, the learned and ambitious patriarch of Constantinople, belongs to the ninth century. This writer has preserved the only portions that remain of the Persian and Indian history of Ctesias, who, as we shall see, gives a nearly contemporaneous testimony to Herodotus. The Myriobiblon of Photius consists of notices and

s

abridgments of two hundred and eighty works which he had read, and it affords therefore much information available in determining questions of literary antiquity. Many works were extant in the ninth century—at Constantinople especially, which disappeared in the following age; and Photius, who had free access to the extensive libraries of that city, wanted no advantage which might fit him for the task of reviewing the literature of the preceding ages. When therefore he quotes and describes a work, and speaks of it confidently as having been long known in the world, and generally received as a genuine production of the author whose name it bears, his evidence carries up the proof to a still more remote age; for no *spurious* work, recently produced, could have been so mentioned by a critic of great learning and sound judgment. In the Myriobiblon, besides some incidental references to Herodotus, we find the following account (Art. 60) of him:—" We have perused the nine historical books of Herodotus, bearing the names of the Nine Muses. This writer uses the Ionic dialect, as Thucydides employs the Attic. He admits fabulous accounts, and frequent digressions, which give a pleasing flow to the narrative; though indeed this manner of writing violates the strict proprieties of the historical style, in which the accuracy of truth ought not to be obscured by any mixtures of fable, nor the end proposed by the author to be long lost sight of. He begins the history with the reign of Cyrus—the first of the Persian kings—narrating his birth, education, elevation, and rule; and he brings it down as far as the reign of Xerxes—his expedition against the Athenians, and his flight. Xerxes was indeed the fourth king from Cyrus—Cambyses being the second, and Darius the third; for Smerdes the Mage is not to be reckoned in the line of kings, inasmuch as he was a usurper who possessed himself of the throne by fraud. With Xerxes, the son and successor of Darius, the history closes (the close of the war with Greece), nor indeed is it carried to the end of his reign; for Herodotus himself flourished in those very times, as Diodorus the Sicilian, and others relate, who mention the story that Thucydides, while yet a youth, was present with his father when Herodotus read his History in public, on which occasion he burst into tears; which being observed by Herodotus, the historian turned to the father and said, 'O! Olorus, what a son have you, who thus burns with a passion for learning!'"

This description of the work, although concise, is abundantly sufficient to prove the existence of the text (as now extant) in the age of Photius, whose testimony establishes also the fact that it had then been long known and reputed as a genuine production of Herodotus, while the exceptions made against certain fabulous digressions contain an explicit acknowledgment that the history was generally received as authentic.

Stephen of Byzantium, author of a geographical and historical lexicon, flourished in the middle of the sixth century. He very frequently refers to Herodotus. Art. *Thurium*, he quotes an epigram relating to him; and under the following words references to him occur:—*Abarnus*, a city, region, and promontory of Pariana, which Herodotus in his fourth book, says, is called *Abaris*. *Arisbe*—

Herodotus and Jason call it *Arisba*. *Archandroupolis*, a city of Egypt, according to Herodotus, in his second book. *Assa*, a city near Mount Atho, mentioned by Herodotus, in his seventh book. *Thalamancei*, a nation subject to the Persians. *Inycum*, a city of Sicily, called by Herodotus, *Inychos*. Herodotus appears to have been one of the principal authorities of this writer, and his citations are usually correct.

Marcellinus, a critic of the sixth century, in his "Life of Thucydides," mentions Herodotus descriptively, and compares him on many points with his rival. Omitting many less direct allusions, the following may be mentioned. He commends the impartiality of Thucydides, who did not allow his personal wrongs to give any colouring to his narrative of facts—a degree of magnanimity uncommon, he says, among historians—"For even Herodotus, having been slighted by the Corinthians, affirms that they fled from the engagement at Salamis." Describing the lofty style of Thucydides, he compares it with that of Herodotus, which, he says, "is neither lofty like that of the Attic historian, nor elegant like that of Xenophon." On the ground of authenticity also, he compares the two historians, giving the advantage in this respect to the younger; while he charges the former with admitting marvellous tales, citing, as an example, the story of Arion and the dolphin: and, towards the close, he repeats the incident already mentioned, said to have taken place when Herodotus read his History in public.

Procopius, the historian of the reign of Justinian, wrote about the middle of the sixth

century. He cites Herodotus in precise terms:—
"Now Herodotus the Halicarnassian, in the
fourth book of his History, says, that the earth,
though distributed into three portions—Africa,
Asia, and Europe, is one; and that the Egyptian
Nile flows between Africa and Asia." (Gothic
Wars, b. IV.)

Stobæus lived a century earlier than the last-
named writer. In illustration of various ethical
topics, he collects the sentiments of a multitude
of authors, and amongst the number, of Herodotus. Short sentences from the historian are
adduced in four or five places, and there is one
of some length.

The Emperor Julian makes several allusions to
our author:—thus, in his first oration in praise of
Constantine, he says, "Cyrus was called the father,
Cambyses the lord of his people." In the
exordium of his Epistle to the Athenian people,
several distinct allusions to the history of the
Persian invasion occur; and in the Misopogon the
story of Solon and Crœsus, as related by Herodotus, is distinctly mentioned. In mentioning the
principal Greek authors (Epist. XLII.), Herodotus
is included. And in an epistle not now extant,
but quoted by Suidas (Art. *Herodotus*), the apos-
tate, as he is there called, cites the historian as
"the Thurian writer of history."

Hesychius, the Lexicographer, lived in the
third century. He makes several quotations from
our author—as thus:—"*Agathoergoi*—persons
discharged from the cavalry of Sparta—five every
year, as Herodotus relates." "*Basilees*—judges;
according to Herodotus, the avengers of wrong."
"*Zeira*—a zone, according to Herodotus." "*Cana*-

mis, Tiara—the bonnet of the Persians, according to Herodotus." *Zalmoxis*—the account given of the Getæ, is quoted at length.

Athenæus, a critic of the second century, quotes our author in the following, among other instances: "Herodotus, in his first book, writes that the Persian kings drink no water except that which is brought from the Choaspian spring at Susa, which is carried for their use wherever they travel." "Herodotus, comparing the Grecian entertainments with those of the Persians, relates that the latter pay a peculiar regard to their natal day." "Herodotus, in his seventh book, says that those Greeks who entertained Xerxes on his way, were reduced to such distress, that many of them left their homes." "Herodotus relates that Amasis, king of Egypt, was accustomed to jest very freely with his guests."

Longinus, the celebrated secretary of Queen Zenobia, quotes our author several times in his treatise on the Sublime. "Was Herodotus alone an imitator of Homer?"—the address of Dionysius to the Phocæans is quoted, " Our affairs, Ionians! have reached a crisis—we must be free or slaves;" he quotes with high commendation a passage, in which our author describes the course of the Nile between Elephantine and Meroe. There is a quotation from the first book, also the story of Cleomenes in the fifth book is quoted:—
" Cleomenes devoured his own flesh."

Diogenes Laertius, author of the " Lives of the Philosophers," brings the line of testimonies up to the time above mentioned : he makes the following references to our author. In his Preface, he refers to the assertions of Herodotus relative to the Mages, and to Xerxes, whom he affirms to have lanced darts at the sun, and to have thrown fetters into the sea. In the *Life of Pythagoras*, a passage is quoted relative to Zamolxis, who was worshipped by the Getæ.

It is obvious that if the testimonies which are next to be adduced are full and conclusive, they will, in point of argument, supersede those which have been already brought forward; for if it can be satisfactorily proved that the now-existing text of Herodotus was known more than two thousand years ago, it cannot be necessary to prove that it was extant at any intermediate period. Nevertheless the above-cited authorities do not merely serve the purpose of completing our chain of evidence, but they are important in proving that the work, far from having been lost sight of in any age, was always familiarly known to scholars. We may therefore feel assured that copies were to be found in most libraries—that the work was frequently transcribed; and that, as the existing manuscripts indicate, we are not dependent upon the accuracy of one or two copyists only, for the integrity of the text.

We have now to show that the history of Herodotus was in existence, and was known to a succession of writers from the age of the writer last mentioned, up to his own times—or about B.C. 440.

A period of six or seven hundred years, ending in the second century of the Christian era, includes the brightest times, both of Grecian and of the Roman literature. Evidence of the most conclusive kind on all questions of literary history may therefore be collected in abundance from the writers of those ages. Innumerable quotations from all the principal authors are found on the pages of almost every prose writer whose works have descended to modern times. The critics and historians, especially, furnish abundantly the evidence we are in search of. We begin this second series with—

Pausanius, who, in his historical description of Greece, has frequent occasion to cite the authority of Herodotus. Of these citations the following may be mentioned:—In a digression relating to the Ethiopians, he quotes from the second, and from the fourth book; "For the Nasamones, whom Herodotus considers as the same with the Atlantics, and who are said to know the measure of the earth, are called by the Libyans, dwelling in the extreme parts of Libya, near Mount Atlas —Loxi." "Agreeably to this Herodotus tells us that in Scythia shipwrecked persons sacrificed bulls to a virgin, called by them Iphigenia, the daughter of Agamemnon." The story of Io is referred to: he quotes from Herodotus a prediction of the Delphic oracle; he authenticates a story told by our author; "these particulars as they are accurately related by Herodotus, it would be superfluous for me to repeat." He refers to the orthography of a name: "and Herodotus in his History of Crœsus informs us that this Labotas was under the guardianship of Lycurgus, who gave laws to the Lacedæmonians; but he calls him *Leobotas*." In this form, in fact, the name now stands in the Greek text:—minute correspondences of this kind vouch for the correct transmission of ancient books. He affirms that at Tænarus was to be seen " Arion the harper, sitting on a dolphin. And the particulars respecting Arion and the dolphin Herodotus relates, as what he himself heard, in his account of the Lydian affairs." Book X. 32, " As to the name of the city, I know that Herodotus, in that part of his History in which he gives an account of the irruption of the Persians into Greece, differs from what is asserted in the oracles of Bacis."

Lucian of Samosata devotes some pages to Herodotus, whose style he characterises and commends; and he relates particularly the mode adopted by the historian for making his work known to the Greeks, so that wherever he appeared all might say—That is Herodotus who wrote the history of the Persian war in the Ionian dialect, and who so gloriously chanted our victories.

Hermogenes, the rhetorician and the contemporary of Lucian, gives the following description of the historian's style: "The diction of Herodotus is pure, easy, and perspicuous. Whenever he introduces fables he employs a poetic style. His thoughts are just, his language graceful and noble. No one excels him in the art of describing, after the manner of the poets, the manners and characters of his different personages. In many places he attains greatness of style, of which the conversation betwixt Xerxes and Artabanus is an example."

Aulus Gellius, a miscellaneous writer, abounds with references to authors of every class. In his Attic Nights, Herodotus is frequently mentioned, as for example—he quotes at length the story of Arion. Again: " Yet Herodotus, the historian, affirms, contrary to the opinion of almost all, that the Bosphorus or Cimmerian Sea is liable to be frozen." There is a verbal quotation from the third book, relative to the lioness, and another, of the fable of the Psyllians.

The evidence of Plutarch is sufficiently ample and conclusive to bear alone the whole burden of our argument. The writings of Plutarch, having in every age enjoyed the highest reputation, have descended to modern times, abundantly authenticated :—among them there is a small treatise (if it be genuine, which is very questionable) entitled "Of the Malignity of Herodotus." The historian, in his account of the Persian invasion, affirms the conduct of the Bœotians on various occasions to have been traitorous and pusillanimous. Now Plutarch was a Bœotian, and he felt so keenly the infamy attached by Herodotus to his countrymen, that, with the hope of wiping out the stain, he endeavoured if possible, to destroy the reputation of our author, by advancing against him the heavy charge of a malignant falsification of facts throughout his history. To effect his object, he reviews the entire work, bringing to bear upon every assailable point the utmost efforts of his critical acuteness, and all the stores of his learning. The specific charges advanced against Herodotus in this treatise must, to a modern reader, appear for the most part extremely frivolous. So far as they may seem to be more serious, they have been fully refuted by several critics. But our business, at present, with Plutarch's treatise, is to derive from it a proof of the genuineness and general authenticity of the work which is the subject of our argument. In the first place then, this treatise, by its many and exact references to all parts of the History, proves beyond a doubt that the Greek text, as now extant, is substantially the same as that read by Plutarch—or rather by this writer who assumes his name, at the time now in view. In the second place, Plutarch's tacit acknowledgment of the work as the genuine production of Herodotus, may be taken as affording alone a sufficient proof of that fact;—for if it had been at all questionable—if any obscurity had rested upon traditionary history, this writer, whose learning was extensive, could not have been ignorant of such grounds of doubt; nor would he have failed to take the short course of denying at once the authenticity of the book. The five hundred years which intervened between the times of Herodotus and of Plutarch, were ages of uninterrupted and widely-diffused intelligence and erudition;—much more so than the last five hundred years of European history: and Plutarch had more ample means of ascertaining the genuineness of the History attributed to Herodotus, than a critic of the present day possesses in judging of the genuineness of Froissart, or of Abulfeda. In the third place, this small treatise yields an implicit testimony in support of the general truth of the history itself; for in leaving untouched all the main parts of the story, and in fixing his criticisms upon minor facts, and upon the mere colouring given to the narrative, this critic virtually acknowledges that the principle facts are unquestionable. It may be affirmed that he has in fact, on the whole, rather established the authenticity of the History against which he levels his critical weapons, than succeeded in destroying its credit.

Josephus quotes and corrects Herodotus—in the Jewish Antiquities; and in his reply to Apion he mentions him descriptively more than once, as where he enumerates the Greek historians; a few pages further, he notices the remarkable fact that "neither Herodotus nor Thucydides nor any of their contemporaries make the slightest mention of the Romans." Presently afterwards he quotes Manetho in opposition to Herodotus, in his account of Egyptian history: and some pages further, he makes an exact quotation from the second book.

Quintilian compares Herodotus with Thucydides: "Herodotus, sweet, bland, and copious." "In Herodotus, as I think, there is always a gentle flow of language." "Nor need Herodotus scorn to be conjoined with Livy."

Strabo, the most learned, exact, and intelligent of the ancient geographers, very frequently cites our author, upon whose statements he makes some severe criticisms; yet without impugning the general authenticity of the History. Art. *Halicarnassus*. "Among the illustrious men born at this place is Herodotus, the historian, who is called the Thurian, because he joined himself to a colony at that place." "It was not improperly said by Herodotus, that the whole of Egypt, at least the Delta, was a gift of the river." Strabo refers to the account given of the voyage round Africa, attempted by the order of Darius. He refers to, and quotes the authority of Herodotus, who affirms that at Memphis in Egypt there was a temple of Neptune.

The last-named writer brings our series of testimonies up to the commencement of the Christian era. In passing up the stream of time, we meet next with—

Dionysius, the countryman of Herodotus, and author of the "Roman antiquities," and of several critical treatises. In one of these, entitled "The Judgment of Ancient Writers," and in another, addressed to Cn. Pompey, Dionysius gives a minute account of the style, method, and comparative merits of our author. In the book on composition, he makes a long and literal quotation from the first book. In giving the character of Thucydides, he thus speaks of Herodotus :— "Herodotus the Halicarnassian, who survived to the time of the Peloponnesian War, though born a little before the Persian War, raised the style of writing history: nor was it the history of one city or nation only that he composed; but included in his work the many and various affairs both of Europe and Asia. For beginning with the Lydian kingdom, he continues to the Persian War—relates whatever was performed by the Greeks and Barbarians during a period of 240 years—selecting whatever was most worthy of record, and connecting them in a single history; at the same time gracing his work with excellencies that had been neglected by his predecessors." Several descriptive commendations of a similar kind might be adduced from the critical writings of this author.

Contemporary with Dionysius, though a few years his senior, was Diodorus the Sicilian. This learned and laborious historian passes over much of the same ground with Herodotus, to whom he makes several allusions. In discussing the question relative to the inundations of the Nile, he states and controverts the opinion advanced by Herodotus on that subject. Further on, he rejects as fabulous the accounts given by Herodotus and others of the remote history of Egypt, and professes to follow the public records of the Egyptian priests; yet he had before eulogised our author as a writer "without a rival, indefatigable in his researches, and extensively learned in history." Diodorus states the various opinions of writers relative to the Median empire, and among these, Herodotus: "Now Herodotus, who lived in the time of Xerxes, affirms that the Assyrians had governed Asia during a period of 500 years before it was subjugated by the Medes."

Our author was known to the Roman writers. Cornelius Nepos evidently follows him in some passages, though he professes to adhere chiefly to the authority of Theopompus, Thucydides, and Xenophon. Cicero bestows upon him high commendation in several places, declaring that "so far as his knowledge of the Greek language permitted him to enjoy it, the eloquence of the historian (whom he terms 'the Father of History') gave him the greatest delight:"—that his language "flows like an unobstructed river:"—and that "nothing can be more sweet than his style."

Pliny the Elder refers to Herodotus frequently; as thus—"If we credit Herodotus, the sea once extended beyond Memphis, as far as the mountains of Ethiopia:" speaking of the inundation of the Nile, he quotes our author—"the river, as Herodotus relates, subsides within its banks on the hundredth day after its first rise." Passing references occur in many places:—"Herodotus, more ancient and a better authority than Juba;" "Herodotus says that ebony formed part of the tribute rendered by the Ethiopians to the kings of Persia;" "this author composed (corrected) his History at Thurium in Italy, in the 310th year of Rome."

Scymnus of Chios, of whose writings some fragments only remain, professes, in his Description of the Earth, to report what "Herodotus has recorded in his History." This writer is believed to have flourished in the second century before the Christian era.

Aristotle cites Herodotus as an example of the antiquated, continuous style. "If the works of Herodotus were turned into verse, they would not by that means become a poem, but would remain a history." In his History of Animals he charges our author with an error, in affirming that "at the siege of Ninus, an eagle was seen to drink;" but no such assertion is to be found in the works of the historian: probably a passage of some other writer was quoted by Aristotle from memory, and erroneously attributed to Herodotus; or possibly he quoted some work of this historian which has since perished. The ambiguous reply of the Pythian to Crœsus is quoted, though not explicitly from Herodotus.

Ctesias, an abstract of whose works is preserved by Photius, is very frequently quoted by ancient authors. He was a Greek physician, who accompanied the expedition led against Artaxerxes by his brother, the younger Cyrus. Though a few years younger, he was contemporary with Herodotus: his testimony therefore brings the series of evidences up to the very time of our author.

Ctesias, having fallen into the hands of the Persians at the battle of Cunaxa, was detained at the court of Artaxerxes as physician, during seventeen years; and it seems that, with the hope of recommending himself to the favour of "the great king," and of obtaining his own freedom, he undertook to compose a history of Persia, with the express and avowed design of impeaching the authority of Herodotus, whom, in no very courteous terms, he accuses of many falsifications. The jealousy and malice of a little mind are apparent in these accusations. Nothing can be much more inane than the fragments that are preserved of this author's two works—his History of Persia, and his Indian History; yet, though possessing little intrinsic value, they serve an important purpose, in furnishing a very explicit evidence of the genuineness and general authenticity of the work which Ctesias laboured to depreciate. If the account given by Herodotus of Persian affairs had been altogether untrue, his rival wanted neither the will nor the means to expose the imposition. But while, like Plutarch, he cavils at minor points, he leaves the substance of the narrative uncontradicted.

Thucydides, the contemporary and rival of Herodotus, whose writings are said to have kindled in his young mind the passion for literary distinction, makes only an indistinct allusion to the History; yet this allusion is such as can hardly be misunderstood. Book I. 22, in explaining the principles by which he proposed to be guided in writing his History, he glances sarcastically at certain writers, who, in narrating events that had taken place in remote times, mix fables with truth, and who seem to have aimed rather to amuse than to instruct their readers. He then immediately mentions the Median war, which forms the principal subject of his rival's work, and of which that work was the well-known record. But if this allusion may not be admitted in evidence, our chain of proof is complete without it.

Citations or allusions similar to these might be brought forward almost without number; but every purpose, both of illustration and of argument—if argument were needed, is accomplished as well by a few as by many. From the entire mass of testimonies, if we were to select, for example, those of Photius, of Dionysius, and of Diodorus, we have proof enough of the genuineness and integrity of the work; for the existence of these testimonies could not be accounted for on a contrary supposition, in any reasonable manner. And when we find the work reflected, as it were, more or less distinctly, from almost the entire surface of ancient literature, no room is left for doubt. The writers of every age, from the time of the author, speak of the work as being well known in their times:—none of them quote it in any such terms as these, "an ancient history, said to have been written by Herodotus:"—or, "a history which most persons believe to be genuine;" for they all refer to it as a book that was in every one's hands. If, therefore, the History had been produced in any age subsequent to that of Herodotus, the author of any such spurious work must have had under his control, for the purpose of interpolation, not only a copy of every considerable work that was extant in his time, but every copy of every such work:—he must in fact have new created the entire mass of books existing in the eastern and western world at the time; and he must have destroyed all but his own interpolated copies; otherwise, some copies of some of these works would have reached us in which these interpolated quotations from Herodotus were wanting. Although such suppositions are extravagant, yet let us attempt to realise one or two of them.

We may imagine then that this History, pretending to be an ancient work, was actually produced in the ninth century, by some learned monk of Constantinople. On this supposition, we must believe that the copyists of that time, in all parts of the Greek empire, having been gained over by the forger to favour the fraud, issued new and ingeniously interpolated copies of the following authors:—namely, Procopius, Stephen, Stobæus, Marcellinus, Julian, Hesychius, Athenæus, Longinus, Laertius, Lucian, Hermogenes, Pausanias, Aulus Gellius, Plutarch, Josephus, Strabo, Dionysius, Diodorus, Aristotle, Ctesias, and many others that are not cited above. Then to this list must be added many works that were extant in the ninth century, but since lost. All the previously existing copies of these authors must have been gathered in, and destroyed; but even this would not be enough; for the Byzantine writers must have had the concurrence of the Latin copyists, throughout the monasteries of western Europe; otherwise, the works of Cicero, and of Quintilian, and of Pliny, would not have contained those references to the History which we actually find in them. Now to effect all this, or a twentieth part of it, was as impracticable in the middle ages, as it would be for us to alter the spots in the moon—for the things to be altered were absolutely out of the reach of those whom we suppose to have made the attempt. But as to these supposed interpolations, it was not formal sentences, or distinct paragraphs—wedged in where they seem to have little fitness, but citations or allusions of an incidental kind, proper to the connection in which they occur, and perfectly congruous with the text.

Let it next be supposed that the genuine History of Herodotus—referred to as we have seen by earlier writers, had perished, or was supposed to have perished, about the seventh century; and that some writer of the ninth century composed a work which should pass in the world for the genuine History. Now, to effect this, he must have had in his memory, as he went along, the entire body of ancient literature, both Greek and Roman; or otherwise he could not have worked up all the references and quotations of earlier authors, so as to make them tally, as we find they do, with his spurious production: and if any of these authors were unknown to him, or forgotten, then we should find discrepant quotations that could not be verified. Moreover, as the genuine work was certainly in existence and widely diffused in the *sixth* century, no writer wishing to make such an attempt could think himself secure against the existence of some copies of the genuine work, which, if brought to light, would at once expose his own to contempt.

Or if a forgery had been attempted at a time nearer to that of the alleged author, then, in proportion as we recede from difficulties of one kind,

we run upon those of another kind. For if, to
avoid the absurdity of supposing that a hugh
mass of books, scattered through many and distant countries, were at once called in, and
re-issued with the requisite interpolations, we
imagine that the work was forged at an earlier
time, when fewer testimonies needed to have been
foisted into existing books; then we come to a
period when learning was at its height—at Alexandria—throughout Greece, and its colonies—
when every fact connected with the history of
books was familiarly known; when many large
libraries existed—when, therefore, no standard
work could disappear, or could be supplanted by
a spurious one; much less could a work which
had never before been heard of, create to itself the
credit of a book long and familiarly known: how
could the learned in the east and the west be persuaded that a work, newly produced, had been in
their libraries for a hundred years? Though the
knowledge of books is more widely diffused in
modern, than it was in ancient times, yet among
those who addict themselves to literature, there is
not now more of erudition, of intelligence, of discrimination, than were displayed in the three or
four centuries of which the Augustan age formed
the centre. To issue a voluminous history, and
to persuade the world that it had been known
during the last two hundred years, is an attempt
not more impracticable in the present day, than
it would have been in the times of Dionysius, of
Cicero, of Quintilian, or of Plutarch.

If we carry our supposition still higher, that is
to say, till we get free from all the difficulties
above-mentioned, then we gain nothing. The

fact principally important as an historical question is granted, namely, that the History was actually extant at, or very near the time, commonly supposed; and then the only point in dispute is the bare name of the author, which, so far as the truth of the history is involved, is a question of inferior consequence. Yet let us pursue this doubt a step further;—If Herodotus the Halicarnassian, were a real person, known in his time as a writer, then some self-denying forger made over to this Herodotus all the glory of being the author of so admirable a work; and this Herodotus accepted the generous fraud, and acted his part to give it credit. But if the name and designation be altogether fictitious—the real author concealing himself; then how happened it that the Greeks of that age should speak of Herodotus as of a real person whom they had known, honoured, and rewarded? In preference to any such impracticable hypothesis, who would not rather accept as true the affirmation which the work bears upon its front?

But now we take up another supposition. After tracing as we have done, the history of the work in question, up through a continued series of quotations, in the Greek and Latin writers, and obtaining by that means a conclusive proof of its antiquity, we may imagine that there is in existence a Persian translation of the History of Herodotus, which, by the peculiarities of its style, as well as by external evidence, is ascertained to have been executed in the time of Artaxerxes. Another translation of the same work is then brought forward in the language of ancient Carthage, which, except in this (supposed) translation has been long extinct. And there is another in the Coptic, or ancient language of Egypt; and another in the Latin, of the time of Plautus and Terence. If these several translations had each descended to modern times, through some independent channel, and if each possessed a separate mass of evidence in proof of its antiquity; and if, when collated among themselves, and with the Greek original, they were found to harmonise, except in those variations which must always belong to a translation; then, and in such a case, we should possess an instance of that sort of redundant demonstration which in fact does belong in full to the Jewish and Christian Scriptures; but to no other writings whatever.

Let it now be granted as *possible* that a writer of a later age, who was a perfect master of the Greek language, who possessed an endless fund of various learning, and who was gifted in a high degree with the imitative faculty, might produce nine books like those of Herodotus, which, supposing there were no external evidence to contradict the fraud, might pass as genuine. To affirm that a forgery such as this is *possible*, is to allow the utmost that our knowledge of the powers of the human mind will permit to be granted; and much more than the history of literary forgeries will warrant us to suppose: for all the attempts of that sort that have been detected, either abound with manifest incongruities; or if executed by men of learning and ability, they have been formed upon a small scale, and have excluded, as far as possible, all exact references to particular facts.

But the work before us is of great extent; its

allusions to particular facts are innumerable, precise, and incautious; its style and dialect are proper to the age which it pretends :—in a word, it is in every respect what a genuine production of that age ought to be. If then it were to be judged of, on the ground of internal evidence alone, no scholar could for a moment hesitate to decide in favour of its genuineness. The reader will recollect that the supposition of a forgery in a later age is excluded by the evidence already adduced in this chapter.

CHAPTER XVIII.

METHOD OF ARGUING FROM THE GENUINENESS, TO THE AUTHENTICITY OF THE HISTORY OF HERODOTUS.

THAT the Greek text of Herodotus, such as it now appears—small verbal variations only excepted, was extant and well known in Greece, at least as early as the commencement of the Peloponnesian War (B.C. 431), is the conclusion that is warranted by the evidence already adduced. It now remains to inquire how far this proof of the antiquity and genuineness of the work carries with it a proof of the general truth of the History.

In a civilised community, where a free expression of opinion is allowed, and where opposing interests actually exist, a writer, who professes to compile an authentic account of transactions that are still fresh in the recollection of the people, can move only within certain limits, even if he might wish to misrepresent facts.—Circumstances, known only to a few, may be falsified—motives may be maligned—actions may be exaggerated—wrongs and sufferings may be coloured by rhetorical declamation—fair characters may be defamed, and foul ones eulogised:—these are nearly the boundaries of falsification. But if personages altogether fictitious are made the heroes of the story—if invasions, battles, sieges, conspiracies, are described which never happened—if, in a word, the entire narrative is a fiction, then it ranks in a different class of productions, nor could it ever gain credit as an authentic account of real, and recent events. The same evidence, therefore, which establishes the existence of an historical work at a time near to that of the events it records, establishes also the *general authenticity* of the narrative;—for the work is not only mentioned by contemporary writers, but it is mentioned *as a history*. This character granted to the book by the author's contemporaries contains, by condensation, the suffrages of the whole community. In substance, we hear the people of Greece assenting to the historian in relation to those principal portions of his narrative, at least, of which they were qualified to form an opinion, and relative to which no writer would attempt to deceive them.

Equity demands that we treat an historian conformably with his own professions. When he narrates events as well known to his contemporaries as to himself, he is not to be considered as sustaining any other responsibility than that of telling his story well:—in such instances we may ask for proof of his impartiality, or of the soundness of his judgment, but not of his veracity, which is not taxed. But when he relates incidents of a private or remote kind;—when he makes a demand upon the confidence of his contemporaries by affirming things in relation to which *they* could not generally detect his misstatements if he erred;—then, and in such cases, we may fairly search for evidence bearing upon the historian's character, and circumstances, and his means of information. This is an important distinction, never to be lost sight of in reading history;—and the inference it contains is this—that a history of *public* transactions, published while many of the actors were still living, and while the events were familiarly remembered by a large number of persons, and which was commonly received as authentic, must be accepted, as to its principal facts, as true, even though there should be reason to suspect the impartiality, the veracity, or the judgment of the writer; but if in these respects, he is entitled to a common degree of confidence, then nothing more than a few errors of inadvertency can, with any fairness, be deducted from the narrative.

Every historical work, therefore, needs to be analysed, and to have its several portions separately estimated.—Whatever is remote or particular will claim our credence according to the opinion we may form of the historian's veracity, accuracy, judgment, and his means of information; but the truth of narratives relating to events that were matters of notoriety in the writer's time, rests altogether upon a different ground; being necessarily involved in the fact that the work was published and accepted as authentic at such or such a date. The strength of this inference will best appear by examining a particular instance.

In adherence to the distinction above mentioned, we must detach from the History of Herodotus the following portions (not as if they were proved to be false, or even improbable; but simply because the truth of them cannot be *directly inferred from the fact of the genuineness of the work*). First—Geographical and antiquarian descriptions of countries remote from Greece: Secondly—The early history of such countries, and indeed the early history of Greece itself: Thirdly—Events or conferences said to have taken place at the Persian court during the war with Greece; and lastly, many single incidents, reported to have happened among the Greeks, but which rest upon suspicious or insufficient evidence. After making deductions of this sort, there will remain—all those principal events of the Persian invasion which were as well known to thousands of the author's countrymen and contemporaries as to himself; and in describing which his responsibility is that of an *author* only, who is required to digest his materials in the best manner he cannot that of a *witness*, called to give evidence upon a matter of doubt.

The leading events which we may accept as vouched for by the antiquity and genuineness of the work are these—The invasion of Greece by a large Asiatic army, about five-and-forty years before the publication of the History:—the defeat of that army by the Athenians and Platæans on the plains of Marathon:—a second invasion of Greece ten years afterwards, by an immense host, gathered from many nations:—the desertion of their city by the Athenians:—an ineffectual contest with the invaders at the pass of Thermopylæ: —the occupation of Athens by the Persians:— the defeat of the invading fleet at Salamis:—the retreat of the Persians, and their second advance in the following year, when the destruction of Athens was completed; and—the final overthrow of the Asiatic army at Platæa and Mycale. That these events actually took place—assuming the

History to be genuine—will appear if the circumstances of the case are examined. At the time when, as it has been proved, the History of Herodotus was generally known and received as authentic, the several states of Greece were marshalled under the rival interests of Athens and Sparta; and an intestine war, carried on with the utmost animosity, raged by turns in all parts of this narrow territory. Such a period, therefore, was not the time when flagrant misrepresentations of recent facts, tending to flatter the vanity of one of these rival states, at the expense of the honour of others, could be endured, or could gain any credit. The Athenians gloried, beyond all bounds of modesty, in having, with the assistance of the Platæans only, repelled the Median invasion on the plains of Marathon. But would this boast have been allowed—would the account of the battle given by Herodotus have been suffered to pass without contradiction by the other states, if no such invasion had actually taken place, or if it had been much less formidable than is represented by the historian; or if the other states had in fact been present on the field? Our author affirms that the Lacedæmonians, though fully informed of the danger which threatened the independence of Greece, persisted in a scrupulous adherence to their custom of not setting out upon a military expedition till after the full moon. In the meantime the battle took place, and a body of two thousand Lacedæmonians, afterwards despatched from Sparta, reached the field of battle only time enough to gratify their curiosity by a sight of the slaughtered Medes. This absence of their allies was ever afterwards made matter of arrogant exultation by the Athenians; and the historian, in giving his support to their boast, dared the contradiction of one half of the people of Greece.

The second invasion of Greece, conducted by the Persian monarch in person, took place ten years after the defeat of the first at Marathon; or about five-and-thirty years before the publication of the History: many individuals, therefore, were then living who took part in the several battles and engagements; and every remarkable event of the war was then as well known and remembered in Greece as are the circumstances of the French Revolution by the people of Europe at the present time (1828).

Our immediate purpose does not demand that we should examine the credibility of the description given by Herodotus of the Asiatic army; for even if it were proved that the numbers stated by him are exaggerated, the principal facts would not be brought into doubt; nor would even the credit due to the historian be much impeached; for in all these particulars he is careful, again and again, to remind the reader that he brings forward the best accounts he could collect—not vouching for their absolute accuracy. That he did avail himself of authentic documents in compiling this description is rendered evident by the graphic truth and propriety of all the particulars. Indeed the picture of the Persian army, and of its discipline and movements, is strikingly accordant with the known modes of Asiatic warfare. The army of Xerxes consisted of a small body of brave and well-disciplined troops—Medes, Persians, and Saces,

which, if it had been ably commanded, and
unencumbered, might very probably have succeeded in their enterprise; but being impeded
and embarrassed by the presence of a vast and
disorderly mob of half-savage or dissolute attendants, they were, at every step, surrounded by a
wide-spreading desolation—more fatal than the
enemy, which rendered the advance of the army
in the highest degree difficult, and its retreat
desperate. To all this, parallel instances may
be adduced from almost every page of Asiatic
history.

When speaking of the twenty Satrapies of
Darius, Major Rennell, in his Essay on the Geography of Herodotus, avails himself of the information contained in our author's description
of the army of Xerxes, to which he attributes a
high degree of authority. Now it is evident that
unless Herodotus had possessed authentic and
accurate documents, it would have been impossible for him to have given the consistency of
truth to two distinct accounts of nations and of
people, so various and so remote from Greece.
"Although," says this writer, "there are some
errors in the description, as there must necessarily
be where the subject is so very extensive, yet
it is on the whole so remarkably consistent, that
one is surprised how the Greeks found means to
acquire so much knowledge respecting so distant
a part. It is possible that we have been in the
habit of doing them an injustice, by allowing
them a less degree of knowledge of the geography
of Asia, down to the expedition of Alexander,
than they really possessed; that is, we have, in
some instances, ascribed to Alexander, certain

geographical discoveries which perhaps were made
long anterior to his expedition . . . We shall
close the account of the Satrapies, and our
remarks on the armament of Xerxes, with some
additional ones on the general truth of the statement of the latter, and on the final object of the
expedition. Brief as the descriptions in the text
are, they contain a great variety of information,
and furnish a number of proofs of the general
truth of our author's history; for the descriptions
of the dress and weapons of several of the remote
nations, engaged in the expedition of Xerxes,
agree with what appears amongst them at this
day; which is a strong confirmation of it; notwithstanding that some attempts have been made
to ridicule it by different writers. Herodotus had
conversed with those who had seen the dress and
weapons of these tribes during the invasion; and
therefore we cannot doubt that the Indians
clothed in cotton, and with bows made of reeds
(*i.e.*, bamboos), were amongst them: of course,
that the great king had summoned his vassals and
allies, generally, to this European war: a war
intended, not merely against Greece, but against
Europe in general, as appears by the speeches of
Xerxes, and other circumstances. . . . The evident cause of the assemblage of so many nations
was that the Europeans (as at the present day)
were deemed so far superior to Asiatics as to
require a vastly greater number of the latter to
oppose them. This is no less apparent in the
history of the wars of Alexander, and of the wars
made by Europeans in the East in modern times.
However, we do not by any means believe in
the numbers described by the Greek historians;

because we cannot comprehend, from what is seen
and known, how such a multitude could be provided with food, and their beasts with forage.
But that the army of Xerxes was great beyond
all example, may be readily believed, because it
was collected from a vastly extended empire,
every part of which, as well as its allies, furnished
a proportion; and if the aggregate had amounted
to a moderate number only, it would have been
nugatory to levy that number throughout the
whole empire; and to collect troops from India
and Ethiopia to attack Greece, when the whole
number required might be collected in Lower
Asia."

It seems impracticable, from the existing evidence, to ascertain how great a deduction ought
to be made from the calculations of Herodotus,
as to the numbers of the invading army; but it
is easy to believe that his authorities, which
unquestionably were authentic in what relates to
the description of the forces, might lead him
astray, without any fault on his part. Or probably,
as the numbers exceeded the facilities of common
computation, some conjectural mode of calculation
was adopted by the contemporary Greeks, which
might easily exceed the truth.—For example, the
length of time occupied by the barbarian train in
passing certain defiles:—or the very fallacious
mode of reckoning employed by the Persians was
perhaps followed:—this, as Herodotus describes
it, consisted in counting ten thousand men, who
were packed in a circle as closely as possible,
and a fence formed round them: they were then
removed, and the entire army, in turns, was made
to pass within the enclosure: the whole was thus

counted into ten thousands. But how probable is it, that, by the inattention of the persons who conducted this process, the successive packages were less and less dense.—Seven thousand men might easily seem to fill the space in which ten had been at first crammed. Nor is it at all safe to argue *à priori* on the supposition that so many could not have been supported on the march. The power which drew a large levy of men from twenty-nine nations, might also drain those nations of their grain. A vast fleet of flat-bottomed barges attended the army along the coast; and as soon as this fleet was separated from it, all the extremities of famine were suffered by the retreating host. This armament is not fairly compared with those which, in later times, have traversed the continent of Asia; for in these instances the aid of an attendant fleet was not available. Without this aid the distant movement of five hundred thousand men is scarcely practicable; with it, three or four times that number might with little difficulty be led a distance of three or six months' march. This important difference has not been duly regarded by those who have discussed the questson. If then such a deduction from the army of Xerxes is made as may readily be accounted for from the inaccurate mode of computation employed by the Persians or the Greeks; and if the attendance of so large a fleet of store ships is considered, we may well hold Herodotus excused from the charge, either of deliberate falsification, or of intended exaggeration.

If it were alleged that Herodotus discovers an inclination on every occasion to place the conduct

of the Athenians in the most advantageous light,
it may be replied that, if such a disposition is
charged upon him, then his substantial impartiality, and the authenticity of the narrative are
convincingly proved, by his allowing to the
Spartans the undivided and enviable glory of
having first encountered the invaders at the pass
of Thermopylæ. In relating this memorable
action he affirms that all the allies under the
command of Leonidas, excepting only a small
body of Thebans and of Thespians, retired from
the pass as soon as it was known that they were
circumvented by the Barbarians; and he plainly
attributes this desertion to the prevalence of
unsoldier-like fears. This statement therefore—
like many others in the History—challenged
contradiction from the parties implicated in the
dishonour.

In recounting the naval engagements which
took place in the Eubœan straits, the historian
contents himself with affirming that, after a
doubtful contest, each fleet retired to its station;
and he attributes the final success of the Greeks,
not so much to their valour and skill, as to a
divine interposition, which, by a violent storm, so
far diminished the Persian fleet that the two
armaments were reduced to an equality.

The ill-success of the Greeks in attempting to
oppose the advance of the Barbarians at Thermopylæ, and the losses they had sustained in several
naval engagements, having reduced them almost
to despair, the Athenians, thinking it impracticable to defend Attica, abandoned their city, and
took refuge on board their ships, and in the
neighbouring islands. The invader therefore was

allowed, without opposition, to execute his threat —that he would retaliate upon the Athenians the burning of Sardis. Here then we arrive at a definite fact, which may be considered as forming the central point of the History. If this fact be established, most of the subordinate incidents must be admitted to have taken place, as they were nothing more than either the proper causes, or the effects, of this main event.

Within so short a period as five and thirty, or forty years, it could not be a matter of doubt or controversy among the Athenians, or indeed with any of the people of Greece, whether Athens had been occupied by a foreign army—its halls and temples overthrown or burned—its sacred groves cut down, and its surrounding gardens and fields devastated. But while several thousand citizens were still living, who had attained an adult age at the time of the alleged invasion, and while the structures of the new city were in their first freshness, or were scarcely completed; and while, if it had actually taken place, the marks of this destruction must have been everywhere apparent, a history is published, and is universally applauded, in which this invasion of Attica, and this destruction of Athens are particularly described. Can then this fact be reconciled with the supposition that no such events had really taken place—that these arrogant citizens had never been driven from their homes? Can we believe that, for the sake of assuming to themselves the glory of having repelled such an invasion, the entire people of Athens would have given their assent to a fictitious narrative, which every one of them must have known had no foundation in truth? or, if such an infatuation had prevailed at Athens, would their neighbours—the Corinthians, and the Bœotians, have left such a falsehood uncontradicted?

It is evident that, unless a powerful invasion of Greece had taken place, Athens—the principal city of Greece, could not have been occupied and destroyed; and unless that invasion had been speedily repulsed, Athens could not have regained that wealth, and power, and liberty which, on other evidence, it is known to have possessed in the first years of the Peloponnesian War. Here then, if the truth of the History of Herodotus were to be argued, the question must come to its issue. If it were denied that such an invasion of Greece happened at the time affirmed by our author, then the fact of the general diffusion, and the high credit, of the History of Herodotus, throughout Greece, must be shown to consist with that denial. On the other hand, an apologist for Herodotus, having established the antiquity and genuineness of the work, must not be required, either to defend the veracity of the historian, or to adduce corroborative evidence in proof of the fact, until the difficulty which rests upon the contrary hypothesis has been disposed of.

The account given by Herodotus of the subsequent events of the Persian War—that is to say—the defeat of the Asiatic fleet at Salamis—the retreat of Xerxes—the second occupation of Athens in the following spring by the Persians under the command of Mardonius; and the final discomfiture and destruction of the Barbarian army at Platæa and at Mycale, follow of course, as substantially true, if the preceding facts are established. It must however be observed that a peculiar character of authenticity belongs to this latter portion of the History: for though the issue of the war was indeed highly gratifying to the vanity of the Greeks, one would almost think that the historian wished, as far as possible, to check their exultation, or to balance the vaunts of each of the states by some circumstances of dishonour. For instance—no veil is drawn over those almost fatal contentions for precedency by which the counsels of the confederates were distracted; nor are the treasons and the interested conduct of the chiefs concealed or excused. The pusillanimity of some, and the fears of all are confessed: indeed so much of infamy or of discredit is thrown by Herodotus upon individuals, and upon the whole community, that his boldness in publishing such statements, and the candour of the Greeks in admitting them, are alike worthy of admiration. Nor can we believe otherwise than that a full conviction of the substantial truth of these statements at once inspired the writer with this courage, and compelled his hearers to exercise this forbearance. It cannot seem surprising that, in later times, some writers jealous for the honour of Greece at large, or of some particular state, should attempt to remove these blots, by impugning the credit of the historian. Yet even in making this attempt, they venture no further than to call in question his account of a few particular transactions, or to dispute those portions of the work which relate to remote times, and distant nations.

We have seen that the history of the Persian invasion, as given by Herodotus, is in its main circumstances, established by the mere fact that the work was known, and had been accepted as authentic, within forty years of the events it records. This then is not an instance in which the veracity of the historian needs to be vindicated, or in which our faith in its veracity must be dependent upon other evidence. Yet it is natural to look around for such other evidence as may be found to bear upon the history. We have a good right to suppose that events of such magnitude as those which Herodotus relates, would be mentioned, more or less explicitly, by other writers of the same age—whether philosophers, poets, orators, or historians. And this in fact is the case in the instance before us; for almost every writer—contemporary with Herodotus—whose works are extant, makes allusions of a direct or indirect kind to the Persian invasion. Some of the authors already adduced in proof of the antiquity and genuineness of the history, must now be recalled to give evidence as to the matter of fact.

Pindar, the prince of lyric poets, is reported to have died at the age of eighty, and was born about B.C. 521, and was in mid-life at the time of the Persian invasion. The odes now extant were recited in Greece before the history of Herodotus was composed. The subject of these compositions are the praises of the victors at the Olympic, the Isthmian, the Pythian, and the Nemean games; and in extolling his heroes, the poet finds occasion to refer to the glories of the cities to which they belonged: they contain therefore many allusions to the events of Grecian history; and as these odes were recited at all the great festivals, the allusions were such as the mass of the people could not fail to understand. This sort of incidental and brief notice of public events, intended to kindle the enthusiasm of the audience, must of course rest upon the knowledge or the convictions of those to whom they were addressed. In the first of the Pythian odes, a rapid sketch is given of the principal events of the Persian war.—Such defeat as they suffered by the Syracusan prince, who, manning the swift ships, with the youth, delivered Greece from heavy servitude.—I would choose the praise won by the Athenians at Salamis:—or I would tell at Sparta the fight near Mount Cithæron, in which the Medes with their curved bows (ἀγκυλότοξοι) were oppressed.—The Medean bow as seen in the bas-reliefs of Persepolis, is very properly described by this epithet—it is very long, and much curved, even in its extended state.

These allusions may be explained by referring to those places in Herodotus, where it is related, that, while Xerxes was advancing towards Greece, the Athenians and Lacedæmonians sent an embassy to Gelon, tyrant of Syracuse, to ask his aid against the Barbarian: this he refused to grant, except upon conditions with which the Greeks could not comply. Yet he fitted out a fleet, and engaged and defeated the Carthagenians, commanded by Amilcar, who had been incited by the Persians to join in the war upon the Greeks: by this victory Greece was delivered from the danger of an attack which must have proved fatal to its liberties; for if the Carthagenian fleet had arrived in the Archipelago, and had joined the Persians, the Greeks could hardly have withstood so vast a combination. The next allusion is to the engagement at Salamis, in which the Athenians, as Herodotus affirms, took the principal part: and the last, is to the final defeat of the Barbarians near Platæa, at the foot of Mount Cithæron. In this battle the Spartans were the most distinguished. In the fifth Isthmian ode, another allusion to Salamis occurs—where men innumerable met their death, as by a hail-storm of destruction.

Æschylus, the father of tragedy among the Greeks, had reached manhood at the time of the first invasion of Greece, and took part in the battle of Marathon: he was present also in the engagement at Salamis, and again at the battle of Platæa. Seven only of his seventy tragedies have descended to modern times :—one of these is entitled " The Persians." The scene is laid at Susa, in Persia, and the time supposed is during the absence of Xerxes in Greece. The play is opened by a chorus of elders, who discourse anxiously concerning the fate of the expedition ; —All Asia is exhausted of men: wives count the days, and mourn the long absence of their warrior-consorts—Atossa the queen enters dejected, and recounts a portentous dream :—a messenger then arrives from Greece: he reports the defeat of the Persian fleet, and the retreat of Xerxes :— in relating the particulars, he glances at the circumstances which preceded the engagement at Salamis, as mentioned by Herodotus—That a messenger (sent by Themistocles) informed Xerxes that the Greeks were about to disperse; to prevent which he imprudently surrounded them : —an engagement ensued, of which Xerxes was a spectator from a neighbouring hill:—the Persians are defeated;—those who occupied the island (of Psyttalea) were all slain. The army, in its retreat, suffers the extremity of cold, hunger, and thirst. On hearing this, the queen invokes the shade of Darius, which appears.—Atossa repeats the story of his son's defeat :—The shade predicts the fatal battle of Platæa, and the destruction of the army. In the closing scene, Xerxes himself arrives, bewailing his misfortunes, and bringing back nothing but an empty quiver. The only material point in which Æschylus differs from Herodotus, is in reckoning the Greek fleet at three hundred, instead of seven hundred sail :— this is evidently a poetic deviation from fact, intended to enhance the glory of the victory.

Of all the Greek historians, none bears so high a character for authenticity and for exactness in matters of fact as Thucydides : his impartiality, his laborious collection, and his judicious selection of materials, and his rejection of whatever seemed to rest on suspicious evidence, are apparent on almost every page of the history of the Peloponnesian war. This history was published about sixty years after the expedition of Xerxes. Thucydides had conversed with many of those who had taken part in the battles described by Herodotus. Many allusions to the events of the Persian invasion occur in the course of the work, and they are all of that kind which is natural, when an historian refers to facts which he supposes to be fresh in the recollection of his readers. The introductory sections of the history contain an outline of Grecian affairs, from the earliest times to the commencement of the war between

Athens and Sparta. In this preliminary sketch, the leading circumstances of the invasion, as related by Herodotus, are mentioned; such as—the war and conquests of Cyrus and Cambyses—the subjugation of the Greeks of Asia Minor—the naval power of Polycrates, tyrant of Samos—the Median war, the reigns of Darius and of Xerxes, and the conduct of Themistocles.—The expulsion of the Pisistratidæ from Greece, the battle between the Medes and the Greeks at Marathon, and, ten years afterwards, the second invasion of Greece by the Barbarians—the desertion of their city by the Athenians, and their taking refuge on board their ships.—Not many years after the expulsion of the tyrants from Greece, happened the battle between the Medes and the Athenians at Marathon; and ten years after that battle, the Barbarians arrived with a great armament, intended to reduce the Greeks to bondage. In this imminent danger, the Lacedæmonians, who were more powerful than the other states, took the command in the war. The Athenians, as the Medes advanced, having resolved to abandon their city, collected all their goods, and went on board their ships, and from that time became a maritime people. After, by their united efforts, the Greeks had repulsed the Barbarians, the several states, as well those which fell away from the king, as those which had fought with the Greeks, took part, some with the Athenians, and some with the Lacedæmonians.—Again, Thucydides refers to—the late Median war—which, he says, was quickly terminated in two battles and two naval engagements. The battle of Marathon, and the burial of the slain upon the field, are afterwards mentioned; and in a funeral oration pronounced by Pericles (whether really so or not is of no consequence to the argument) the exploits of the Athenians in repelling the Barbarians are spoken of as being too well known to need to be particularised; and again, the conflict at Thermopylæ is mentioned;—the battle of Platæa, and the engagement at Artemisium. The defeat of the Medes, the devastation of Athens, and its restoration are narrated. The distance of time, namely, fifty years, between the defeat of Xerxes, and the commencement of the Peloponnesian war, is mentioned.—All these actions which took place either among the Greeks, or between them and the Barbarians, were included within a period of nearly fifty years, reckoning from the retreat of Xerxes, to the commencement of the present war.

These, and some other allusions to the events of the Persian invasion, coinciding as they do with the more ample narrative given by Herodotus, and coming from an historian who made it his boast that he admitted nothing into his work which was not supported by satisfactory evidence, and who, moreover, was disposed rather to detract from the credit of his rival, than to confirm it, must be held to furnish the most conclusive kind of independent testimony. Indeed, the express affirmation of Thucydides that Athens was destroyed by the Persians, affords alone a sufficient proof of the fact; for no such affirmation as this could either have been made, or tolerated, within sixty years after the event, unless it were universally known to be true.

Lysias the orator, at the early age of fifteen

years, it is said, accompanied Herodotus and other Athenians to Thurium: after a long residence in Italy, he returned to Athens, where he distinguished himself by his eloquence. In a funeral oration, pronounced in honour of the Athenians who fell in the Corinthian war, he speaks of the Persian war.—The king of Asia, unsatisfied with his present greatness, and actuated by a boundless ambition, prepared an army of 500,000 men, hoping by this mighty force to reduce Europe under his subjection. . . . With such rapidity was the victory (at Marathon) accomplished, that the other states of Greece learned by the same messenger the invasion of the Persians, and their defeat; and without the terror of danger, felt the pleasure of deliverance. It is not surprising, then, that such actions, though ancient (about eighty years) should still retain the full verdure of glory, and remain to succeeding ages the examples and the envy of mankind. . . . Many causes conspired to engage Xerxes, king of Asia, to undertake a second expedition against Europe. . . . After ten years preparation, he landed in Europe, with a fleet of 1,200 sail, and such a number of land forces, that it would be tedious to recount even the names of those various nations by whom he was attended. . . . He made a journey over land, by joining the Hellespont, and a voyage by sea, by dividing Mount Athos. The orator then briefly mentions the engagements at Artemisium and Thermopylæ, the abandonment of Athens, and the removal of the citizens to Salamis:—their city was deserted, their temples burnt or demolished, their country laid waste.

Isocrates flourished a few years later than

Lysias, yet he was contemporary with Herodotus. One of his orations, pronounced in praise of the Athenians, contains passages to the same effect. They first (the Athenians) signalised their courage against the troops of Darius (at Marathon). . . . The Persians, a short time after renewed their attempts, and Xerxes himself, forsaking his palace and his pleasures, ventured to become a general. At the head of all Asia he formed the most towering designs. For who, though inclined to exaggeration, can come up to the reality? The conquest of Greece appeared to him an object below his ambition.—Designing to effect something beyond human power, he projected that enterprise, so celebrated, of making his army sail through the land, and march over the sea; and he carried this idea into execution by piercing Mount Athos, and by throwing a bridge over the Hellespont. Against a monarch so proud and enterprising, who had executed such vast designs, and who commanded so many armies, the Lacedæmonians, dividing the danger with Athens, drew themselves up at Thermopylæ. With a thousand of their own troops, and a small body of their allies, they determined in that narrow pass to resist the progress of all his land forces. While our ancestors (the Athenians of the *last* generation) sailed with sixty galleys to Artemisium, and expected the whole fleet of the Barbarians. . . . The Lacedæmonians perished to a man; but the Athenians conquered the fleet they had undertaken to oppose. Their allies were dispirited. The Peloponnesians, occupied for their own safety, had begun to fortify the Isthmus. . . . The enemy approached Attica with a fleet of twelve hundred sail, and with land forces innumerable. . . . The Athenians assembled all the inhabitants of their city, and transported them into the neighbouring island.—And where shall we find more generous lovers of Greece than those who in its defence abandoned their abodes, suffered their city to be ravaged, their altars to be violated, their temples to be burned to the ground, and all the terrors of war to rage in their native country? . . . Athens, even in her misfortunes, furnished more ships for the sea-fight off Salamis, which was to decide the fate of Greece, than all the other states together; and there is no one, I believe, so unjust as to deny, that by our victory in that engagement the war was terminated, and the danger removed.

Ctesias, as we have seen, affords a testimony conclusive in favour of the antiquity of the history attributed to Herodotus. We have now to adduce his evidence on the subject of the Persian invasion —reminding the reader that his history of Persia was composed with the avowed design of invalidating the account given by Herodotus of Persian affairs: he thus speaks of the expedition of Xerxes:—Xerxes, having collected a Persian army, consisting, besides the chariots of war, of eight hundred thousand men, and a thousand galleys, led them into Greece by a bridge which he had caused to be constructed at Abydos. It was then that he was accosted by Demaratus the Lacedæmonian, who passed with him into Europe, and who endeavoured to dissuade the king from attacking the Lacedæmonians. Xerxes arriving at the pass of Thermopylæ, placed ten thousand men under the command of Artapanus, who there

engaged Leonidas—chief of the Lacedæmonians.
In this conflict a great slaughter of the Persians
took place, while not more than three or four of
the Lacedæmonians were slain. After this Xerxes
sent twenty thousand men to the field; these also
were overcome, and though driven to fight by
blows, were still vanquished. The next day he
sent forward fifty thousand men; but as these
also failed in their attack, he no longer attempted
to fight. Thorax the Thessalian, and Calliades
and Timaphernes, princes of the Trachinians,
were then present (in the Persian camp) with
their troops. These, with Demaratus, and Hegias
of Ephesus, Xerxes called into his presence, and
from them he learned that the Lacedæmonians
could by no means be vanquished unless they were
surrounded and attacked on all sides. Forty
thousand Persians were therefore despatched under
the command of these two Trachinian leaders,
who traversing a difficult path, came behind the
Lacedæmonians. Thus surrounded, they fought
valiantly, and perished to a man. Again Xerxes
sent an army of one hundred and twenty thousand
men, commanded by Mardonius, against the
Platæans: it was the Thebans who incited the
king against the Platæans. Mardonius was met
by Pausanias the Lacedæmonian, at the head of
not more than three hundred Spartans—one thousand of the people of the country—and about six
thousand from the other cities. The Persian army
being vanquished, Mardonius fled from the field
wounded. This same Mardonius was sent by
Xerxes to pillage the temple of Apollo; but to
the great grief of the king, perished in the
attempt by a hail-storm.

Xerxes next advanced with his army to Athens; but the Athenians having fitted out one hundred and ten galleys, fled to the island of Salamis; he therefore entered the deserted city, and burned it, except only the citadel, which was defended by a few who remained; but they retiring by night, he burned that also. The king then advancing to the narrowest part of Attica, called Heracleum, began to construct a mole towards Salamis, with the intention of marching his army on to the island. But by the advice of Themistocles the Athenian, and of Aristides, a body of Cretan archers was brought up to obstruct the work. A naval engagement then took place between the Persians and the Greeks, the former having more than a thousand ships, commanded by Onophas—the latter seven hundred. Yet the Greeks conquered, and the Persians lost five hundred ships. Xerxes, himself, by the counsel and contrivance of Themistocles and Aristides, fled:—not fewer than one hundred and twenty thousand men having perished on the side of the Persians in the several actions. Passages to this effect occur in the Myriobiblon of Photius.

In those particulars in which this account of the Persian invasion differs from that of our author, no one who carefully compares the two, can hesitate to give his confidence to Herodotus rather than to Ctesias, not only because he lived some years nearer to the events; but because his narrative displays more judgment, more consistency, and more probability, and is also better supported by other evidence. It is enough for our present purpose that this writer affirms the same great events to have taken place—that the Persian king led an immense army into Greece, where he met a total defeat.

Of the authors whom we have cited, the first two—Pindar and Æschylus, had reached maturity at the time of the Persian invasion, and were personally concerned in its events, and composed the works to which we have referred while Herodotus was yet a youth. Though poets, they represent the victories of the Greeks as recent facts, well known to their hearers, and the slightest allusion to which was enough to kindle the national enthusiasm. The other writers—Thucydides, Lysias, Isocrates, and Ctesias, were also contemporary with Herodotus; and two of them were his professed rivals. From their evidence it is apparent that the events of the Persian invasion were matters of common knowledge and conversation, and were the themes of writers in every class among the Greeks, in the very age in which they are said to have taken place.

It follows therefore that the historian of these transactions is not to be regarded as if he were the author of a narrative for the truth of which he is individually responsible, and in which we cannot confide until we have proof of his veracity. He is rather the collector of facts that were universally acknowledged by his contemporaries:—and the truth of the history rests upon the fact that it was published, and was accepted, while the individuals to whom the events were known were still living.

If we look to the Greek writers of the next and of the following age, we find the same general facts affirmed or alluded to—orators, poets, and historians, hold the same language, and assume it as certain that their ancestors gloriously repulsed an innumerable Asiatic army. But historical proof of a *traditionary* kind differs essentially from that which it is just now our intention to display; we therefore do not bring it forward in the present instance.

In a preceding chapter (XV.) we have referred to the mass of evidence, confirmatory to the *written* testimony of ancient Historians, which might be brought forward from the treasures of the British Museum. In many instances the *general* truthfulness of Herodotus, and his exactness also, are vouched for in the most substantial and convincing manner, by objects of various kinds, to which the reader may have access any day in that vast collection. Yet in relation to such instances there may be room for a cautionary remark; and it is of this kind.—

There is a tendency in the mind to relieve itself from the labour of *thinking*, by accepting, without inquiry, any sort of proof that offers itself to the senses—to the eye and to the touch. In this manner we may fall into the habit of forgetting, or of neglecting, the direct and proper evidence of *written* and authentic testimony, while we are occupied with that which *seems*, although it may not be so in reality, to be more convincing, or to be less precarious; as for example: after giving attention to the evidence that has been adduced in the preceding chapters, we may feel assured of the fact—that the Greeks and Persians did fight on the plains of Marathon. There is then shown to us a seal, which, on good evidence, we know to have been picked up upon the very spot that still bears that name in Greece: the device upon this gem is manifestly Persian :—the winged lions are almost a copy of the bas-reliefs still existing on several ruins in Persia: we conclude therefore that this relic of antiquity belonged to a chief of the Persian army, and we accept it as a palpable proof of the truth of the historian's narrative: and though that narrative thus gains, in our view, a confirmation, it does so by losing something of its proper weight; and we are afterwards inclined to think, that if the *tangible* proof were withdrawn, the *written* proof would stand less firmly than it did before.

Then again, in relying upon the evidence of gems, inscriptions, or sculptors, not merely as illustrations of history, but as proofs of its truth, we may sometimes substitute the worse kind of evidence for the better.—The relics of ancient art, in very many instances, derive their meaning, and draw their historic value from the concurrent testimony of *written* history: the entire *proof* is a product of the *two* taken together. Then it must not be forgotten that the *traditionary* history of the relic is often of doubtful authenticity—resting perhaps upon the word of those who had a commodity of indefinite value to sell;—or the workmanship may be of a later age than the antiquary is willing to admit;—or the inscription may have been placed by authority out of the reach of that opinion to which an historian is always amenable. An arrogant republic, or a vain-glorious tyrant, might, without fear, stamp bold lies upon coins, or engrave impudent untruths upon the entablatures of temples; and the brazen or the marble record may receive from the modern antiquary a degree of respect which it never won from contemporaries. Herodotus mentions some instances of this kind. An intelligent inquirer into the truth of remote facts will usually give more confidence to the explicit assertions of one with whose character and qualifications he is in some measure acquainted, than he does to positive averments that come from a party altogether unknown. Now an historian is a person concerning whose veracity, discretion, and intentions we have the means of forming our own opinion; but in admitting the evidence of inscriptions and coins, we receive a testimony—knowing perhaps nothing of the witness.

CHAPTER XIX.

EXAMPLES OF IMPERFECT HISTORICAL EVIDENCE:—HERODOTUS.

The object of the preceding pages has been to display, in its several parts, that chain of evidence by means of which a high degree of certainty in matters of antiquity is attainable. And it appears that there are cases in which the proof of remote facts rests, as it were, in our own hands, so that, irrespectively of the veracity, or accuracy, or impartiality of the witnesses, our assent is demanded on the ground of the constancy of the laws of the social system. In such cases, a consideration of distance of time does not enter into the argument; for the proof remains from age to age unimpaired; or rather, we are carried by this proof up to the times of the events in question, and are now as competent to judge of the validity of the evidence as we could have been if we had lived in that age.

The real difference between this absolute proof and every other sort of historical evidence, will be best exhibited by adducing some instances of a different kind; and in taking our examples from the same author—Herodotus, we place both kinds of evidence upon the same level, so far as the personal qualites and the merits of the historian are concerned in the argument.

The distinctive character of all such historical evidence as ought to be called *imperfect*, is this—that it comes to us through some *medium*, upon the trustworthiness of which we must more or less implicitly rely. Ordinarily, this medium is the veracity, or the accuracy—the learning, or the impartiality, of the historian. In such instances the *immediate proof* stands beyond our reach; and instead of being able to handle and inspect it for ourselves, we can only inspect it at a distance, and, by the best means in our power, estimate its probable value. This secondary evidence may indeed sometimes rise almost to absolute certainty; in other cases it may possess scarcely an atom of real weight. The first book of Herodotus will furnish examples of both sorts, and some in every degree between the two extremes.

In the introductory sections of his history, Herodotus refers to those mutual aggressions which were ordinarily assigned by the authors of his times as the origin of the animosity which had so long raged between the Greeks and the people of Asia: thus he mentions the abduction of Io from Argos by the Phœnicians—of Europa from Tyre—of Medea from Colchis, and of Helen from Sparta; which last act of violence, produced, he says, the Trojan war, and which the Persians, as he affirms, were wont to allege as a perpetual justification of every enterprise they might attempt against the Greeks.

These events took place—if at all—from thirteen to eighteen hundred years before the time of Herodotus: the last of them, the Trojan war, may well be regarded as substantially true on the authority of the poems of Homer, which bear the character of history too strongly to be treated as mere fiction. As to the abductions abovementioned, they are to be regarded as samples of the manners of the times:—such circumstances, and many others to which neither poets nor historians have given celebrity, no doubt took place on the shores of the Ægæan sea—favourable as these have ever been to piratical enterprises. Yet if we can believe that Herodotus actually examined for himself the writings of the "Persian historians" whom he quotes, and if he there found coincident narratives of the above-mentioned outrages, these vague traditions would then acquire something like the authority of history.

There is a fact affirmed by the historian in the outset of his history which deserves a passing notice:—he says, that "the Phœnicians, coming from the shores of the Red Sea (the Persian Gulf, or the Indian Ocean) settled upon the borders of *this* sea (the Mediterranean) in the country they now inhabit; whence they made distant voyages, carrying on the commerce of Egypt and Assyria, with the surrounding countries." This emigration of the Phœnicians—which in itself is by no means improbable—the distance between the two seas being not great, and such emigrations being frequent in ancient times—is mentioned by several ancient authors, though denied by Strabo; nevertheless it provoked the ridicule of Voltaire, who asks, "What does the father of history mean in the commencement of his work, when he says that, 'the Persian historians relate that the Phœnicians were the authors of all the wars; and that they came from the Red sea to ours'? It seems then that they embarked on the Gulf of

Suez—passed through the straits of Babel Mandel—coasted along the shores of Ethiopia—crossed the Line—doubled the Cape of Tempests, since called the Cape of Good Hope—ascended the sea between Africa and America, which is the only way in which they could come—re-crossed the Line, and entered the Mediterranean by the Pillars of Hercules, which would have been a voyage of more than four thousand marine leagues, at a time when navigation was in its infancy!"

This passage is a sample of this writer's ignorance and audacity in dealing with history; and it is an instance of the ease with which a charge of absurdity or falsification may be made out against an historian by a writer who is at once destitute of learning and of candour. "M. Voltaire," says Larcher, "would have spared himself this criticism, had he possessed even a moderate knowledge of the Greek language. If Herodotus had intended to intimate that the Phœnicians came by sea, he would have employed another Greek idiom. Besides, he would not have added, that 'they *then* undertook long voyages;' as, on the supposition of their having come by sea, they had already made a voyage much longer and more perilous than any they afterwards undertook. But if there remained any doubt as to the meaning of the passage, the author removes it in another place (Polymnia, 89): 'These Phœnicians, as they themselves say, formerly inhabited the shores of the Red Sea, whence *passing over*, they now occupy the maritime part of Syria.'"

The History—properly speaking—commences

with the story of Crœsus, king of Lydia, who reigned at Sardis about a century before the time of Herodotus. The Greeks, especially those of Asia Minor, maintained a frequent intercourse with the Lydians, and must therefore have had some general knowledge of their history; and it is evident that our author made himself acquainted, by personal researches, with such records and traditions as he could find at Sardis. But between his time and the reign of Crœsus, that city had once and again been pillaged, its government overthrown, the manners of its inhabitants changed, and probably, most of the ancient families had been banished, exterminated, or reduced to poverty; their places being supplied by Persians and Greeks. It must therefore be believed, that the authentic records of the state had to a great extent been dissipated, and that little better than vague reports remained to be collected when Herodotus visited Sardis. We are not therefore to be surprised if we find an air of the fabulous in the story of Crœsus and of his predecessors, the kings of Lydia. Nevertheless, some of the leading facts were authenticated by those gifts, of various kinds, that had been consecrated by the Lydian kings at Delphi, and many of which were preserved in the temple of Apollo, at that place, in the time of Herodotus: these gifts, by the inscriptions they bore, served to verify the accounts elsewhere received. At Delphi, Herodotus not only inspected vessels of gold and silver, preserved in the temple where the oracles were given, but he received from the priests *their own copies* of the many responses which he quotes in the course of his work. In these vaticinative verses the craft of the priests who composed them is often sufficiently apparent: and whatever they may be, their *genuineness* rests entirely upon the honesty of the Delphian priests, from whom our author received them. Yet the subject of the ancient oracles should not be passed by without acknowledging that, amidst all the glaring frauds, and the frivolous evasions, and the interested compliances with the wishes of the applicants, which characterise these responses, there is apparent also in some of them a knowledge of contemporary—though remote events, and of a sagacity in relation to the future, which is not satisfactorily explained without admitting the interposition of a superhuman agency. An absolute denial of any such intervention, while it is unsupported by a true philosophy, does violence to the principles of historical evidence; nor is it demanded by any argumentative necessity.

The interlocution between Crœsus and Solon—the Athenian legislator, as related by Herodotus, may fairly be numbered among those dramatic embellishments with which ancient writers—and our author not less than others—thought themselves at liberty to relieve the attention of their readers. It need not be questioned that Solon visited Sardis; and it is not improbable that some rebuke of the Lydian king's preposterous vanity—really uttered by the Grecian sage, may have formed the text of this long conversation.

The story of Adrastus, the Phrygian refugee, and of Atys, the son of Crœsus, if founded in fact, are evidently much indebted to the ingenuity of the narrator. Though these incidents may seem puerile to a modern reader, we ought to carry ourselves back to the author's times, before we pronounce them to be altogether improper in the place where they appear. A student of history who reads only modern compilations will fail to obtain that just and exact idea of antiquity which these excrescent parts of the works of ancient historians convey.

The history of Crœsus is interrupted by a long digression, in which our author gives a sketch of the early history of the Athenians and Lacedæmonians. On these points he could be at no loss for traditions, or other sources of information; and here also he was open to correction from his contemporaries, who were as well informed as himself in matters of Grecian history. Yet the reader should not lose sight of the *dates* of the events severally mentioned, in forming his opinion of the value of the evidence. It is the manner of Herodotus to relate unimportant circumstances which took place—if at all—five hundred, or a thousand years before his time, with as much minuteness of detail, and as much confidence, as when he is describing recent events. Frequently, it may be supposed, he followed what he deemed authentic documents; but as we have no sufficient means of forming an opinion on the subject, such recitals are not to be admitted among the established points of history, unless they are confirmed by a coincidence of authorities.

The narrative of the war between Crœsus and Cyrus, which ended in the final dissolution of the Lydian kingdom, is resumed, sect. 69. The leading events of this war could not fail to be well known at the time in Greece; for besides that the intercourse between Greece and Asia was frequent,

Crœsus was on terms of friendship with the Lacedæmonians, and was everywhere celebrated for the magnificence of his offerings to the Delphic god: moreover, the fall of Sardis, and the consequent conquests of the Persians in Asia Minor, brought a formidable enemy to the very door of Greece, and obliged the several states to inform themselves much more exactly than heretofore, of the affairs of their Asiatic neighbours. We may therefore place the conquests of Cyrus in Asia Minor among the authenticated facts of history. Yet from the details, as given by Herodotus, some considerable deductions must be made; for there is an air of dramatic embellishment apparent throughout the narrative. Sardis was taken by Cyrus about one hundred years before Herodotus wrote his history: it is not therefore probable that he had the opportunity of verifying his authorities by consulting any living witnesses of the event: it is more likely that he worked up, in his own manner, some floating traditions received from the Asiatic Greeks.

Crœsus, confounded by misfortunes which seemed to give the lie to the Delphic god, whose favour and advice he had courted by gifts of unexampled richness, requested permission of Cyrus to send the fetters he had worn, to Delphi, to be laid on the threshold of the temple;— directing the messenger to ask the Grecian god— If it was his custom to delude those who had merited the best at his hands. This request was granted; and the Lydian messenger brought back a reply which, whether or not it may be considered as genuine, is curious, if taken as a specimen of the policy and style of the Pythian :—

When the Lydians arrived and delivered their message, the Pythian is said to have replied— That even the god could not avert the decree of fate. That Crœsus, the fifth in descent, suffered for the sin of his progenitor, who being a servant of the Heraclidæ, consented to the guile of the woman, and slew his master; taking possession without right, of his place and honour. That yet Apollo *had endeavoured* to defer the fall of Sardis till the next generation; but that *he had not been able to move the Fates*, who would no further yield to his solicitation than, as a special favour to Crœsus, to place the taking of Sardis three years later than otherwise it would have happened. Let Crœsus therefore know that he is a captive three years later than the Fates had decreed; and then remember that Apollo rescued him when about to be burned. As to the response, Crœsus had no right to complain; for the god had foretold that if he invaded the Persians, he would overthrow a great empire; and if upon this he had wished to be better informed, he should have inquired again, whether his own empire, or that of Cyrus was intended. Wherefore, as he had neither understood the oracle, nor asked for its meaning, he might take the blame to himself.

Having dismissed the Lydian affairs, Herodotus proceeds to give a sketch of the history of the Assyrians, Medes, and Persians, and to relate the story of the elevation of Cyrus to supreme power in Upper Asia. That he had visited Persia cannot reasonably be questioned; nor need it be doubted that he diligently availed himself of every means in his power to acquire information. Whether he was master of any of the eastern

languages does not certainly appear; for though
he frequently refers to the Persian historians, and
though, in one place (139), he makes a philological
remark on a peculiarity of the Persian language,
we must ask more direct proof than this of his
possessing an accomplishment so rare among the
Greeks. We must however believe, that, at least
by means of an interpreter, he had consulted the
Persian writers. In commencing the history of
Cyrus, he says—I shall follow those Persian
writers who, without endeavouring to exaggerate
the exploits of Cyrus, seem to adhere to the
simple truth;—yet not ignorant that three different
accounts of him are abroad.—Whether these three
accounts are in fact those given by himself, by
Ctesias, and by Æschylus, cannot be ascertained.
It is evident that exaggerations and errors
abounded among the oriental historians: the
Greeks therefore, having at best a very imperfect
access to these discordant authorities, must be
perused with caution: it would be unsafe to rely
with confidence upon any of these narratives; or
to found upon them objections to statements
which we derive from sources that are much
more credible.

A general conformity with facts is all that we
ought to expect from the Greek historians when
they speak of the remote history of Asia. Herodotus at Babylon, or at Susa, must have been
almost entirely dependent upon the good faith of
the learned men with whom he happened to form
acquaintance; and even if we give them credit
for as much honesty as is usually practised on
similar occasions towards foreigners—and him for
a great measure of diligence and discretion, we

shall scarcely find reason for considering these portions of the work to be true, otherwise than as to the general outline of events. Herodotus must however be allowed to rank above Xenophon, on the ground of authenticity; for the Cyropædia is only a political romance. Diodorus Siculus had access to sources of information that were not open to Herodotus; and the statements of the later may be admitted in correction of those of the earlier historian. Justin, or rather Trogus, seems to follow our author in his incidents, varying from him only in the order of some events. Josephus, in his reply to Apion, treats the Greek historians with contempt when they presumed to speak of Asiatic affairs; urging against them their many contradictions, and their want of really ancient and authentic documents, and quoting, as of higher authority, several works of which these citations are almost the only remaining fragments. Without impeaching the character of Herodotus, we may peruse the earlier portions of his history as an entertaining narrative, held together by a connected thread of truth, and supporting a series of incidents which, though characteristic of the times, are of very questionable historical authority. Of this kind is the story of the birth and early adventures of Cyrus, in which the art of the narrator in working up his materials, is apparent.—Probably some popular tales communicated to our author in Persia, were adapted by him to the taste of the Greeks. In his account of the manners, usages, habits, and buildings of the nations he visited, and of the features and productions of the countries through which he travelled, our author is deserving of a high degree of confidence; and though a few particulars,—plainly fabulous, are mingled with these descriptions, they must be admitted to take a place among the most valuable of the remains of ancient literature.

The narrative of the subjugation of the Ionians and Æolians of Asia Minor, by the Persians, stands, for the most part, upon a higher ground of authority than those which precede, and those which immediately follow it; not only because the transactions were comparatively recent; but because the affairs of these Asiatic Greeks were, at all times, well known to those of Europe.

The capture of Babylon by Cyrus was an event too remarkable in itself, and in the extraordinary circumstances attending it, to leave room for much diversity among the accounts of it which were transmitted to the next age. The Greek historians differ but little in relating this memorable event, and their testimony, independent as it is, when collated with the circumstantial predictions of the Hebrew prophet, deserves peculiar regard. If the history of Herodotus had no other claims to attention, it would have claim enough by affording, as it does, in several signal instances, an unexceptionable testimony in illustration of the fulfilment of prophecy.

The expedition of Cyrus against the Massagetes, a Scythian nation, in which he perished, closes the first book of the history. Here again there may be reason to suspect a want of authentic information. The scene of action was remote, not merely from Greece, but from Persia, and the survivors of the Persian army told, when they returned, each his own tale of wonder: nor is it probable that any other account of the war was extant in the time of Herodotus than what had been received from these persons.

The instances that have now been mentioned, occurring in the first book of Herodotus, may serve as examples of the different degrees of authority which may belong to different portions of an historical work—dependent both upon the means of information possessed by the writer, and upon his liability to contradiction and correction from his contemporaries. It is enough if we keep in view the general principles stated above (chap. XIII.), in adhering to which, we have a sufficient guidance in perusing a work like that of Herodotus, combining as it does, materials of all kinds, more or less valuable and authentic. As to some of the facts he relates, we may regard them as absolutely certain, others as doubtful, improbable, or unreal. With the worst intentions, and the meanest qualifications, an historian of recent events, whose writings are received in his own times as authentic, can seldom be charged with glaring falsifications of facts; on the other hand, the most cautious, industrious, and scrupulous writer, who compiles the history of remote times, and of foreign nations, may innocently wander very far from the path of truth. It would subserve no useful purpose to adduce a larger sample of instances in illustration of these obvious principles. We may now give some account of those who have signalised themselves as the assailants of this great writer.

Herodotus, as we have already said, was severely reprehended by several ancient writers, especially by Ctesias, Manetho, Diodorus Siculus, Strabo,

Josephus, and, above all, by Plutarch, or by the angry writer who assumes his name. The grounds of exception taken by these writers are, in a few instances just; in most cases, the influence of prejudice or petty jealousy is apparent; yet none of these criticisms affect that part of the history which alone we allege to be unquestionably authentic. But modern authors also have attacked the reputation of the historian, and we may briefly notice some of these more recent criticisms; for if it is affirmed of a portion of this history, that its truth is absolutely certain, it ought to be shown that the facts in behalf of which so high a claim is advanced have never been called in question—or never, with any degree of plausibility.

Certain critics, of the fifteenth and sixteenth centuries, taking offence at some of the less authentic portions of this work, and especially at some ill-understood descriptions of animals and plants, speak of the historian as a compiler of fables: thus Ludovicus Vives, a learned Spaniard, well known in England during the reign of Henry VIII., speaks of the books of Herodotus as abounding in things untrue. Another says, "Herodotus, that he might not seem to have omitted anything, brought together, without selections, matters of all kinds; of which the greater part were derived, not from ancient records, but from the fables of the vulgar. And although his style is agreeable, and even elegant, he forfeits the confidence of those who exercise a sound and impartial judgment; for such readers cannot give credence to a work so crammed with various narrations.—By some indeed he is called the 'father of history;' but by others he is justly named the 'father of fables.'"

Bodin, in his "Method of History," says, "I wonder that Cicero should have designated Herodotus alone as the father of history, whom all antiquity accuses of falsehood; for there cannot be a greater proof that an historian is unworthy of credit, than that he should be manifestly convicted of error by all writers. Nevertheless I do not think that he ought to be wholly rejected; for besides the merit of eloquence, and the charm of the Ionic sweetness, there is in him much that holds forth antiquity, and many things in the latter books of his history, are narrated with an exact adherence to truth."

Wheare, in his "Method of reading History," thus speaks of our author: "Although Herodotus gives some relations that are not much better than fables, yet the body of his history is composed with eminent fidelity, and a diligent pursuit of truth. Many of those less authentic narratives he himself introduces by saying that he reports not what he thinks true, but what he had received from others."

"It would be absurd," says Isaac Vossius, "to confide in Herodotus alone, in what relates to Persian and Babylonian affairs; seeing that he was unacquainted with the Persian language, and unfurnished with the records of any of the nations of the east." Bishop Stillingfleet speaks of the historian very much in the same strain as the authors above quoted. He has also been uncourteously treated by some later writers; of these Voltaire is the most distinguished. Whenever occasion presents itself he labours to cast contempt upon the father of history. Of this writer's ignorance and flippancy in commenting upon Herodotus, we have already adduced an example: others of a similar kind might easily be cited. Thus, he represents the historian as *affirming*, in a number of instances, what he professes only to report; as the story of Arion, and that of the Lydians who are said to have invented various games to allay the pains of hunger. He denies as utterly incredible the account given by Herodotus of the dissolute manners of the Babylonians: "that which does not accord with human nature, can never be true." Yet the customs alluded to are expressly affirmed to have prevailed there by Strabo, and are distinctly mentioned by a writer whose evidence in such a case need not be suspected—Baruch, VI. 43; and usages not less revolting are known to have been established in many ancient cities.

In several instances, either from ignorance or malice, Voltaire mistranslates Herodotus, in such a manner as to create absurdity or impropriety which does not exist in the original; and sometimes he cites passages that are nowhere to be found in our author. Herodotus, (Thalia, 72) affirms that it was the custom of the Scythians to impale a number of persons, having first strangled them, as a part of the funeral rites with which their kings were honoured. But Voltaire makes the historian affirm that the victims of this barbarous custom were impaled alive; and he then finds occasion to deny the truth of the story. If there are any, who, at this time, think Voltaire's criticisms upon the Scriptures worthy of any regard, they would do well to examine, with some care, the grounds of his remarks upon Herodotus. If in the case of a Greek historian, towards whom we may suppose him to have entertained no peculiar ill feeling, we find him displaying ignorance, indifference to truth, and a senseless flippancy—what may we expect when he attacks those writings towards which he avows the utmost hostility of intention?

Under all these attacks Herodotus has not wanted apologists; and while the writers above mentioned, taking an unfair advantage of some doubtful, or evidently fabulous passages, for the truth of which the historian does not pledge himself, have accused him of a want of veracity; others, more candid, have entered into the details of these accusations, and have shown, either that the author's credit is not really implicated in the narratives he brings together; or that these accounts are much better founded than, at first sight, they may appear. The editors and translators of Herodotus—such as Aldus, Camerarius, Stephens, Wesseling, Gronovius—have undertaken his defence; in some instances establishing the disputed facts; in others excusing the author from the charge of falsification. These discussions relate, for the most part, to those portions of the history which we have excluded from our present argument; and with which therefore we have here no immediate concern.

"Few writers," says Larcher, "have united in so eminent a degree as Herodotus the various excellences proper to an historian. Let us in the first place speak of his love of truth. Whoever reads his history with attention, easily perceives that he has proposed to himself no other

object but truth; and that when he entertains a
doubt he adduces both opinions, leaving it to his
readers to choose which they please of the two.
If any particular seems to himself unauthentic
or incredible, he never fails to add that he only
reports what has been told him. Among a
thousand examples I shall cite but two.—When
Neco ceased to dig the canal which was to have
led the waters of the Nile into the Arabian Gulf,
he despatched from this gulf certain Phœnicians,
with orders to make the circuit of Africa, and to
return to Egypt by the Pillars of Hercules, now
known as the Straits of Gibraltar. These Phœnicians returned to Egypt the third year after their
departure, and related, among other things,
that in sailing round Africa, they had had the
sun (rising) on their right hand. Herodotus did
not doubt that the Phœnicians actually made the
circuit of Africa; but as astronomy was then in
its infancy, he could not believe that in this
voyage they had really seen the sun on the right
hand:—'this fact,' says he, 'appeared to me by
no means credible: yet perhaps there are those to
whom it may seem so.'

"Another point which has not been duly
attended to is, that very often he commences his
narrative thus—The Persians—The Phœnicians—
The Egyptian Priests, have told me this or that.
These narrations, which sometimes extend to a
considerable length, are, in the original, throughout, made to depend upon this word $\phi\alpha\sigma\iota$—
they say, either expressed or understood. The
genius of our modern languages obliging us to
retrench these phrases, it often happens that
Herodotus is made to say in his own person what

in fact he reports in the third person. Thus things have been attributed to him, for the authenticity of which he is very far from vouching.

"He travelled in all the countries of which he has occasion to speak, he examined with scrupulous attention the rivers and streams by which they are watered—the animals which belong to them—the productions of the earth—the manners of the inhabitants—their usages, as well religious as civil;—he consulted their archives, their inscriptions, their monuments; and when these means of information failed him, or appeared to him insufficient, he had recourse to those among the people who were reputed to be the most skilled in history. He even carried his scrupulosity so far, that though he had no just reason for distrusting the priests of Memphis, he repaired to Heliopolis (Euterpe, 3), and then to Thebes, in order to discover if the priests of the latter city agreed with those of Memphis.

"One cannot refuse confidence to an historian who takes such pains to assure himself of the truth. If, however, notwithstanding all these precautions, it has sometimes happened to him to be deceived, I think he deserves in such instances rather indulgence than blame. Herodotus is not less exact in all matters of Natural History than in historical facts. Some ancient writers have dismissed, as fabulous, some particulars which have since been verified by modern naturalists—much more learned than the ancients. The celebrated Boerhaave did not hesitate to say, in speaking of Herodotus—'modern observations establish almost all that great man's assertions.'"

Some English writers also, wishing, as it seems, like Voltaire, to bring all history under suspicion, by endeavouring to prove that the best authenticated facts may, with some show of reason be questioned, have impugned the testimony, not of Herodotus alone, but of all the Greek historians. In recent times all this ground has been so well and thoroughly explored by writers eminently qualified for the task, that it would be quite a superfluous labour to refute those whose criticisms have passed into oblivion.*

Writers who, on general grounds, have laboured to show that Herodotus vastly exaggerates the power, valour, energy, of the Greeks, as compared with the Asiatic nations, have forgotten that, in estimating his testimony in this case, we are abundantly furnished with independent evidences —touching, as well the Asiatic, as the European civilisation, at the times in question. These existing monuments on the one side, leave no room to doubt that the soil of Greece, during a long course of time, supported a numerous people, eminently endowed at once with the physical qualities of strength, beauty, alacrity, and courage, and with a mental conformation, combining the ratiocinative and imaginative faculties in the happiest proportions. There is proof before us that these advantages, inherent in the race, were improved; that a very high degree of civilisation in almost all its branches, and of refinement, was attained; that the resources of an extensive commerce were possessed, and a large amount of political power acquired, by the Greeks; or to

* Some of these were named in the first edition of this book; but it would be a waste of space to bring them forward anew.

express all at once—that the Greeks were then, what the nations of western Europe are now, as compared with the nations of Asia.

Even if it could be made to appear probable that, in the first ages of the world, Asia—and in Asia, Persia, was the centre of civilisation, yet it must be granted, that, so far as authentic history reaches, the picture of the Asiatic nations is uniform in its character and colouring. Asia has indeed produced some races distinguished by a fierce energy, by romantic courage, by loftiness and richness of imagination. But in no people of Asiatic origin that has displayed at once, and in combination, the effective energy, the high intelligence, the taste, the well-directed and sustained industry, which belong to the more advanced of the European nations:—never have its hordes risen to that level on the scale of intelligence at which men become at once desirous of political liberty, and capable of enjoying so great a good.

The relation which modern European armies— those of the Portuguese, the Dutch, the French, and the English, have always borne to the native forces of India, is very much the same as that which history affirms to have existed in all ages between the people of the East and of the West. Though the latter have not driven the former before them like sheep, they have at length prevailed over them, as courage conquers rage, as mind subdues mere force, and as skill is more than numbers. It is, in substance, the same story that we read, whether the page of history presents us with the exploits of Clive in India, or of Pompey in Parthia and Syria, or of Miltiades at Marathon, or of Alexander in Persia.

The narrative of Herodotus is therefore substantially the first chapter of the history of the enduring conflict between Asia and Europe; and this commencement of the story is in harmony with all its subsequent events. On the one side is seen a reckless despotism, seated on the shoulders of a boundless population, and which, at the instigation of a puerile or a ferocious ambition, lets forth a deluge of war, the course of which was as little directed by skill, as it was checked by humanity. On the other side are seen much smaller means, employed with incomparably greater intelligence; and excepting only the partial events of war, the general issue has ever been the same.

CHAPTER XX.

RECENT EXPLORATIONS, CONFIRMATORY OF THE TRUTH OF ANCIENT HISTORY: HERODOTUS AND BEROSUS.

WHAT we are now doing is to adduce a few samples of the means that are available for establishing the truth of the more remote facts of ancient history, according to those general principles which have already been explained—taking Herodotus as our first, and Berosus as our second instance. In the tenth chapter (p. 106) a brief reference has been made to those statues, busts, monuments, inscriptions, whence ancient historians drew a portion of their materials. But more than a few of these solid vouchers for the truth of written history have come down to modern times, and are accessible, either on the sites of ancient cities, or in museums. In the twelfth chapter (pp. 133-149), these now-extant evidences are again, and more particularly referred to. In the fifteenth chapter a glance at the contents of the British Museum brings this species of evidence yet further into notice, and we there (p. 208) make a passing reference to Herodotus, as one amongst those writers—indeed, the foremost of them, whose testimony finds confirmation in the sculptures of the Grecian, the Assyrian, and the Egyptian saloons.

To this particular subject, therefore, we now
return; but shall think it sufficient to name, at
hazard, a few among the very many instances
which might be adduced, of a similar kind, and
which possess, in different degrees, the same
historic value. The reader will understand that
nothing more can be attempted within the limits
of a volume like this, than to state the general
principles of historic evidence, and to illustrate
such statements by a few examples. This has
been done at large, in the instance of Herodotus
(as we have just now said) by several eminent
writers of modern times, namely, the editors of
the Greek Text; and still more effectively by
some of later date—French and German. Among
English writers we should mention Sir John Ker
Porter, in his travels in Persia; Major Rennell,
in his Essay on the Geography of Herodotus;
Mr. Layard, in his "Nineveh and its Remains,"
and his later work, "Discoveries in the Ruins of
Nineveh and Babylon." To the same purpose
much of illustrative and incidental discussion
finds a place in Grote's "History of Greece," and
in Mure's "Critical History of the Language and
Literature of Greece." More specifically these
subjects come forward in the Papers and Essays
of Dr. Hincks, and of Sir H. Rawlinson, and in
many of the elaborate notes, and the subjoined
essays of the now forthcoming work, "The History of Herodotus: a New English Version," by
Mr. Rawlinson, Sir H. Rawlinson, and Sir J. G.
Wilkinson. In these works—accessible to the
English reader, and which are found in most
libraries—ample and precise information may
easily be obtained, of the same kind as that of

which a few instances only are here adduced. Major Rennell's Essay on the Geography of Herodotus, has already been referred to (p. 302), and it might here again be brought forward, for furnishing instances attesting the fact that the Greek historian, not content with collecting materials at second hand, and at home, had actually visited most of the countries of which he gives any particular account, and certainly Mesopotamia and Egypt, and to some extent Scythia, and Northern Africa also, beside the southern parts of Italy; and it may be affirmed, as to this great extent of lands, that, in their now actual natural features, their products—animal and vegetable, the customs and usages of the people, and especially in those enduring architectural monuments which attract the attention of modern travellers, these countries furnish visible and tangible vouchers in support of the reputation of Herodotus—giving evidence, as they do, of his industry, intelligence, and, generally, of the exactness of his reports and descriptions.

Sir Robert Ker Porter[*] finds frequent occasion to name this same authority in illustration of existing antiquities. "How faithfully," he says, do these vestiges agree with the method of building in Babylon, as described by Herodotus! . . . the bricks intended for the walls were formed of the clay dug from the great ditch that backed them; they were baked in large furnaces, and in order to join them together in building, warm bitumen was used; and between each course of thirty bricks, beds of reeds were laid interwoven

[*] Travels in Georgia, Persia, Armenia, Ancient Babylonia, &c. Two vols. quarto, 1821.

together. The bitumen was drawn from pits near the Euphrates, which pits exist at this day." Since the time (1821) of Sir R. Ker Porter's explorations in Babylonia, so much has been done in these regions that we turn of course to more recent authorities: these, although they do not deprive his writings of all value, supersede them to a great extent. Chiefly within the last ten years, and entirely within these thirty years, unexpected progress has been made in deciphering the inscriptions that abound among the remains of this region; and it may now be affirmed that the dark unknown of remote Asiatic history stands revealed before us. This recent revelation —this solving of what had been regarded as inscrutable mysteries—has taken effect in various degrees, upon the existing written histories of Assyria, Babylonia, Persia, Scythia—confirming much—correcting much; and utterly demolishing the credit of some portions of this hitherto-accepted history. It is thus that the tangible and the visible remains of remote ages, as now *interpreted*, have effected an extensive reform in this department of human knowledge. If, in a few words, we were to state what has been the general result of these discoveries, it would be in this way—The recent interpretation of the inscriptions heretofore, or recently known, and which are found upon bricks, upon slabs and sculptured surfaces, and upon the face of rocks, has, in several remarkable instances, furnished evidence confirmatory of Hebrew Scripture history; it has given a *general* support to the statements of Herodotus, as well as to those of Diodorus, the Sicilian; at the same time correcting those statements in various particulars; it has irrecoverably annihilated the testimony of Ctesias—the rival and the bitter enemy of Herodotus; and on the other hand it has, to a great extent, given authentication to what is extant of the Chaldæan writer—Berosus. To this last instance we must presently revert.

In mentioning (Chapter XI.) the exceptions to which the testimony of ancient historians may be open—without impugning their veracity, we have of course claimed indulgence for them in relation to events remote, both in time and place from themselves, and for a knowledge of which they must have been dependent upon precarious sources of information. Nevertheless there are many instances of this very sort which have received from the industry of modern travellers very remarkable confirmation. One such instance comes before us in an early, or, as we may call it, the preliminary portion of the history of Herodotus. In speaking of Lydia and of its people, he says that it contains little worthy of note—less, indeed, than other countries—yet it has one structure of enormous size, to which nothing is comparable, after we have excepted the buildings of Egypt and of Babylon: this is the tomb of Halyattes, the father of Crœsus, the foundation of which consists of immense blocks of stone, and otherwise of a mound of earth. This structure has now outlasted the revolutions of two thousand four hundred years, or more, and lately it has, with sufficient certainty, been identified by modern travellers. It is found upon the northern bank of the river Hermus, in the plain between Mounts Temnus and Siphylus. Mr. Hamilton thus describes the principal tumulus, generally desig-

nated as the tomb of Halyattes:—" It took us
about ten minutes to ride round its base, which
would give it a circumference of nearly half a
mile. Toward the north it consists of the natural
rock, a white, horizontally stratified, earthy lime-
stone, cut away so as to appear as part of the
structure. The upper portion is sand and gravel,
apparently brought from the bed of the Hermus.
Several deep ravines have been worn by time and
weather in its sides, particularly on that to the
south; we followed one of these as affording a
better footing than the smooth grass, as we
ascended to the summit. Here we found the
remains of a foundation nearly eighteen feet
square, on the north of which was a huge circular
stone, ten feet in diameter, with a flat bottom,
and a raised lip or edge, evidently placed there as
an ornament on the apex of the tumulus."

The Prussian consul at Smyrna, M. Spiegenthal,
has examined this monument with more care, and
has explored the interior. He gives the average
diameter of the mound as 281 yards, which would
require a circumference of about half a mile, as
roughly estimated by Mr. Hamilton. " Carrying
a tunnel into the interior of the mound, he discovered a sepulchral chamber composed of large
blocks of white marble, highly polished, situated
almost in the centre of the tumulus. The chamber
measured about 11 feet by 8, and was 7 feet in
height. It was empty, and contained no inscription or sarcophagus. This chamber, no doubt,
had been entered and ransacked in remote times,
and its treasures, whatever they may have been,
carried off. There can be little doubt that this
marble chamber was the actual resting place of

the Lydian king, who died according to our chronologies, B.C. 568." This structure, when seen by Herodotus, was a recent work—say about 130 years had passed over it: it is now a mound, crumbling into a formless mass:—meantime the description of it—even this page of Greek—in my view—is, as to its historic and its literary integrity, as fresh and as perfect as it was two thousand years ago—yes, and it is as imperishable as anything mundane can be. This Greek text will cease to exist—never—unless a deluge of water, of fire, or of universal barbarism shall come to wrap this planet in its pall.

As nothing is attempted in this volume beyond the illustration of the method or process of historical evidence, we take only a glance at those visible confirmations of our author's testimony, which are now directing the curiosity of the learned men of Europe, toward the levels of Mesopotamia—the banks of the Tigris and Euphrates. The mounds, the basement works, the gigantic sculptures, the inscriptions, combine to give evidence concerning Nineveh, and Babylon, and Persepolis, and in doing so shed a light upon remote antiquity, which, while it extends the limits of what is called "the historic period," avails also at once to correct and to corroborate the extant written materials of history. Heretofore the existence of very many contradictions in these literary materials, and the suspicious aspect of portions of it, had thrown a vague uncertainty over the whole. But the course of inquiry, at this time, has a discriminative tendency, and it will, in its results, undoubtedly enable those who shall be competent to the task, to set off the true and certain, from the false and the doubtful, throughout the entire range of ancient history. Far more important than the determination of any particular problems in the Assyrian, or Babylonish, or Persian history, such as the disputed date of wars, or the succession of monarchs, is the exclusion of those loose modes of thinking and of writing, the aim and *intention* of which has been to bring all history under suspicion, and thus to divert attention from the *past* universally, and to fix the thoughts of men upon the things of the day, and the objects of sense.

Between the written history which has reached modern times, in the modes that have been mentioned in the preceding chapters, and the now extant substantial monuments of the same times, there is a correspondence which can in no way be accounted for, otherwise than by assuming the genuineness and the authenticity of the former.

"The great temple of Babylon, regarding which the Greeks have left so many notices, is beyond all doubt to be identified with the enormous mound which is named *Mujellibéh* by Rich, but to which the Arabs universally apply the title of *Bábil*. In the description, however, which Herodotus gives of this famous building, he would seem to have blended architectural details which applied in reality to two different sites; his measurement of a stade square, answering pretty well to the circumference of Babil, and his notices, also, of the chapels and altars of the god, being in close agreement with the accounts preserved in the inscriptions of Nebuchadnezzar, of the high place of Merodach at Babylon; while, on the other hand, the elevation of seven stages, one above the other, and the construction of a shrine for the divinity at the summit of the pile, must necessarily refer to the temple of the Planets. of the Seven Spheres at Borsippa, now represented by the ruins of Birs-Nimrud."—SIR H. RAWLINSON: *Herodotus*, vol. i. p. 321.

"On the whole, we may conclude with tolerable confidence, that in the great northern mound of Babylon, we have the remains of that famous temple which Herodotus describes so graphically, and which ancient writers so generally declare to have been one of the chief marvels of the eastern world. Its bricks bear the name of Nebuchadnezzar, who relates that he thoroughly repaired the building; and it is the only ruin which seems to be that of a temple, among all the remains of ancient Babylon."—*Idem.*

In the course of these recent explorations, an instance has presented itself which, in a very peculiar manner, illustrates our proper subject in this volume, namely—the trustworthiness of that mode of transmission which has brought ancient books into our hands.

Berosus, or Ber Oseas, a Chaldean priest and historian, flourished and wrote at Babylon in the times of Alexander's immediate successors. His work—the History of Babylonia, has failed to come down to modern times; but it was extant in the early centuries of the Christian era; and it was very frequently mentioned, and cited at length, by writers of those times. This history is confidently appealed to, and is quoted by Josephus; and passages drawn from it are found in Tatian, Eusebius, Clemens, Alexandrinus, Athenæus, Agathias, and others. Altogether, when these variously derived quotations are brought together, they form a mass—broken indeed into fragments, but yet sufficient for subserving highly important purposes in clearing up the ancient history of the East. In converting this remarkable instance to our purpose in this argument, we have *first* to point out the illustration it affords of the reality, and the truthfulness of that system of quotation to which, again and again, we have directed the reader's attention. Here we have before us a case in which fragmentary citations, and incidental references—made by a number of writers, are found so to consist, and to agree one with another, as to authenticate at once the writer who is quoted, and the writers who quote: it is a mutually corroborative testimony. But in the next place, these fragments have lately received a kind of authentication that was little looked for, and which indeed deserves peculiar regard. What we here refer to is the trilingual Rock-Inscription which recently has received its interpretation. In referring to this instance, and in converting it to our present purpose, we must be understood to assume, what we believe ought not to be doubted, namely, the validity of that system of interpretation which has at length given us the English of these inscriptions. A few passages we now quote are from Rawlinson's Herodotus. The following (vol. ii. p. 590) describes the Rock-Inscriptions of Behistun.

"Behistun is situated on the western frontier of the ancient Media, upon the road from Babylon to the southern Ecbatana, the great thoroughfare between the eastern and the western provinces of the ancient Persia. The precipitous rock, 1,700 feet high, on which the writing is inscribed, forms a portion of the great chain of Zagros, which separates the high plateau of Iran from the vast plain watered by the two streams of the Tigris and Euphrates. The inscription is engraved at the height of 300 feet from the base of the rock, and can only be reached with much exertion and difficulty. It is trilingual: one transcript is in the ancient Persian, one in Babylonian, the other in a Scythic or Tartar dialect. Col. Rawlinson gathers from the monument itself that it was executed in the fifth year of the reign of Darius, B. C. 516."

In these inscriptions, covering a large surface of the native rock, Darius, the great king, tells the world who he is, what he has done, what wars he has waged, what countries he has conquered, and what structures he has raised:—

"I (am) Darius, the great king, the king of kings, the king of Persia, the king of the (dependent) provinces, the son of Hystaspes, the grandson of Arsames the Achæmenian."

We have mentioned (p. 246) what was the usage of the copyists in commending their labours to the care of the men of after times, and in attaching tremendous anathemas to the crime of destroying, or of alienating the book. Here, now, a curious coincidence presents itself; for this great king, in bringing this sculptured record of his reign to a close, thus utters his will:—

"Darius the king says,—If seeing this tablet, and these images, thou injurest them, and preservest them not as long as my seed endures, (then) may Ormazd be thy enemy, and mayest thou have no offspring; and whatever thou doest, may Ormazd curse it for thee."

As to the available value of these inscriptions. Mr. Rawlinson thus writes (vol. i. p. 432):—

"Until quite recently the most obscure chapter in the world's history was that which related to ancient Babylonia. With the exception of the Biblical notices regarding the kingdom of Nimrod, and the confederates of Chedor-laomer, there was nothing authentic to satisfy, or even to guide research. . . . The materials accumulated during the last few years, in consequence of the excavations which have been made upon the sites of the ruined cities of Babylonia and Chaldæa, have gone far to clear up doubts upon the general question. Each succeeding discovery has tended to authenticate the chronology of Berosus, and to throw discredit upon the tales of Ctesias and his followers. . . . The chronology which we obtain from the cuneiform inscriptions in this early empire, harmonises perfectly with the numbers given in the scheme of Berosus. . . . It is evident that the chronological scheme of Berosus . . . is, in a general way, remarkably supported and confirmed. . . . As to the chronology of Ctesias, it is irreconcileable with Scripture, at variance with the monuments, and contradictory to the native historian, Berosus, whose chronological statements have recently received such abundant confirmation from the course of cuneiform discovery. . . . It may therefore be discarded as a pure and absolute fiction; and the shorter chronology of Herodotus and Berosus may be followed. The scheme of these writers is in tolerable harmony with the Jewish records, and agrees also sufficiently well with the results at present derivable from the inscriptions."

Our object here is not to determine disputable points in ancient history, but merely to exhibit, in its several parts, the method, or process, of historic proof. With this view, only, before us, we need not do more than bring forward these *samples* of this method, in its several kinds. It would be easy, if useful, to go on—from book to book of the History of Herodotus—finding confirmations or corrections of his narratives and descriptions, and much that would be pertinent, derived from the pages of modern travellers, or from the contents of museums. But to do so would lead us far, and indeed would fill bulky volumes. The facts, thus far briefly adduced, furnish the intelligent and studious reader with *suggestions* for prosecuting inquiries, on this ground, to any extent to which his taste or his purposes may lead him onward.

CHAPTER XXI.

INFERENTIAL HISTORIC MATERIALS.

A BOOK may come into my hand which contains no narrative of events—no allusion to the persons or transactions of the author's times—in a word, nothing, from the first page to the last, which in a direct manner should enable me to assign a date to it. Nevertheless, such a book may actually possess much historic significance, and it may take its place among those materials of which a writer of history will eagerly avail himself. This assertion may need some explanation; as thus:—

Each nation, as distinguished from other nations, its contemporaries, and each period in the world's history, as compared with periods anterior to it and subsequent, has its characteristics, its moral tone, its intellectual range, and its tastes; it has its principles, its modes of reasoning, and especially its condition as a season, either of progress and expansion, or of decay and decline. Now these characteristics are important in themselves, and they are often highly so, in clearing up historic problems.

Nevertheless historians seldom afford *direct* information illustrative either of the moral or the intellectual condition of ancient nations; nor indeed is this deficiency much to be regretted, for such subjects are too indefinite to be treated in the style proper to history; and when historians philosophise, they bring the simplicity of their testimony into just suspicion. Besides, the mental condition of a people can be fairly estimated only by being placed in comparison with that of others; and few writers, how extensive soever may be their acquaintance with facts, are qualified to arbitrate between their contemporaries, and their predecessors, or between their own countrymen and their neighbours.

Yet although information of this sort may not present itself on the pages of historians, it may be derivable from other sources; for when the literary monuments of an ancient people are in existence, the knowledge we are in search of may be collected with a high degree of certainty therefrom. Yet the process may be nice and difficult, inasmuch as the indications from which it is to be gathered are more or less recondite. For this very reason the conclusions we obtain by a course of inferences and comparisons, may be the more exempt from suspicion. The pages of historians may be swelled with descriptions of the resources, the foreign influence, the population, and the polity of empires; meantime an intelligent inquirer may obtain—from the casual hints and allusions of writers of a less pretentious class, a true knowledge of the taste and the morals of a people.

It is obvious that we are not to attach much value, in this sense, to the embittered sarcasms of misanthropes, or to the epigrams of satirists, who hold up to view the two corrupted extremes of a social system—namely, the pampered favourites, and the desperate outcasts of fortune. Nor should we listen, without caution, either to the dreams of poets, from whose pictures the ills of reality have been discharged, or to the averments of philosophers, who are often less true to nature than even the poets.

Inferences, in an inquiry of this kind, may be drawn from what is recorded of—the modes of life, and the domestic usages, and the amusements of a people; or from the characteristics of their worship; or from the popular feeling, whether of approbation, surprise, or abhorrence, that is excited by the actions of public persons.

Valid information also is to be gathered from the enactments of a people whose moral condition is under inquiry. This sort of material is either that which is fixed, and has been consigned to the executive, by legislative authority; or that which floats at large in those ethical writings which have taken a permanent place in the literature of the country. In deriving inferences from the first—namely, the sanctioned laws of a people, several distinctions must be observed; for we must not bring forward antiquated laws; and in examining recent enactments, the political circumstances of the time must not be forgotten, for the momentary interests of parties, or of individuals, not seldom produce legislative decisions that are altogether anomalous, as to the condition of the people. Often mere chance has had sway in senates, and may have exercised more influence in the grave business of law-making than the sage and solemn forms of the place would seem to bespeak.

But it must be with the last-named source of

information only that we shall now have to do.
What we say is this—That, with due caution,
substantial information relative to the moral and
intellectual condition of a people, may be collected from the ethical writings that have been
accepted and approved among them. This proposition carries several important consequences,
and it may be well to illustrate it by some
examples.

Every hortatory composition contains, explicitly
or by implication, two fixed points, which it is
the business of the inquirer to ascertain. One of
these is much more readily found than the other;
yet there exists a means of measuring the distance
between the two; so that the one being determined, the other also may be discovered:—for
example, The first point ascertainable in an
ethical composition is—the system of morals, or
the standard of excellence which the author has
imagined, and which he recommends and enforces.
This point may be termed *the ideal level of the
writer's mind* in morals, and it is in most cases
quite easy to be fixed. The second, and less
obvious point, and that which is the very object
of our inquiries, is—the actual state of morals
among those whom the writer addresses, and
which may be called *the real level of popular morals*.
Our business then is to find this last or unknown
point, by measuring the distance between the two.
Now this distance is more or less distinctly indicated by the tone of every ethical composition.
We have then in our problem three terms: one
known, one demanded, and a middle term, connecting the two, which remains to be worked out of
the materials before us.

The distinctness of the indications from which our middle, or *measuring term*, is to be formed, will vary greatly in different cases. In works of a philosophical cast they will be extremely faint, and perhaps not available for our purpose; while in treatises that are of a simple and popular character, and which consist of precise exhortations—reproofs and advices—there will be little difficulty in drawing the inferences we are in search of. It will be found, also, that serious writers are more safe guides than those that indulge in satire; for the satirist seeks for extremes.

We say that writings of a philosophic or moral cast, and in which there occurs no allusion to events or to individual persons, may nevertheless be made available as the materials of history.— Two or three instances will show what we mean. We take our first example from a book which is as abstract in its form and style as any that could be found; and give, in brief, the purport of a section on Magnanimity, in Aristotle's Ethics.

Magnanimity, says Aristotle, is a quality conversant with what is great. But what things are these? He then may properly be termed magnanimous who deems himself worthy of great things, and who is so, in truth. For he who thus deems of himself without cause is a fool. He whose merits are equal only to a humble station, and who thus thinks of himself, is called wise, not magnanimous; for magnanimity belongs to what is actually great. In like manner, as handsomeness belongs only to height of stature; those who are small, may be comely, or symmetrical,

but not handsome. On the other hand, one who
falsely deems himself to possess great merit, is
called vain—a term which can never properly
belong to those who are truly great. Again;
one who under-rates his merits is mean-spirited,
whether his real deserts be great, moderate, or
slender; since he still thinks that less than he
possesses is his due: especially is he pusillanimous
who thus disparages great qualities in himself;
for what would such a man do if destitute of that
merit? He, therefore, who is truly magnanimous,
is of necessity a good man; and whatever there is
great in any virtue belongs to him. It befits not
him to flee, wringing his hands, nor to do wrong
to any one; for why should he commit unworthy
actions to whom nothing great can be added?—
Wherefore this greatness of soul seems to be a
sort of ornament to all the virtues—enhancing all
of them, and not, by any means, consisting without them. True greatness of soul is therefore
rare, since it demands the perfection of probity
and goodness. Magnanimity is peculiarly displayed both in honour and in disgrace; for the
great man, when surrounded by opulence and by
assiduous attendants, experiences only a moderate
happiness; since what he enjoys is not more than
what befits him; or perhaps, not so much; for
virtue can hardly ever be said to possess its due
reward. The honours bestowed upon him he
therefore calmly admits as being, though not
equal to his merits, the utmost that those around
him have to bestow; while ordinary or mean
praises he utterly contemns; for of such he deems
himself undeserving. In like manner he despises
disgrace; for he knows that it is unjustly cast

upon him. Thus, in prosperity he is not elated; in adversity not dejected.

Without attempting to draw inferences too far from a passage like this, it may fairly be said to indicate the existence of popular notions of moral greatness, more refined than those of nations merely warlike; and far exalted above those of a people—merely commercial. The writer must, in his own country, have seen examples of heroic virtue which approached the perfect image he exhibits. One is not surprised to learn that he belonged to the race which produced Aristides, Cimon, Epaminondas, and Phocion. It is observable that Aristotle's magnanimous man is decked only with the honours that befit a *citizen*, or a distinguished leader in a republic—not with the gaudy shows of oriental despotism: it is not deemed a becoming part of his hero's glory that millions of his species should lay in the dust at his feet. We may also fairly remark, that this acute thinker had evidently no idea of that peculiar sentiment which is engendered, in great minds, by an habitual reference to the moral attributes of the Deity: his hero is a purely *mundane* person; or, if we might so accommodate the term—he is *atheistical.* Neither did his notion of moral greatness include that humility which springs from a sense of delinquency, or imperfection, in the sight of the Supreme Lawgiver and Judge. If ideas of this class had at all been known to the Greeks of that age, or if they had come within the writer's view, he would assuredly have included them among his definitions, whether he thought them worthy of commendation, or not so. For his manner is to omit no abstract idea that bears any relation to his topic.

To what extent sentiments like those mentioned by Aristotle were prevalent in his times, it is not easy to ascertain from the passage just quoted; since the treatise in which it appears is of an abstract, not of an hortatory character; yet it contains one expression which, on the principle of our present argument, we should call *a term of measurement*; he says, that true magnanimity is exceedingly rare, or hard to be attained; in other words, that is was much easier to find among the writer's countrymen, an Alcibiades than an Epaminondas. But the historical significance of a passage like this will best appear by bringing it into comparison with a quotation, on a similar topic, from the most eminent of the Roman moralists.

Cicero's Treatise, De Officiis, is abstract rather than hortatory; and yet, compared with the Ethics of Aristotle, it is less metaphysical, and it approaches nearer to the modern idea of a practical work. Without designedly painting the manners, or formally estimating the morals of his times, this great writer furnishes, in his various compositions, many indications from which the state of both may be inferred. Of all social bonds, none, he says, can be found more weighty or more dear, than that which binds each one of us to our country. Dear are our Parents, dear our children, relatives, friends; but in our country are centred the endearments of all—for which, what good man would hesitate to die, if his death might promote its interests? Whence the more detestable is the ferocity of those who, by every crime, rend their country; and who have ever been busied in accomplishing its ruin. Actions performed magnanimously and courageously we are wont to applaud, as it were, with a fuller mouth. Hence the themes of orators on Marathon, Salamis, Platæa, Thermopylæ, Leuctra; hence our Cocles, hence the Decii, hence Cnæus and Publius Scipio, hence Marcellus, and others without number; for the Roman people especially excels in greatness of soul. Indeed, our love of military glory is declared by the fact, that our statues are adorned with the garb of the warrior. But that elevation of soul which displays itself in dangers and labours, if it wants probity—if it contends not for public, but private advantages, becomes a vice. Not merely is it not a virtue, but is rather to be deemed a ferocity—repulsive to human nature. Well therefore is fortitude defined by the Stoics, when they say, it is 'virtue defending right.'—Wherefore no man who has attained the praise of fortitude has been renowned for treachery or mischief; for nothing can be laudable which is unjust. Those, therefore, are to be esteemed valiant and magnanimous, not who commit, but who repress wrongs. That true and wise greatness of soul, which is indeed laudable and consonant to nature, regards deeds more than fame; and would rather be, than seem illustrious. And he is not to be reckoned among great men who is dependent upon the erring opinion of the thoughtless multitude. For lofty spirits, always thirsting for glory, are easily driven on to what is unjust. And it is indeed hard to find one who, while he undergoes labours and dangers, does not seek glory as the wages of his exploits."

In these expressions there is conspicuous that paramount passion—the love of country, which belonged so peculiarly to the Roman people—which was a principal cause of the growth of their power, and which, though then on the wane, was not extinct in the age when the state ceased to be free:—no good man would hesitate to die for his country's good—this was a sentiment more characteristic of the Romans than of the Greeks. The Grecian chiefs not seldom betrayed their country for gold; those of Rome, scarcely ever. Then the military spirit is much more prominent in the one instance than in the other. Cicero's great man is, of course, a warrior; Aristotle's is a statesman: the Roman obtains *glory;* the Greek, *honour, dignity.* The one, if destitute of probity, becomes the factious destroyer of his country, and is regardless of dangers and toils: the other—merely vain. The Greeks addicted themselves to war to defend their liberties, and to determine their intestine quarrels; but the Romans did so from the innate love of combat, and the insatiable desire of conquest. Both moralists make true virtue essential to true magnanimity; but the Greek proves this necessary connexion on abstract principles; the Roman insists that *utility* must be made the ultimate rule of conduct; and this principle is expressive of that practical feeling in which the Romans so much excelled the Greeks. If then, by some error, the passages above quoted were attributed—each to the other writer, a reader well acquainted with the history of the two people, would not fail to detect the incongruity of the sentiments and the phraseology. The two authors hold essentially the same opinions; but the one thinks like the companion of sophists, the other like the friend of soldiers. This perceptible difference between the two is an index to the *historical significance* of both.

We shall now cite a passage on a subject not very dissimilar, from a modern writer; and the reader will perceive that a great change and improvement has taken place in the sentiments of mankind, between the times of the ancient writers and the modern.

The duty (of respecting the natural equality of men) says Puffendorf, is violated by pride or arrogance, which leads a man, without cause, or without sufficient cause, to prefer himself to others, and to contemn them as not on a level with himself. We say *without cause;* for when a man rightfully demands that which gives him pre-eminence over others, he may properly exercise and maintain that advantage—yet avoiding absurd ostentation or contempt of others. As, on the other hand, any one properly renders honour or preference to whom it is due. But a true generosity or greatness of soul is always accompanied by a certain seemly humility, which springs from the reflection we make upon the infirmity of our nature, and the faults which heretofore we may have committed, or which yet we may commit, and are not less than those of other men. . . . . . It is a still greater offence for a man to make known his contempt for others by external signs, as by actions, words, gestures, a laugh, or any other contumelious behaviour. This offence is to be deemed so much the greater, inasmuch as it so excites the minds of others to wrath and the desire of revenge. Thus it is that many may be found who would rather put their life in immediate peril, and much rather break amity with their neighbours, than sustain an unrevenged affront. Since, by this means, honour and reputation are injured, the unblemished integrity of which is essential to peace of mind.

The latter sentences of this passage preclude the idea that the writer lived in times when a sordid, or servile insensibility to reputation had extinguished those sentiments to which so much importance, and so much merit, was attributed by uncient warlike nations. At the same time, the irst part of it contains a corrective sentiment, of which scarcely a trace is to be found in any of the Greek or Roman writers—a sentiment plainly arising from an enhancement of the notion of *moral responsibility*, and from a far higher estimate of the nature of virtue. In other words, the two first quoted writers were polytheists; the last was a Christian.

Our next instance is taken from the Enchiridion of Epictetus. The icy sophism of the Stoics had found some admirers at Rome before the times when the ancient republican severity of manners had disappeared. But *theoretical* stoicism does not reach its perfection till some time after *practical* stoicism has become obsolete. It is a reaction in the *moral* world, produced by the rank exuberance of luxury, sensuality, effeminacy, and the arrogance of preposterous wealth. If, therefore, the date of the Enchiridion were unknown, it would be more safely attributed to the times of Domitian, than to the age of Cincinnatus, or of Cato. In reading the following passage one may readily imagine the lame sage,* wrapping himself in his spare blanket, and his ample self-complacency, as he makes his way—unnoticed, through the insolence and voluptuousness of Imperial Rome.

If it ever happens to thee to turn from thy path with the intent to gratify any one, know that thou hast lost thy institute (*i. e.* forsaken thy *rule*). Let it be enough for thee, on all occasions, to be—a philosopher. But if, indeed, thou desirest to seem a philosopher, look to thyself, and be content with that. Let not such thoughts as these trouble thee—I live without honours, and am no where accounted of. . . . Is some one preferred to thee at table, or saluted before thee, or consulted before thee? If these things are goods, thou oughtest to congratulate him to whose lot they fall; if they are ills, do not grieve because they have not befallen thee. But remember, that as thou dost not pay attention to those things by which exterior advantages are obtained, it cannot be that they should be given thee. For how can he who stays at home fare the same as he who goes abroad?—or can the same things happen to him who is obsequious, and to him who is not?—to him who praises, and to him who praises not? Thou wilt be unjust and greedy if, without having paid the price at which these things are sold, thou dost expect to receive them freely. Now, what is the price of a lettuce?—say a farthing: one therefore pays his farthing, and takes his lettuce; but thou dost not pay, and dost not take. Think not thyself in worse condition than he. For as he has his lettuce, so thou hast the farthing thou

* Servus Epictetus sum natus; *corpore claudus.*
Irus pauperie, deliciæ Superum.

didst not pay. And thus it is in other things.—
Thou hast not paid the price at which an invitation to a feast is sold: for he who makes a feast sells invitations for flattery—for obsequiousness. Give then the price, if thou thinkest the bargain to thy advantage. But if thou likest not to afford the cost, and yet wouldst receive the things, thou art at once greedy and foolish. And hast thou then nothing instead of the feast? Yes, truly; thou hast this, that thou didst not commend one whom thou didst not approve; nor hast thou had to bear his insolence on entering his halls.

Many admirable sentiments are to be found in the writings of Epictetus; though, for a portion of them, there may be reason to believe he was indebted to Christianity, of which obligation he makes no acknowledgment. The treatise from which this passage is derived furnishes an example of that laborious and unsuccessful conflicting of pride with pride, which is natural to men of superior intelligence, who occupy an inferior condition, and are surrounded by vulgar insolence, servility, and profligacy. There was evidently a *class* of persons in the author's time in circumstances like his own—that is to say—intellectualists, who, as a defence against the scorn of worldlings, put on a mail of steely logic.

The Enchiridion, if regarded as *a material of history*, may fairly support the inference that, in the writer's time, wealth and luxury had triumphed over stern principles and severe manners;—that the philosophical character had ceased to command general respect, as it did at Athens in the age of Plato;—and that philosophy itself, having passed its prime, was fast becoming palsied and querulous.

A comparison, at once curious and instructive, might be drawn between two writers who, at first sight, may seem too unlike to be named together —Epictetus and Thomas à Kempis. Yet quotations from the Enchiridion, and the De Imitatione, might be adduced in proof of a real affinity. There is even a similarity in the form of the two works; for both writers, in a style of severe and laconic simplicity, address their pointed aphorisms —now to themselves, now to their half-refractory disciple, much in the manner of a nurse, upbraiding a pettish child. A *monotony*, both of *principle* and of *topics*, pervaded both books. Both authors compel Wisdom to ascend the summit of a snow-girt peak, where she can be neither approached, nor even heard, by the mass of mankind. Both writers were in fact, though on widely different principles, not only recluses from the ordinary walks of human life, but recusants of the common emotions of our nature. And both, by an implicit contrast, exhibit the falling condition of the social system of their times. Yet there is this difference between the two, that while the Stoic presents to view the darkness of paganism, enlivened by a glimmer from Christianity, the Monk holds forth the brightness of Christian truth, dimmed by the errors of superstition.

The moral treatises of Plutarch are of a practical, more than of a philosophical kind, and they yield therefore abundant indications, as well of the opinions, as of the manners of his age. In truth, the student of history would hardly need other aid in ascertaining the religious and moral sentiments of the times of Trajan, than he may find in the pages of this writer. Among this author's moral pieces there is one that is curious, and valuable too, as a material of history—namely, the tract on Superstition—*the dread of dæmons*. With great force of language and aptness of illustration, he depicts the mental torments of the man who believes the gods to be malignant, inexorable, and capricious; and he contrasts this unhappy temper with the comparatively harmless error of those bolder spirits who cast away altogether the belief and fear of supernal beings; and while he recommends "the mean of piety," he decidedly prefers atheism to superstition.

What say you?—The man who thinks there are no gods is impious? But is not he who thinks them to be cruel and malignant, chargeable with an opinion that is much more impious? For my own part, I would rather that men should say, 'There is no such person as Plutarch,' than that they should affirm that Plutarch is a man capricious, instable, prone to wrath, revengeful of accidental affronts, pettish; one who, if you have neglected to invite him with others to a feast, or if, being otherwise engaged, you have failed to salute him at your gate, will devour you, or seize and torture your son; or will send a beast, which he keeps for the purpose, to ravage your fields.

Plutarch speaks of four states of mind, as known and existing in his times—namely, 1. The wise piety, which he recommends, and which forms the medium between superstition and atheism.—2. The joyous or *festive* worship of the gods, in which he sees nothing to reprehend.—

3. A bold rejection of all religion, which he thinks *an error*, though an innocent error :—and 4. Superstition, which is not merely an error, but a practical evil of the worst kind. Of the first he says almost nothing ; nor does he offer a single hint explanatory of the mode in which the gods and goddesses of the Greek mythology might be made the objects of a devout and reasonable piety : and yet piety without a god, must be an unmeaning term. Plutarch's piety is a vague sentiment, which he feels to be proper to human nature, and highly beneficial ; but which was absolutely destitute of solid ground, or certainty ; for no invisible being or beings were known to him whom he could both love and fear. Even if the philosopher, by a course of doubtful reasonings, might work out for himself an idea of the Deity, such as might keep alive the sentiment of piety, no such abstruse notion could be brought within the apprehension of the vulgar. What is there then left to the vulgar ?—not atheism—for that is an error :—not superstition ; for that is a tormenting mischief :—nothing remains but the festive worship of the gods ; and this, with all its impurities, and all its follies, was the only portion that could be assigned to the millions of mankind :—Plutarch knew of no alternative on which to found the religious sentiments of men. Yet on another occasion he expresses his opinion strongly as to the necessity of religion for the support of the social system.—It seems to me that it were easier to build a city without a foundation, than to construct or to preserve a polity, from which all belief of the gods should be removed. Yet how great soever were the evils of atheism, he deemed

those arising from superstition to be greater. According to his testimony, when the only theology known to the Greeks took possession of timid minds, it rendered life intolerably burdensome.—Of all kinds of fear, none produces such incurable despondency and perplexity as superstition. He who never goes on board a ship, does not fear the sea; nor he the combat, who is not a soldier; nor he the robbers, who stays at home; nor does the poor man fear informers, nor he who is low, the eye of envy; nor he who inhabits Gaul, earthquakes; nor the Ethiopian, the thunderbolt. But the man who dreads the gods, dreads all things;—the earth, the sea, the air, the heavens, darkness, light, noise, silence, dreams. The slave in slumber forgets his master, the captive his chain, the wounded and the diseased their anguish:—kind sleep, friend of the sufferer, how sweet are thy visits! But superstition admits not even this solace; it accepts no truce, it gives no breathing time to the mind, nor permits the spirits to rally or to dispel its harsh and grievous surmises. But like the very region of the wicked, so the dreams of the superstitious man abound with terrific apparitions, and fatal portents: and this passion, always inflicting punishments upon the distracted spirit, scares the man from sleep by visions. And he—self-tortured, believes himself obliged to comply with fearful and monstrous behests. Such a man, when he awakes, instead of contemning his dreams, or smiling with pleasure in finding that what had disturbed him has no reality, still flies before an innoxious shadow, while at the same time he is substantially deluded by falling into the hands of conjurors and impostors, who strip him of his money, and impose upon him various penances.

The tortures inflicted upon timid spirits by the Grecian polytheism are depicted with not less force by the observant Theophrastus.—Superstition is a desponding dread of divinities (dæmons). The superstitious man, having washed his hands in the sacred font, and being well sprinkled with holy water from the temple, takes a leaf of laurel in his mouth, and walks about with it all the day. If a weasel cross his path, he will not proceed until some one has gone before him, or until he has thrown three stones across the way. If he sees a serpent in the house, he builds a chapel on the spot. When he passes the consecrated stones, placed where three ways meet, he is careful to pour oil from his cruet upon them: then falling upon his knees, he worships, and retires. A mouse, perchance, has gnawed a hole in a flour-sack: away he goes to the seer, to know what it behoves him to do; and if he is simply answered, 'Send it to the cobbler to be patched,' he views the business in a more serious light, and running home, he devotes the sack as an article no more to be used. He is occupied in frequent purifications of his house; saying that it has been invaded by Hecate. If in his walks an owl flies past, he is horror-struck, and exclaims—Thus comes the divine Minerva. He is careful not to tread upon a tomb, or to approach a corpse; saying that it is profitable to him to avoid every pollution. On the fourth and seventh days of the month, he directs mulled wine to be prepared for his family; and going himself to purchase myrtles and frankincense, he returns, and spends the day in crowning the statues of Mercury and Venus. As often as he has a dream, he runs to the interpreter, the soothsayer, or the augur, to inquire what god or goddess he ought to propitiate. Before he is initiated in the mysteries, he attends to receive instruction every month, accompanied by his wife, or by the nurse and his children. Whenever he passes a cross-way, he bathes his head. For the benefit of a special purification, he invites the priestesses to his house, who, while he stands reverently in the midst of them, bear about him an onion, or a little dog. If he encounters a lunatic, or a man in a fit, he shudders horrifically, and spits in his bosom.

The four centuries that had intervened between Theophrastus and Plutarch, during which a philosophical atheism had spread widely among the educated classes, had not, it appears, lessened the terrific influence of the Grecian polytheism over melancholy minds. On the contrary, it seems to have been enhanced, rather than diminished; for the language of Plutarch is stronger than that of Theophrastus. The verisimilitude of both descriptions, and their accordance, leave no room to doubt that this effect of the religious belief of the Greeks was of frequent or ordinary occurrence among them. Indeed there is reason to think that few persons of serious temper, even though imbued with the spirit of the sceptical philosophy, could free themselves from the burdensome scrupulosities and the horrific fears which attend every form of polytheism, and from which neither the refinement, nor the scepticism, nor the voluptuousness, nor the frivolity, nor the good taste, nor the subtle reasonings of the Greeks, could emancipate the devotees of their religion. The philosophic Julian might be named in illustration of this assertion. Beside his hatred of Christianity, his conduct was evidently influenced on many occasions by a very honest dread of the capricious dæmons whose falling interests he so zealously upheld: witness his magical practices.

It will be seen that passages such as those above quoted, possess a substantial value, when brought to their place among the materials of history. Ethical writers reflect the image of the principles and the manners of their times. In some instances we may infer too much; in others may mistake a partial for a general representation; but if, with due caution, we review a wide field of ethical literature, the *general result* of such an induction cannot differ much from truth.

If, for example, from the entire series of Greek writers, all passages of a purely ethical kind were to be extracted, and were arranged in chronological order, the collection would afford the means of ascertaining, not only the system of morals and religion that was known to that people, but also the actual state of morals and manners, as it varied from age to age. With such materials before us, there would be less room for conjecture, and less danger of error, in determining the moral condition of the people, than is found in ascertaining the extent of their political power, or the amount of their national wealth. Upon ethical passages, such as those we have adduced above, one fact presents itself—namely, that in the profane authors there is little of direct admonition or reproof, and rarely an appeal to a recognised standard of right. The reason is obvious. The Greek and Roman ethical writers discuss questions of morality in the tone proper to a learned disquisition, each saying the best things in the best manner he could:—no man was authorised to do more than propose his opinion: no feeling of official responsibility, no high solicitude, gave seriousness or force to his manner. Morals were not founded upon religion: on the contrary, an ethical treatise, containing the expression of reason and conscience, was at once a virtual refutation of the national theology, and a sarcasm upon the gods. Especially it is to be observed, that the instruction and reformation of the mass of mankind entered not into the contemplation of moralists and philosophers, who, while they amused one another with eloquent disquisitions, were not troubled by the thought that the millions of their fellow-men remained, from age to age, untaught in wisdom and virtue.

Not so was it with the people of Palestine. Not philosophy, but morality, was paramount; and morality was taught in its dependence upon religion. And it was not to a small class in the community, but to the people at large, that ethical writings were addressed:—and it was not for amusement, but for reproof, that they were so addressed:—and these writers, instead of propounding their individual opinions, and supporting those opinions by abstract reasonings, took the short course of appealing to a known standard of right and wrong. They speak to their fellowmen as from on high, and in the tone of authority; and each acquits himself, with gravity, of a weighty responsibility. From the writers of Palestine the modern Western nations have learned the style of instruction, admonition, and reproof, and this can have its origin, and derive its force, and maintain its influence, only from a Divine Revelation, entrusted to the administration of human agents.

But our present object leads us to remark that, whether or not this peculiarity of the Jewish and Christian writings be attributed to their Divine origination, it renders them far more available as historical documents, than are the writings of other ancient nations. For inasmuch as these compositions unite the several qualities of being *authoritative, hortative,* and *popular,* they leave nothing to be wished for in ascertaining, either the moral level of the writer's mind, or the actual level of manners in his times. It is evident that an appeal to a fixed standard, and an admonitory application of its known rules to the existing practices of the people, completes the requisite *data* of the historical problem above-mentioned. In the standard we have a known quantity; and in the hortatory forms of address, we have a mean of measurement, by which the actual state of morals may be ascertained.

An inquiry of this kind, if pursued in its details, would prove the existence and operation of an ethical system, so pure and perfect, that all after nations to whom it has been made known, have found nothing left to them but to admire and adopt its principles. What can the modern moralist do but work up the materials which he finds ready to his hand in the New Testament? To devise a new theology, or to invent a new morality—which should recommend itself to the common sense of mankind, would be as impracticable as to propose a new set of mathematical axioms. Truth is single and simple; and when once discovered, it must be adopted and followed. As a matter of history, it appears that the writers of ancient Palestine have taken possession of the regions of religion and morality.

But it would be practicable to ascertain, not only the system of morals taught by the Jewish and Christian writers; but the actual state of morals among those whom they immediately addressed. The Hebrew prophets furnish ample means for pursuing such an inquiry; but the unstudied earnestness of the Apostles, and especially the epistolary form of their compositions, would render the task of the inquirer easy, and conclusive in its results. In an argument of this kind we should not be entitled to conclude that the persons addressed were blameless in their lives—because their teachers address them as "Saints"—a conventional term. Our inferences must be of a less ambiguous kind. We must assume nothing but what is necessary to give consistency to the writer's assertions:—in other words, we are to assume just as much as is found to be safe and reasonable in the interpretation of any ancient author.

In the Epistles to the Galatians and the Corinthians, we find proof that Paul was not the man to spare the faults or errors of those to whom he wrote; and each of his letters affords some evidence as well of his quick-sightedness, as of his sincerity. Men will more easily bear to be charged with vices, or with evil tempers, than to be reproached for dulness of apprehension:

but in an Epistle addressed, as it seems, to the better-informed class of his own nation, he does not hesitate to blame their inaptitude and non-proficiency. (Heb. v. 11, 14.) Instances of a similar kind are the characteristics of the writer's manner.

If a father in writing to a son addresses him in the language of approving affection; and if his admonitions relate only to the graces of an amiable deportment and temper, it is fair to conclude that the character of the son is unstained by grievous vices; for such a letter would not be addressed by a wise parent to a son who was "wasting his substance in riotous living." This inference would be confirmed, if we found the same father writing to another son in terms of mingled affection, remonstrance, and severe reproof; and that he urged upon him, with pungent persuasions, the virtues of justice and temperance. Now it is an inference of this kind that we are entitled to draw from Paul's Epistles. In some of them he discharges the painful duty of administering stern reproof on points of common morality; and in these instances he carries the requirements of virtue as far as can be imagined possible; and he enforces his injunctions by the most awful sanctions. Such is the writer, and such is his system of morals. But the same moralist, in addressing other societies, writes in the style of a happy father to an exemplary son. The Epistles to the Philippians, the Thessalonians, and the Ephesians are of this kind; and the inference is this—that these societies were in a state not far below the writer's own standard of morals. In every society there will be a diversity of character, and in every numerous society there will be those to whom a wise teacher will address strongly-worded cautions, on the prime articles of morality. So it is in these Epistles; and the passages are vouchers for the writer's consistency and faithfulness. These more serious admonitions are, however, manifestly addressed to *a minority*, or to an individual; or they are directed to persons who are not within the pale of the society.

A passage so often quoted (Phil. iv. 8) might be compared to the last sedulous touches of an accomplished artist, who having completed an excellent piece of work, reluctantly withdraws his hand while it seems yet possible to add a higher lustre to its polish. Passages like these, from such a writer, whose discrimination and whose sincerity are proved, afford the best kind of evidence in attestation of purity of manners among the Christians of Philippi.

Other of the Epistles of Paul, as well as those of James, Peter, and John, furnish instances to the same effect. The result of bringing them forward would be proof irrefragable, that the teaching of the apostles had produced a high degree of conformity to that new and refined standard of morals which they promulgated:—it would show that, in many cities of the Roman world, where, formerly, nothing had been seen but shameless dissoluteness, and abominable idolatries; or, at the best, Jewish sanctimoniousness, or philosophical pride, societies were formed, which had been collected chiefly from the humbler classes, and in which the full loveliness of virtue was suddenly generated and expanded, and produced its fruits. Not only were the gods expelled by the new doctrine, but the vices also.

Facts and inferences of this kind have often been brought forward by writers who have taken up the Christian argument: we in this place are not taking up that argument as if it were our subject and purpose in this volume. The facts above briefly referred to, and the inferences that are thence derivable, fairly challenge for themselves a place as belonging to a summary of the method or process of historical proof. For if we affirm that various passages occurring in the ethical writings of Aristotle, and of Cicero, and of Epictetus, and of Theophrastus, and of Plutarch, are highly significant, as materials of history, it must be proper also to show that the apostolic Epistles—ethical as they are—come within the same range, and should be duly regarded as authentic evidences, touching the moral condition of the community within which they were circulated, and involving therefore the truth and the excellence of the religion which then spread itself throughout the Roman world.

CHAPTER XXII.

THE MODERN JERUSALEM—A VOUCHER FOR THE LITERATURE OF ITS ANCIENT OCCUPANTS.

In the twelfth chapter of this volume, and particularly at p. 133 and to the end, we have referred to those monuments of ancient art—buildings, sculptures, coins, which, as materials of history, are available in confirming or correcting the statements of ancient writers; and again in the twentieth chapter, we have brought forward (as samples only) some instances in which the existing remains of antiquity may be appealed to, as vouchers for the truthfulness of one of these writers—Herodotus.

Then in the fourteenth chapter we have seen what is the relative strength of that evidence which vouches for the genuineness and for the authenticity of the Holy Scriptures, as compared with that on the ground of which classical literature is accepted as real, and trustworthy. The superiority which we have claimed for the canonical writings results from:—1. The number of copies that have come down to modern times. 2. The high antiquity of some of these extant manuscripts. 3. The extent of geographical surface over which copies were diffused at an early date. 4. The importance attached to them by their possessors. 5. The reverential care with which manuscripts were executed. 6. The separation, and the mutual hostility of those in whose custody the books were conserved. 7. The visible influence of the writings upon the conduct and opinions of nations, from age to age. 8. The mass, and the intricacy of quotations from them. 9. The existence of ancient versions. 10. The vernacular extinction of the languages in which the books were written. 11. The means of comparison with spurious and imitative books. 12. The strength of the inference derivable from the genuineness of the books, to the credibility of their contents. The facts referred to under these twelve heads well deserve the reader's careful attention, and with this view they are here recapitulated.

But now there is one ground of comparison, quite proper to an argument of this sort, to omit all allusion to which might seem to indicate a consciousness of weakness; for, on the ground which is now in view, there is an apparent advantage largely on the side of classical literature, and profane history. Let us then look into this defective portion, as it may seem, of the Biblical evidence, and measure its actual importance.

With this purpose in view, we return, for an hour, to the British Museum. In passing through these saloons we find ourselves visibly confronted with the memorials of each of the principal developments of ancient civilisation; and with some also of those that were very limited, and obscure, and temporary. Ample and multifarious, and admirable are the monuments—in marble and in metal, of what the men of other countries have been, and of what they have done, in ages so long gone by. Here, for instance, is the Egypt of three or four thousand years ago—its people, and their employments; and here its despotisms, its dynasties—so many—are set forth in their gigantic semblances; and we may actually touch surfaces that were chiselled and polished at the time when —or before that time, Abraham was journeying from Mesopotamia towards Canaan. Here also is the Assyrian despot, and here the Babylonian and the mighty builder, and the lord of fifty nations— here they now hold their court, and show us before what glories, and what terrors it was that millions of men bent the knee and kissed the dust, in the times of Samuel, and of Solomon, and of Hezekiah. Here are substantial displays of the earliest developments of the human mind, under wholly different conditions—physical, social, political. Here are the earliest conceptions of Greek taste, intelligence, and free ideality; all these are vouched for; and mementos are before us of the Lycian people also, and of the Lydian, and of the Etruscan; and as we come down to later times, Greek art, and Roman art, bring us into familiar correspondence, not only with national characteristics, but with the individual persons of those ages. Now, during those times, the people of Palestine were passing from the lower to the upper culminating point of their national existence. Where, then, in this great assemblage of the nations of antiquity—where is Palestine? Are there none here to represent her, and to challenge a place for a people whose literature has pervaded the civilised world? The books of the people of Palestine are in every home—in every sacred edifice—they are found in palaces, and in cottages, and they are treasured near to the hearts of the good—high and low, and are extant in the memories of all. Why then should not the men of Palestine, and why should not its religious rites, be represented in the marbles, and in the metals, of our museums?

It may indeed be said that the ancient Palestine is not altogether absent from the museums of Europe; for among tens of thousands of samples of the mintages of antiquity, there are found a few coins of the Maccabean times, with their innocent and homely symbols; and in the series of the Imperial coins there are some vouchers for the fact of the overthrow of the Jewish state; there is the woman seated by the palm—the representative of the Judæa Devicta. Need we ask the reason of this absence of sculptured memorials of this one among the nations of antiquity? The want of sculpture is, in truth, this people's glory; the absence of the vouchers we might look for is indeed a voucher, attesting the noblest of all distinctions—that of having so long possessed and maintained, a free social polity, and a true theology.

If at this time an order were given to remove from the British Museum all memorials of the cruel tyrannies, and of the sensual idolatries of Egypt, and of Assyria, and of Greece, and of Rome—if every article were expelled that gives evidence of the oppressive despotisms, or of the vicious religions of ancient nations, how meagre an exhibition would remain after such a clearance had been effected! It is therefore this people's glory—a glory unrivalled—that no sculptures are extant to represent it in the museums of Europe! Nevertheless, there are monuments of its history to be found, if we look for them where it is reasonable to make the search ; namely, in Palestine itself, and at Jerusalem especially.

A few—say five or six—of the principal cities of antiquity, have continued to be inhabited from the very earliest times to this time;—such are—Damascus, Constantinople, Athens, Rome, and Jerusalem. The consequences of this uninterrupted occupation of the same sites, have been—more or less so in each instance—such as these—the preservation of some of the most ancient basement structures; the superposition of the structures of each age, in layers or deposits resembling the strata of the earth's crust; the commingling of older materials with the more recent buildings in the mason's work; and, generally, the creation of a modern town, lifted up, as one might say, upon the head and shoulders of the ancient city. Such cities, in exploring which we find evidence of their having undergone these several conditions, may fitly be called—HISTORICAL CITIES; and from these sources alone—or if there were none else available—we might gather abundant materials adapted to the purpose of illustrating the *written history* of nations, and of giving to it the most conclusive confirmations.

The briefest exemplification of what we here affirm, taking up two or three instances only, would occupy a great space. The educated reader does not need to be told what has actually been done, in this way, in regard to Athens and Rome. Something of the same kind has, also, within a few years, been effected in relation to Jerusalem;

but in this instance very much remains to be done; and much will undoubtedly be effected, at no distant time, when the Turkish guardianship of Palestine shall have ceased; or when Mahometan jealousy shall have given way to European intelligence. We advert to this instance, in concluding this volume, because it properly brings into view —at once, the several kinds of facts and statements which belong to our argument.

It is thus, then, that we bring the modern Jerusalem into our prospect. Two short periods excepted—after the capture and overthrow of the city—Jerusalem has been inhabited, *continuously*, throughout a period of three thousand years; and during all that length of time a written history has attended its fortunes, even from the earliest age, to this present time. If in this place indulgence might be given to a metaphor—and to such a metaphor—we should say that, looking at the entire mass of authentic history as an organic body, Jerusalem—the same hard material from age to age—is the vertebral stay of all history; or, in homely phrase, that this one city is the very back-bone of chronology. This is certain, and it has become more and more evident from year to year of late, that in every instance in which the leading events of the Hebrew and Jewish history may be ascertained with precision, such fixed points send forth ribs which give support to the loose matters of Egyptian, and Assyrian, and Persian, and Macedonian history.

It is peculiar to this one ancient city to have passed under the hand, and to have been for a length of time in the occupation of each of the great empires that have had a place and a name

in the world, during the course of three thousand
years. Each of these powers has solidly monu-
mented itself within, and about its walls. A
narrow space indeed is this to contain the archi-
tectures of ten empires: or, to be more precise, of
seven empires, and of three royal holdings. Yet
so it is; and in attestation of the fact, and as a
consequence of it, if at this moment we were
fitting ourselves out for a six or twelve months'
explorative sojourn in the Holy City, we should
think it indispensable to pack our portmanteaus
with books, ancient and modern, which, retrogressively catalogued, would include—I. The
principal modern works or guide-books, which
show what the Franks have done in recent times
in the way of church-building, monasteries,
hospitals, hospices, and private residences. II.
Such records as there may be (if any) of Turkish
doings in the same or similar modes; and much
has been done by the pashas in the repairs of the
walls, and in alterations and repairs within and
around the Haram. III. The Arabic writers
(they are more than a few), the post-Islamic, and
the ante-Islamic—such as Abulfeda, and others,
in whose writings incidental notices, at least,
occur of the Saracenic structures of their "Al
Kuds." There is much relating to the mosque of
Omar, and of Al Aksa. IV. The entire mass of
the crusading histories—the writers who are
brought together in that bulky folio, the "Gesta
Dei per Frankos." With these there must come
very many writers of the fifteenth and following
centuries, who treat of the topography of Palestine,
such as Adrichomius, in the "Theatrum Terræ
Sanctæ." V. The Byzantine writers who touch

upon the churches and monasteries of the Holy Land; with Procopius, and his account of the buildings of Justinian; the early Itineraries, Greek and Latin; and among these Jerome must find his place. VI. Some of the Greek Fathers—Cyril of Jerusalem and Eusebius. VII. The Greek and Roman profane historians, in series; from whom we learn all that can be known of the fate and fortunes of the city after its overthrow, and during the years of its desecration, as the Ælia Capitolina, by heathen temples and their impure rites. VIII. Josephus, and the Book of Maccabees, are our authority as to Herod's structures, of which many unquestionable remains are discernible among the ruins of the city. The same writer, and perhaps some of the rabbis, give the evidence that is required for interpreting the existing remains of the Asmonean period; thence-forward, or, we should say, higher up, it is—IX. To the Hebrew prophets and historians that we must look for the light we need, so far as the *written* memorials of the times of Ezra, Nehemiah, Hezekiah, Solomon, David, may afford it.

Thus it appears that, in carrying forward those explorations which already have in part been made, and which are now in progress, and which may be effected hereafter at Jerusalem, what we are doing, and what we shall yet be doing, is this—we are taking up the ancient written records of this city, page after page, and we are verifying each of our authorities by aid of the architectural remains of the same times—even from the remotest periods, down to this age. It is this Jerusalem which, beyond any other ancient site, furnishes the means, and the material, for thus collating and verifying the literary records of a people, by means of its extant monuments.

Architectural remains, such as those are which invite the labours of the antiquary at Athens, and at Rome, and at Jerusalem, require to be examined in relation to four distinguishable subjects;—as first—the *materials* (in a geological sense) that have been employed; and the question to be answered is—Whence have these been drawn—whether from quarries near at hand, or from a remote region? The *second* of these inquiries relates to the style and quality of the *mason's work*—that is to say, we have to note any peculiarity that may belong to the mode of squaring blocks of stone, and of fitting them one to another, and of placing them in layers; or to the manufacture of bricks, if these are in question. The *third* inquiry is properly *architectural*, and it has respect to the decorative style of the structure, and its aspect, and its beauty, considered as a work of taste. There then follows the *fourth*, and it is a most important question—Are these courses of masonry where we now find them—in their original, their primeval position; or have these blocks been dislodged, and overthrown, and scattered, and in some after-time reassembled and made use of by the builders of a later period? This last is often the determinative inquiry, in relation to doubtful points of history; and in the instance just now before us, it has a peculiar significance, inasmuch as there is reason to conjecture that some, at least, of the ponderous masses —the prodigious blocks, whereupon the heterogeneous structures of the modern Jerusalem take their rest—have been dislodged, upheaved, turned about, and again replaced, as at first, more than once or twice in the lapse of ages.

To the first of the above-named questions our answer is easy;—the material of the ancient Jerusalem was drawn from quarries quite near at hand: it is the lime-stone rock of the very site of the city. This has always been supposed; and the fact has lately been more fully ascertained by the explorations of Dr. Barclay,[*] an American physician, and long a resident at Jerusalem. Within the vast caverns that undermine Bezetha, and at a great depth below the surface of the present city, the mother rock shows, beyond a doubt, what masses have been hewn from it, namely, those large blocks, sixty feet in length, which underlie the Haram wall, and the city wall, in many places, and much of the interior of the city. In those caverns, such as we now find them, these blocks were squared, and their edges bevelled, and their surfaces—the upper and the under, were nicely prepared for their adjustments, according to the methods of a highly refined masonic art. As to this art of the *builder*, it is such as could have been practised by none but a people well advanced in practical intelligence, and that were in the enjoyment of the opulence and the tranquility proper to a secure political condition. The mason's work which is peculiar to, and characteristic of, the cyclopean substructures of the Haram, and the ancient city wall, is of a kind that fixes attention when once it has

[*] "City of the Great King."

been seen, and it is such as speaks its remote origin almost as intelligibly as an inscription could do.

The *architectural* characteristics of Jerusalem, as well of the ancient, as the modern city, cannot but be intelligible to those who are conversant with this branch of antiquarian lore. We easily read the various fortunes of the city, indicated right and left, in-doors and out of doors, scattered upon the surface, and deep in wells, tanks, and caverns, built into walls, and confusedly mixed with the chiselled labours of the workmen of other ages. The one source of ambiguity is that which arises from these disorderly commixtures, when a fragment, a capital, an entablature, which is manifestly Roman, or Byzantine, or Norman, stands so transfixed upon a structure whereupon it is embedded, as to conceal what might indicate the chronology of the earlier work. Nevertheless, amid many such indeterminable questions, there can be no question on the general ground, that, in and among the architectural remains of Jerusalem, we are looking at specimens of the builder's art, in all the stages, and in all the styles and fashions that have belonged to it, from the most remote times to the latest.

As to the fourth of the above-named heads of inquiry, full of historic significance as it is, a solution of the problems belonging to it must await a time when this site shall yield itself up, without reserve or restraint, to the industry and intelligence of European antiquarians.

We have need to be reminded of the fact, that, as we become familiar with the books of the Old

Testament in childhood, it is not until years later that we learn to correct the wrong chronological conceptions which have arisen from the misadjudgment of them as to their order of time. These early erroneous notions continue to haunt the imagination, perhaps through life, and we lose sight of, or quite forget the fact that a period of four or five hundred years intervenes between prophets that take their turn to be read, in the mornings and evenings of a week. Under the misguidance of these chronological errors, we are likely to carry forward, into the era of a people's maturity, conceptions which belong only to the age of their patriarchal and nomadic simplicity. Some few instructed readers of the Bible may be quite exempt from any such misconceptions; but probably it is many that are subject to them. Moreover, the grave tones of the inspired writers, and their singleness of purpose, so unlike the conventional and sophisticated manner of other writers, favours the idea that the Hebrew nation continued, from age to age, to live on in a condition of pastoral simplicity.

Such was far from being their condition; and a more attentive perusal of the historical books of the Old Testament, and of the prophets, will suggest, and more than merely suggest the belief, that this ancient people had reached a stage of advancement in the arts of life—substantial and decorative—which places them, at the least, on a level with any people that were their neighbours and contemporaries, or of any that are known to us by their records and by their monuments. It is true that we are used to think of Solomon's temple as a magnificent structure; and yet the descriptions given of it in the Books of Kings and Chronicles, convey an impression rather of its metallic splendour and its richness of decoration, than of the cyclopean style of the masonry that sustained it. Was it, in truth, a great work in an architectural sense? This question admits of a probable answer. The series of prophets, in discharge of their function as the reprovers of national sins, mention and rebuke the sumptuous style and the luxurious manners of those who then were the princes of the people; yet they make no boast, as if they were proud of the wealth, and the arts, and the instructed skill of their countrymen. Nevertheless there occur, in many parts of the prophetic writings, incidental allusions to the splendour of the private structures of the city—houses of hewn stone, houses ceiled with costly woods, decorated with ivory and gold, and fitted up with every device which elaborate luxury might ask for, are spoken of even by some of the earlier prophets. We must believe, therefore, that the Jerusalem of the ancient monarchy was a city of palaces and of princely mansions, in constructing which no cost had been spared.

Here, then, the two portions of an inferential argument come into contact; and it is just at the basement line of the palaces and the mansions of the ancient Jerusalem that they do so. The juncture is of this sort;—we hold in our hand the various literature of an ancient people; this literature has traversed the fields of time in those several modes of conveyance to which, in the preceding pages, we have given attention; it has thus come into our hands *safely*; it stands attested in modes so many and so sure, that now to speak of it as if it were questionable would be a mere prudery and an affectation. Up and down throughout these writings we find incidental notices of the sumptuous style of the upper classes of the people, in their modes of living, and in the decoration of their public and private buildings; at least it is so as to what were the visible parts of such structures. The kings and the nobles of the Hebrew monarchy were men of great wealth; ample revenues were at their command, and they spent their incomes magnificently. Looking to the documents—the parchment rolls—the volumes of the prophets of those ages, such are the inferences we must derive from them.

But what objects are those that present themselves when, with the pick in hand, we go down to the levels of the ancient Jerusalem? What we there find are courses of highly-wrought masonry, with which, as to the dimensions of the single blocks, and the labour that has been bestowed upon them, nothing can be compared unless it be in Egypt and at Palmyra. The inference is valid, namely, that the people of this city—even those whose structures, sacred and domestic, underlie the monuments of eight or nine successive empires or kingdoms—the primeval people—must have been wealthy, and far advanced in the arts, and large also in their conceptions, and bold in their enterprises. They were a people great and well civilised, and they were so at a time when, as the Greek historian tells us, the ancestors of his nation were petty marauders by sea and land, and were feeding upon acorns!

Such are the conclusions which we arrive at after a careful perusal of the literature of the Hebrew people, if now, at this day—and yet it is in a sense which he did not intend—we listen to the invitation of one of its poets, who challenges us to "Walk about Zion, and to go round about her," and to "tell the towers thereof, and to mark well her bulwarks, and to consider her palaces;" for in doing so we shall find the means for confirming ourselves in those convictions, the strength of which concerns each of us in the most intimate manner.

THE END.